VIOLENCE AND GENDER
IN THE GLOBALIZED WORLD

Global Connections

Series Editor: Robert Holton, Trinity College, Dublin

Global Connections builds on the multi-dimensional and continuously expanding interest in Globalization. The main objective of the series is to focus on 'connectedness' and provide readable case studies across a broad range of areas such as social and cultural life, economic, political and technological activities.

The series aims to move beyond abstract generalites and stereotypes: 'Global' is considered in the broadest sense of the word, embracing connections between different nations, regions and localities, including activities that are trans-national, and trans-local in scope; 'Connections' refers to movements of people, ideas, resources, and all forms of communication as well as the opportunities and constraints faced in making, engaging with, and sometimes resisting globalization.

The series is interdisciplinary in focus and publishes monographs and collections of essays by new and established scholars. It fills a niche in the market for books that make the study of globalization more concrete and accessible.

Violence and Gender
in the Globalized World
The Intimate and the Extimate

Edited by

SANJA BAHUN-RADUNOVIĆ
University of Essex, UK

V.G. JULIE RAJAN
Rutgers University, USA

ASHGATE

Published by
Ashgate Publishing Limited
Wey Court East
Union Road
Farnham
Surrey GU9 7PT
England

Ashgate Publishing Company
Suite 420
101 Cherry Street
Burlington, VT 05401-4405
USA

www.ashgate.com

British Library Cataloguing in Publication Data
Violence and gender in the globalized world : the intimate
   and the extimate. - (Global connections)
   1. Women - Violence against 2. Minority women - Violence
   against
   I. Bahun-Radunovic, Sanja II. Rajan, V. G. Julie
   362.8'8'082

Library of Congress Cataloging-in-Publication Data
Violence and gender in the globalized world : the intimate and the extimate / [edited] by Sanja Bahun-Radunovic and V.G. Julie Rajan.
      p. cm. -- (Global connections)
   Includes bibliographical references and index.
   ISBN-13: 978-0-7546-7364-4
   ISBN-10: 0-7546-7364-2
   1. Women--Violence against--Cross-cultural studies. 2. Violence--Social aspects--Cross-cultural studies. I. Bahun-Radunovic, Sanja. II. Rajan, V. G. Julie.

   HV6250.4.W65V56 2008
   305.4--dc22

                                                                    2008002387

ISBN 978 0 7546 7364 4

Reprinted 2009

Mixed Sources
Product group from well-managed
forests and other controlled sources
www.fsc.org Cert no. SGS-COC-2482
© 1996 Forest Stewardship Council

Printed and bound in Great Britain by TJI Digital, Padstow, Cornwall

Contents

Notes on Editors

Sanja Bahun-Radunović is Lecturer in the Department of Literature, Film and Theatre Studies at the University of Essex, UK. Her publications include: *Modernism and Melancholia*: *History as Mourning-work* (forthcoming); *The Avant-garde and the Margin*: *New Territories of Modernism* (Cambridge Scholars Publishers, 2006); *To Icarus, With Love* (Prometej Publishers, 1998); and *On the Atomic Bomb, Pain, Spaghetti, and the Rest* (Promocija Publishers, 1994).

V.G. Julie Rajan is Visiting Assistant Professor in the Department of Women's and Gender Studies, Rutgers University, USA. Her publications include: *Femininity, Nation, and Violence*: *Post-Independence Narratives of Resistance Written by Women Residing in India* (Mellen, forthcoming); *The Phenomenon of Women Suicide Bombers*: *Narratives of Violence* (forthcoming); and *The Home and the World*: *South Asia in Transition* (Cambridge Scholars Publishers, 2006).

Notes on Contributors

Sharon A. Bong is Lecturer in Women's Studies at Monash University, Malaysia. She is the author of *The Tension between Women's Rights and Religion: The Case of Malaysia* (Mellen, 2006) and is currently completing her book-length study entitled, *Knowing through Doing: Rights, Cultures and Religions from a Malaysian Feminist Epistemology* (forthcoming).

Charlotte Bunch is Founder and Executive Director of the Center for Women's Global Leadership in Rutgers University, USA. An activist, author, and organizer in the women's, civil, and human rights movements for over three decades, she has served on the boards of numerous organizations and is currently part of the Advisory Committee for the Human Rights Watch's Women's Rights Division, and on the Boards of the International Council on Human Rights Policy and the Global Fund for Women.

Sealing Cheng is Henry Luce Assistant Professor in the Women's Studies Department at Wellesley College, USA. Cheng's latest book-length study, *Transnational Desires: Filipina Entertainers in US Military Camp Towns in South Korea* (forthcoming), focuses on migrant women who work as entertainers in United States military camp towns in South Korea.

Drucilla Cornell is Professor in Private Law and Research Chair of Customary Law, Indigenous Values, and Dignity Jurisprudence at the University of Cape Town, South Africa. She has published seven books in which she probes the boundaries between feminism, continental philosophy, and legal theory, including *Beyond Accommodation: Ethical Feminism* (Rowman & Littlefield, 1999) and *Transformations: Recollective Imagination and Sexual Difference* (Routledge, 1993).

Marta Fernández-Morales is Lecturer in North American Literature and Contemporary English Theater at the University of the Balearic Islands, Spain. She has published numerous articles on gender violence, feminist theory, and American drama.

Jennifer M. Green is Senior Staff Attorney at the Center for Constitutional Rights, USA, and a former director of the Harvard Law School's Human Rights Program. She has worked for the Center in various capacities since 1991 and has served as a counsel for the plaintiffs in a number of the cases discussed in her contribution: *Doe v. Karadžić*, *Doe v. Unocal*, and *Doe v. Constant*.

Loretta Ihme is Lecturer and Researcher at the Faculty of Cultural Science of the Europa-Universität Viadrina in Frankfurt (Oder), Germany. Her most recent publication is "Europas Gespenster. Frauenhandel, Nation und Supranation" in *Perspektiven für Europa—eine neue Öffnung?/Perspectives of Europe—The New Opening?* (Peter Lang, 2006).

Angéla Kóczé is a member of Roma Women Initiative and she has served as the Chair of the Romaversitas Foundation in Budapest and Board Member of the PAKIV European Roma Fund. Her publications include: "Strategies to Promote the Successful Integration of Romani Students in the School System" in *Separate and Unequal: Combating Discrimination against Roma in Education* (Columbia University Press, 2004).

Valsala Kumari K.B. is a former Secretary to the Government, State of Kerala, India. Her most recent publications include, "Gender and Nation: Tradition and Transition" (*The Croatian Journal of Ethnology and Folk Research*, 40/1 [2003]).

Deborah L. Madsen is Professor of American Literature and Culture, and Co-Director of the program in Gender Studies at the University of Geneva. She has published over 12 books, including *Feminist Theory and Literary Practice* (Pluto Press, 2000) and *Beyond the Borders: American Literature and Post-Colonial Theory* (ed., Pluto Press, 2003).

Rose Shomali Musleh is the General Director of the Women's Affairs Technical Committee in Palestine. She has published studies and activists' reports on the political and socio-economic situation of the Palestinians in the West Bank and Gaza.

Svetlana Slapšak is Professor of Anthropology of Ancient Worlds and Anthropology of Gender, Balkanology, and Dean of Institutum Studiorum Humanitatis, Ljubljana, Slovenia, as well as the author of over 14 books, among which *War Discourse, Women's Discourse: Studies and Essays on Wars in Yugoslavia and Russia* (ISH, 2000) and *Balkan Women for Peace* (co-ed., Transeuropeans, 2003) are most recent. Slapšak has been a dissident and human rights activist since 1968.

Yifat Susskind is Communications Director of MADRE, an international women's human rights organization. She is the author of a number of articles on US foreign policy, appearing in *Foreign Policy in Focus*, *The W Effect: Bush's War on Women* (Feminist Press, 2004), and other publications.

Meredeth Turshen is Professor at the Edward J. Bloustein School of Planning and Public Policy at Rutgers University, USA. Her most recent book is *Women's Health Movements: A Global Force for Change* (Palgrave Macmillan, 2007).

Preface

Feminist Quandaries on Gender and Violence: Agency, Universality, and Human Security

Charlotte Bunch

The chapters in this book, *Violence and Gender in the Globalized World: The Intimate and the Extimate*, reflect both the incredible progress in and the enormous challenges to addressing gender-based violence in the world today. These discussions of gender and violence illuminate the complexities of some of the key debates and dilemmas in feminist theory—the relationship between the universal and the particular, and between women's agency and victimization. And the silences point to areas where more work is needed, such as a feminist approach to global and human security.

The issue of gender-based violence demonstrates the importance of both women's agency and the extent of their victimization historically. Women activists have placed violence against women squarely on the local, national, and global agendas of governments and civil society over the past four decades. This illustrates women's power to describe and name our realities as the basis of changing how those are perceived. But this work has also been done in an area where women are seriously victimized, tortured, terrorized, enslaved, and killed. Thus addressing gender and violence requires moving beyond the dualism of seeing women as either victims or agents to understanding the dynamic tension between both dimensions of women's lives.

In looking at the complex interactions between violence and gender explicated in this volume, it is important to remember that thinking of violence against women and of gender-based violence as categories that include many different forms of violence is relatively new. Different specific types of violence that women suffer have, of course, been addressed in the past; however, as a broad issue reflecting male–female power dynamics and gender constructions that should be altered across the globe, this is a new approach resulting from the international interaction made possible by global networking among feminists since the 1970s.

Perceiving gender-based violence as something that women have in common, even though the forms vary, has made it possible to elevate attention to this issue at the global level in terms of visibility, laws, justice, and human rights. Women activists from all parts of the globe have brought gender-based violence from the grass roots to the global agenda utilizing the UN World Women's Conferences (1975–95) and the Decade for Women (1975–85), which brought donor dollars to women's rights for the first time through development planning. Understanding gender violence as a human rights violation that was the responsibility of states and the international community to punish and prevent only came in the 1990s with women's global organizing. The World Conference on Human Rights in Vienna in 1993 became the milestone of recognition of violence against women as a human rights issue. The UN Declaration on Violence against Women and the creation of the post of UN Special Rapporteur on Violence against Women, Its Causes and Consequences, that followed soon after, were essential building blocks in this understanding. In the short span of 15 years, the standard setting and development of international norms on gender-based violence has been nothing short of remarkable, including among others the integration of gender into the UN human rights bodies on torture, the recognition of rape as a tool of war and the definition of gender-based persecution incorporated into the statutes of the International Criminal Court.

There has been a steady growth in the integration of a gender perspective into much human rights work, and in the use of international human rights law and instruments by women's groups globally. National laws in some 90 countries now address domestic violence specifically, and many spell out other specific forms of violence as well. The UN Secretary General's study on violence against women in 2006 and the World Health Organization's multi-country study on women's health and interpersonal violence in 2005 illustrate how far this issue has moved globally. These studies establish standards on what data is needed and what is the state's responsibility for this issue.

Why does this history matter? Because a volume like this would not have been possible without it. And this volume, by explicating some of the challenges and complexity of looking at gender and violence, contributes to the next critical stage of working toward implementing these universal norms and standards that call for an end to gender-based violence.

Challenges

While the international recognition of gender-based violence and the evolution of human rights standards to address it have expanded rapidly in the past two decades, there is, nevertheless, no discernible decline in the occurrence of such violence or women's insecurity resulting from it. The greatest challenge therefore is the persistence, multiplicity, and ever-growing number of forms of such violence in daily life. As the UN Secretary General's study on violence against women reveals, governments are failing their responsibility and due diligence to address this issue. There is a serious lack of real resources or political will committed to this issue—including a lack of services, of justice system mechanisms, and of attention to data to measure effectively the problem or the impact of practices that seek to diminish it.[1]

The UN calls for an end to impunity for violence against women in the formal legal system, and this is crucial. But impunity is also about the informal sectors of family and community—the culture of impunity for gender-based violence is almost

---

1 United Nations, "In-Depth Study on All Forms of Violence against Women: Report of the Secretary General" (October 9, 2006). <http://daccessdds.un.org/doc/UNDOC/GEN/N06/419/74/PDF/N0641974.pdf?OpenElement>.

universal. Most perpetrators everywhere expect and count upon "getting away with it"—not only legally, but especially in the eyes of the community. Violence thus persists because of cultural acceptance and fears of confronting perpetrators. Most cultures still tolerate violence against women in both contemporary as well as traditional forms. Cultural violence is not some marginalized, exotic "cultural practice" that takes place somewhere else. It is the culturally embedded practice and assumption of domination over women in virtually all societies, and the general acceptance of violence as a means of maintaining that control, even of defending one's masculinity. Rather than label some practices as "cultural and traditional" forms of violence, we need to understand that all violence against women is supported by cultural attitudes, at least as long as the culture—one's family, community, friends, colleagues, and religion—generally accepts it. This is the real cultural challenge of violence against women. Consequently, myths about culture and human rights also need challenging—all human rights work involves changing culture and must be shaped by the specificities of each culture to be effective in doing so. Thus, respect for and attention to diversity and the universality of human rights are not opposites, but two parts of a dynamic that must be made mutually reinforcing in their claims.

To understand gender and violence also requires understanding the dynamic relationship between universality and diversity. Violence against women is one of the most common experiences of women, but it can only be understood and combated by seeing it in all its diversity. Violence is always particular in that it is shaped by the intersection of race, ethnicity, class, sexual orientation, age, physical ability, culture, or other factors with gender in any given time and place. Thus, the naming of various forms of violence and their different convergences with gender and other factors is crucial to making broad claims about violence truly universal in their application to all, as well as to shaping varying strategies to end it in differing contexts. The chapters in *Violence and Gender in the Globalized World: The Intimate and the Extimate* provide grounding for this work.[2] Their impetus is close to one important strategy in work on gender-based violence over the past few years: to describe violence against women in the context of other global forces that are obstacles to women's security and development, such as the rise of religious fundamentalisms, the inequity of resources resulting from globalization, poverty, and HIV/AIDS. This strategy seeks to position work on violence, not in isolation, but as part of other programs and policies. For example, HIV/AIDS programming requires an understanding of questions about gender-based violence that need to be asked in local health clinics and a sensitive approach to implications and dangers of violence against women in disclosure policies for AIDS testing, and similar activities.

---

2 Another creative example is the Companion Report "*Mairin Iwanka Raya*: Indigenous Women Stand against Violence" issued by FIMI (Foro Internacional de Mujeres Indigenas), an international indigenous women's network, on the occasion of the UN Secretary General's study. The Companion Report outlines the particular ways in which indigenous women experience various forms of violence. Foro Internacional de Mujeres Indigenas, "*Mairin Iwanka Raya*: Indigenous Women Stand against Violence: A Companion Report to the United Nations Secretary-General's Study on Violence against Women" (New York: FIMI, 2006).

An area that needs more global attention, however, is the link between gender-based violence and human security. The concept of human security provides an alternative framework to traditional concepts of national security and it approaches security in an integrated way; it views peace, security, equality, human rights, and development as interrelated. This broad framework puts an emphasis on both protection and empowerment, seeing victimization and agency as two parts of reality, each of which needs to be addressed—often simultaneously. Looking at definitions of human security, one can find no better paradigm for human insecurity than violence against women, which directly and indirectly affects a vast number of people. The UN Human Security Commission report, for example, emphasizes that "violence unseats people's security."[3] If you add the fear of violence and lack of control over sex to many women's inability to control when they will become pregnant, you have a very solid core of human insecurity surrounding issues of women's bodies.

Furthermore, it needs to be understood that violence against women is not only an important human security issue in its own right, but also that it is connected to the perpetuation of other forms of domination and insecurity in the world. The way that violence against women in the family is normalized is a key component to creating a culture that accepts the violence of war, militarism, and other forms of domination and conflict. Not only is violence against women exacerbated by war and conflict, but also that violence is part of what perpetuates war and conflict; it feeds acceptance of violence as an inevitable and normal means of dealing with differences.

The climate of impunity for violence against women that persists in most societies feeds the culture of impunity towards violence more generally. Such a culture is reflected in many of the problems addressed by the international community—men demanding sex for food in refugee camps, for example, which has implicated men of all cultures. It also reinforces at the gut level that violence wins and domination succeeds, whether at home or in wars. A disturbing sign of this cultural prevalence in the U.S. is the growing number of girls involved in violent acts because they read the society's message that to be empowered and avoid being victims, they must be violent. Addressing violence at the heart of society, in our families and daily life, is a critical part of laying out the conditions for human security for all—an alternative to the nationalist, military-based security that is fueling so many conflicts and problems in the world today. This volume adds to knowledge needed to advance this urgent work.

Charlotte Bunch
Executive Director, Center for Women's Global Leadership
New Brunswick, NJ
November 2007

---

3 Commission on Human Security, "Human Security Now" (2003), 6. <http://www.humansecurity-chs.org/finalreport/English/FinalReport.pdf> (accessed November 26, 2007).

Bibliography

Commission on Human Security. "The Final Report of the Commission on Human Security: Human Security Now." 2003. <http://www.humansecurity-chs.org/finalreport/English/FinalReport.pdf>.

Coomaraswamy, Radhika. "Are Women's Rights Universal? Re-Engaging the Local." *Meridians*: *Feminism, Race, Transnationalism.* Middletown: Wesleyan University Press, 2002: 1–18.

Ertürk, Yakin. "Intersections between Culture and Violence against Women: Report of the Special Rapporteur on Violence against Women, Its Causes and Consequences." 2007. <http://www.crin.org/docs/SRVAW_07.pdf>.

Foro Internacional de Mujeres Indigenas. "*Mairin Iwanka Raya*: Indigenous Women Stand against Violence: A Companion Report to the United Nations Secretary-General's Study on Violence against Women." New York: FIMI, 2006.

United Nations. "In-Depth Study on All Forms of Violence against Women: Report of the Secretary General." October 9, 2006. <http://daccessdds.un.org/doc/UNDOC/GEN/N06/419/74/PDF/N0641974.pdf?OpenElement>.

Acknowledgements

Our greatest debt is to our contributors whose scholarly work and activist practice has been an inspiration, and whose dedication and patience throughout the multiple stages of this project has been encouraging and stimulating. Furthermore, this book would not be possible without the enthusiasm and active support of the Ashgate's Commissioning Editor, Neil Jordan, who was attentive to the many potentials and specific contexts of such a volume.

The editors are grateful for permission to reprint the extracts from the following copyrighted material: Drucilla Cornell, "A Call for a Nuanced Constitutional Jurisprudence: *Ubuntu*, Dignity, and Reconciliation" (*Suid-Afrikaanse Publiekereg/ South African Public Law* 19 (2004): 666–75); and Drucilla Cornell and Karin Van Marle, "Exploring *Ubuntu*—Tentative Reflections" (*African Human Rights Law Journal* [2005]: 195–220). We are grateful to Karin Van Marle for allowing us to reproduce portions of the latter text which she has co-authored. We would also like to thank Meredeth Turshen who has kindly given permission for the use of two photographs from her field trip to Algeria in April 2001; these appear on the cover-page and on page 86. The cover of the collection displays a mural painted by the children from a primary school destroyed by Islamist fundamentalists in the infamous massacre in Haï Raïs, Algeria, on August 29, 1997. The other photograph was taken by Turshen in the courtyard of the same school and it contextualizes both Turshen's text and the mural itself.

We are indebted to numerous friends and colleagues with whom we have discussed these topics and we are especially grateful to Charlotte Bunch, who has supported this project since its inception. We thank Dušan, Kartik, and Raja, who, in a spirit of genuine inter-gender consideration, understood our absences and brought us joy in the intervals of respite.

Finally, the editors would like to dedicate this book to three women who have fought through the many challenges posed to women in their generations: Subbulakshmi, Muthukannu, and Gordana.

You will always be our inspiration.

Introduction

On Violence, Gender, and Global Connections

To embark on a project of discussing gender and violence in today's world means to summon a great number of hard-to-resolve questions. Current dialogues on gender and violence surface a number of problematic issues across a variety of contexts, the most significant of which are related to, on the one hand, the struggle of scholars in women's and gender studies to theorize femininity in a manner that can address the particularities of an individual's experience as well as women's experiences across global economic divides, and, on the other hand, the gay rights activists' challenge to the framing of sexual rights as purely antithetical, and therefore readable only in the context of heteronormative ideologies. Despite such methodological differences, all contemporary approaches to the relationship between gender and violence are grounded in awareness that the regulation, surveillance, and assumed performance of gender is informed by conventional views of "masculinity" and "femininity" and, further, that those views are premised on historic assumptions of how the gendered production of "male" and "female" bodies have been constructed through the phenomenon of violence. This designation of societal significations to human experiences and activities as "female" and "male" is associated with various forms of violence that constitute a range of physical, psychological, representational, discursive and situational violations of human and, particularly, women rights. Violence against women, the focus of the collection of essays *Violence and Gender in the Globalized World: The Intimate and the Extimate*, is a consequence of the workings of gender difference in patriarchal contexts—a societal dynamic that requires the consistent privileging of masculinity over femininity in an assumed heteronormative framework. Because that privileging is essential to the stability of patriarchy, it is reinforced in the moral frameworks and social processes of all cultural expressions in patriarchal societies to the point of violence. Patriarchal processes understood in this manner are so much part of our global reality that they have mitigated our ability to discern and read this "violence"; consequently, violence against women is often perceived as normative, and even necessary, in the everyday lives of both men and women in international cultural contexts.

Thus the issue of gender and violence encompasses an extraordinarily broad and culturally inflected terrain of political, physical, psychological and cultural acts and actions that delimit—particularly—women's activity and mobility, and threaten their security. In hosting contributions by eminent scholars and activists from around the world, including Germany, India, Malaysia, Palestine, South Africa, the United States, and other countries, this volume purports to account for at least a portion of the global variability of women's experiences of violence; to redefine the critical picture of the subject of gender and violence in the age of globalization by bringing visibility both to uncommonly discussed geo-political sites and the experiences of violence that, for various reasons, have gained little attention; and to emphasize a resonance between women's experiences of violence in the so-called developed and developing contexts by drawing attention to both. As our contributors reiterate in their chapters, the cultural and performative diversity of the acts of gender violence can hardly be subsumed under a single definition or even relegated to a certain epoch or a symbolic moment in time. The discussion of violence in general, and gender violence in particular, is inextricable from a consideration of social sanctions, naturalizations, taboos, customs, and traditions that are as much universal as they are unique for each society. Furthermore, these experiences and behaviors have complex temporality: global peoples also carry with themselves the indices of past and present violence—memories and experiences that render them hybrid expressors of passivity or agency in their own cultural contexts and communities. These experiences and their interpretations have influenced women's positions as recipients, conveyors, and/or perpetrators of gender violence at the beginning of the twenty-first century. In this way, past and present violence historicizes and politicizes female bodies, and acts diversely as a reifying source or a reconstitutive resource of women's various actions, a topic which demands continuous scholarly and activist attention.

It is this ongoing, organic process of focusing on, and the discernment, constitution, and reconstitution of historic, present, and future potential registers of womanhood globally that we identify as a "feminist" approach to the subject of gender and violence in this collection. Hence, to discuss the conceptual hyphen of gender *and* violence in a feminist project appears to the editors to be a task simultaneously more urgent and more complex than that of addressing exclusively the manifestations of the narrowly conceived "gender violence"—for the latter approach all too easily identifies and petrifies the victims and perpetrators, alienating both groups from the context of their activity and reducing the complexity of the phenomenon under discussion. In this light, the present collection interprets the dialectics between gender and violence through distinctions in gender violence, as they are influenced by the identity politics circumscribing each culture at a given moment in time. At the same time, our contributors particularly attend to the comparative contexts of political, economic, and cultural violence that have influenced not only women's well-being, but also the general experience and social production of gender internationally. This global comparative method demands an intersectional and interdisciplinary approach to understanding how patriarchal constructions of gender difference occlude the additional variables of social difference, such as race and language; only such an approach can account for the multi-textured nature of gender violence.

In this light, the core agenda of this volume is to highlight recent transformations in the interpretation of the relationship between women and violence, particularly as it informs the social production of femininity at the beginning of the twenty-first century. Traditionally, femininity has been articulated through an assumed consistency in women's experiences of enduring, witnessing, and mitigating against violence throughout their entire lives—all of which have been enunciated from the cognitive position that defines women specifically as the recipients, and therefore the victims, of violence. Such a definition is supported, for example, by women's tendencies to experience incidences of sexual violence in the situation of conflict and/or domestic violence in their own homes. Recent feminist perspectives have problematized that approach to femininity by drawing attention to how women may be also configured by and implicated in violence. Sealing Cheng's investigation into trafficking in women in South Korea, for example, critiques NGO representations of women only as victims of trafficking by drawing attention to the voices of the trafficked women themselves and their own approach to the phenomenon of trafficking (see Chapter 9). In that vein, an additional agenda of the present volume is to mitigate against conventional constructions of corporeality and social behavior as either "feminine" or "masculine" and to reveal the ways in which these definitions have limited and disrupted the potential interpretations of feminine social agency outside of patriarchal constructs. Some emergent treatises on women militants, for example, demand a more elastic definition of women's social agencies, one that may account for the complex ways in which women can be read as perpetrators of violence. The consciousness of these issues is present throughout our volume.[1] More specifically, our contributors draw attention to how women's decisions to fulfill unconventional feminine roles coalesce with their experiences of being violated within patriarchy in their traditional roles as wives, mothers, and daughters. Our consciousness of those broader implications is reflected in our inclusion of Meredeth Turshen's examination of how the neocolonial politics of the Algerian civil war has informed the violent experiences of both male and female teenagers and consequently has repositioned gender dynamics in that society (see Chapter 5).

Such dialogues remind us that the complexity of women's experiences of violence is a function, not only of the plural experiences of femininity derived from the dialectics between gender and violence, but also of how each of those plural experiences takes on new guises and acquires new meanings with the rise of the global market economy, information technology, disintegration of classical warfare, and the installment of new modes of violence on the global stage.[2] Since the purpose of this project has been to document the current state of scholarship and activism as it responds to particular, historically shaped needs of women worldwide, this volume has taken the shape which reflects how the discourse of gender and violence has informed and is informed by the past two decades of globalization-work: global market economy and its discontents; neo-modern militarism, civil wars, international terrorism, and international interventionism; the emergence of new media and the excess of traditional media coverage; still highly unequal economical relations globally; the steady depletion of health system resources in both developed and developing countries; and, as our own experience as the editors of this volume has testified, the restrictive conditions for education and research work in many parts

---

1 Problematic representations of women suicide bombers are explored in V.G. Julie Rajan's *The Phenomenon of Women Suicide Bombers: Narratives of Violence* (forthcoming).

2 On the phenomenon of new militarism and the rise in collateral damage, as by-products of globalization, see Mary Kaldor, *New and Old Wars: Organized Violence in a Global Era*, 2nd edition (Cambridge: Polity Press, 2006). On these issues as bound to free market economy, see Amy Chua, *World on Fire: How Exporting Free Market Democracy Breeds Ethnic Hatred and Global Instability* (London: Heinemann, 2003).

of the globe. In particular, as the context of accelerated globalization necessitates that every examination of gender and violence starts from a re-examination of the workings of gender violence as it relates to sustainable economy and its impact on woman's well-being and the exercise of cultural, faith and custom-based rights, these topics have been visited by most contributors. One may find one such close assessment of the gender economics of globalization in Valsala Kumari K.B.'s probing of the societal and gender effects of the tools for poverty alleviation such as microcredit, in the context of Kerala, India (see Chapter 3). On the other hand, this collection also recognizes the urgency of addressing one hidden by-product of globalization: the resurgence of racism. The correlations among global and local concerns over race are thus among the primary concerns in the volume, as evidenced in Loretta Ihme's study. Her observation that current representations of the trafficking of women by media and national propaganda in the enlarged European Union resonate with historical racial prejudices against, among other societal productions, the masculinity of darker-skinned men, is relevant for the discussion of gender, race, and violence not only in Europe, but in the global arena (see Chapter 10).

Personal experiences of violence in conflict situations, theoretical postulations of what constitutes a conflict, and the consequences of conflict on societies over time has been the focus of many chapters in the collection. The heightened attention that our contributors pay to this topic testifies to its exigency. The number of civilian deaths and refugees/displaced persons rises every second, and the range of economic and infrastructural damage expands swiftly around the globe. In the view of this state of affairs, the demand for international help in conflict-mitigation and assuring the basic security for civilian population affected by "new wars" is immense. In this context, the issue of human security has been disclosed as pre-eminent in the current discussions of gender and violence, and this is the topic to which Charlotte Bunch pays substantial attention in her Preface.[3] At the same time, there is a pronounced need critically to recognize the implicit or temporally prolonged effects of violent conflict, such as the reconfiguration of social structures and the undermining of the functioning of social institutions, in particular those that are supposed to ensure gender equity and social mobility. Rose Shomali Musleh's timely review of the impact that the ongoing conflict in the region has had on the lives of Palestinian women and their struggle for the improvement of gender relations in Palestinian society discloses the various levels on which the concept of "collateral damage" operates (see Chapter 4). One such "implicit" collateral damage is addressed in Svetlana Slapšak's chapter, in which the author takes us into the "post-conflict"[4] phase of the disintegration of former Yugoslavia and suggests a connection between the abusive representation of women, especially by anti-war oriented intellectuals, and the wider political failure to take responsibility for what happened during the war (see Chapter 6).

---

3 For a more general discussion of these issues, see Mary Kaldor, *Human Security: Reflections on Globalization and Intervention* (Cambridge: Polity Press, 2007).

4 The editors, however, acknowledge the problematic interpretations associated with the term "post-conflict." The term assumes an immediate end to violence after the official conclusion of a conflict situation, and hence does not take into account the many new and the exaggeration of the old forms of visible and invisible violence occasioned by the conflict.

While collateral damage accumulates worldwide, generating an ever-expanding network of media coverage in which the intimate and the extimate collapse, old methodological frameworks are rendered insufficient, and then refuted, reconfigured, and, sometimes, reinvented. In compiling this collection, the editors were conscious of the necessity to address the concrete life experiences, personal narratives, and needs of women in various parts of the globe. Recognized in recent feminist scholarship, the need for research more closely linked and more sophisticatedly attuned to the unique local experiences of women—cultural, political, religious, psychological—and yet appreciative of the ways of global interconnecting and exchanges of knowledge and practice that the accelerating pace of globalization also offers today is a marker of the remarkable evolutionary potential of women's and gender studies.[5] An evidence for this dynamics may be found in Yifat Susskind's piece where the voices of indigenous women in Nicaragua and Kenya reorient our knowledge on the political mobility of indigenous peoples and forge new strategies for combating violence (see Chapter 1). Such reconsiderations of what constitutes women's experiences of violence in their own words give rise to new historiographies concerning the position of women internationally—from the local through the international levels—and create a space in which to consider future horizons of both feminist theory and women's organizing.

These observations highlight yet another agenda of the volume: an exploration of the variables configuring the ambiguous border between feminist theory and women's activism. In different terms, both Susskind's chapter and Angéla Kóczé's assessment of women's gendering of Roma identity politics (see Chapter 11) eloquently call for contextualized re-examination of activist practices. Exemplifying the fusion of activist and academic concerns to which this collection aspires, both Susskind and Kóczé attend to some academic concepts which, in their opinion, need to be saved from slipping into irrelevance: they argue that the methodological frameworks of the conceptual models such as "intersectionality" (Susskind) or "dialogic experience" (Kóczé) should be re-introduced into the everyday activist work in the respective contexts which they discuss in order to make them relevant to the immediacy of women's experiences of violence today. In their analysis, traditional or custom-based legal and methodological frameworks are also reconstituted in the process of devizing local strategies to address the reality of feminine experience.

In a similar vein, both Drucilla Cornell's probing of the constitutional and activist relevance of the traditional South African law *ubuntu* (see Chapter 7) and Sharon A. Bong's discussion of the work of religious rights feminists in Malaysia (see Chapter 2) demonstrate how the methodologies and contexts traditionally denounced as "patriarchal" may hide major liberatory practices for both women and men. While

---

5 Various recent texts emphasize women's voices and experiences. One such example is Ritu Menon and Kamla Bhasin's *Borders and Boundaries: Women in India's Partition* (New Brunswick: Rutgers Press, 1998), which interprets the 1947 Partition of British India through the personal accounts of women survivors of the Partition. Furthermore, for a number of important theorizations of the interplay of local and global perspectives in recent scholarship, see *Feminist Theory Reader: Local and Global Perspectives* (ed.), by Carole Ruth McCann and Seung-Kyung Kim (New York and London: Routledge, 2003).

Bong argues that fusional practices, such as religious rights feminist activism, may offer the best ground-level based response to gender violence, Cornell's promotion of the seemingly patriarchal law *ubuntu*, a view she shares with some of the most prominent feminist activists in the legal spheres in South Africa, is based on the belief that this traditional law offers an important critique of the Western legislative systems. In this way, the continuity between the local/particular and the global/ universal is disclosed, and its active ingredients are critically probed to allow for a broader examination of women and violence in a wide range of cultural contexts. This continuity is particularly visible in the discussions of international legislation, such as Jennifer M. Green's assessment of the litigation of international human rights violations in the USA and the European Union courts (see Chapter 8).

Thus, our volume also identifies some positive consequences of globalization: the rise of "new humanitarianism"; the work of reconciliation and reconstitution; new visions for alleviating poverty; recuperative societal work; a renewed awareness of diverse ethnic, sexual, occupational, religious and politic identity choices for women globally; the development of alternative, less-hegemonic legislative frameworks for the future; and the increased importance of one specific response to the issues of gender and violence—art. In Deborah L. Madsen's assessment of the recent Chicana writing (see Chapter 12) and Marta Fernández-Morales's study of the V-Day movement (see Chapter 13), literature, theater, and art emerge as not only an alternative to the old discourses on gender and violence and the (still) superior catalysts of healing process, but also as a new form of global connecting. The situation in which an artistic project such as the V-Day can convene hundreds of thousands of people in Africa, Asia, Europe, and America over the common aim to battle gender-related violence and initiate the awareness-raising programs in almost 700 universities globally, assures us of the continued relevance of these alternative responses at the dawn of the new millennium.

The final product of these varied discussions is a multi-layered volume that can be described as "newly feminist" in its inclusion of variegated discursive, testimonial, and activist snapshots of the status of women globally at present. Through the juxtaposition of these discourses, unforeseen global connections are forged: a "both- and" attitude is endorsed as a basis for a new ethics of activism and legislation in the case-studies dealing with such different parts of the world as South Africa (Cornell) and Malaysia (Bong); the urgent need to prevent the epistemological violence which media and NGO discourses exert on female sex workers is voiced from Germany (Ihme) and South Korea (Cheng); the call for alternative methodologies binds the consideration of indigenous peoples in Kenya and Nicaragua (Susskind) and that of the Roma (Kóczé); and so on. As a result, this book testifies to the productive multitude of approaches to gender in a world in which the shrinking of time and space has generated unprecedented modi of violence but has also offered new historical possibilities for its record and reparation. This variety of themes and interpretative systems bears witness to a new, *heterogeneous and interdisciplinary* form of global connecting that has been consolidating in recent years.[6] It is thus not incidental

---

6 See, for one account, Valentine M. Moghadam, *Globalizing Women: Transnational Feminist Networks* (Baltimore and London: Johns Hopkins University Press, 2005).

that, for all the variety of their subjects and methodologies, all the chapters featured in *Violence and Gender in the Globalized World: The Intimate and the Extimate* emphasize one specific issue: the need for a global cooperative strategy to promote security—from local, through national, to international levels; a strategy that, even as it is expandable and, hence, widely applicable, should nevertheless be capable of adjusting to specific contexts in order to highlight the variant terrain that grounds the discourse of gender and violence at the beginning of the twenty-first century.

Sanja Bahun-Radunović, London, and V.G. Julie Rajan, Philadelphia
October 2007

Bibliography

Chua, Amy. *World on Fire: How Exporting Free Market Democracy Breeds Ethnic Hatred and Global Instability*. London: Heinemann, 2003.

Kaldor, Mary. *New and Old Wars: Organized Violence in a Global Era*. Cambridge: Polity Press, 2006.

—— *Human Security: Reflections on Globalization and Intervention*. Cambridge: Polity Press, 2007.

McCann, Carole Ruth, and Seung-Kyung Kim (eds), *Feminist Theory Reader: Local and Global Perspectives*. New York and London: Routledge, 2003.

Menon, Ritu and Kamla Bhasin. *Borders and Boundaries: Women in India's Partition*. New Brunswick: Rutgers Press, 1998.

Moghadam, Valentine M. *Globalizing Women: Transnational Feminist Networks*. Baltimore and London: Johns Hopkins University Press, 2005.

Rajan, Julie V.G. *The Phenomenon of Women Suicide Bombers: Narratives of Violence*. Forthcoming.

PART I

Revealing the Gaps

The chapters in this part highlight and explore the significance of what has been perceived as "gaps" in the critical cultural and theoretical scholarship of gender and violence. The existence of many discrepancies in knowledge concerning femininity attests to a number of such gaps in the mapping of gender studies. Traditionally, such gaps have been viewed negatively, as a reminder of the still nascent manifestation of women's and gender studies on the seasoned stage of intellectual thought. In addition, the visibility given to such tensions often has necessitated ongoing debates as to the legitimacy of any one position. Yet, such debates and the attentiveness to hermeneutic gaps are beneficial for any production of knowledge.

The editors assembled the pieces in this part, "Revealing the Gaps," intentionally to surface such gaps and reorient our knowledge about them. As editors, we hope that Yifat Susskind's activist piece on indigenous women's voices in Nicaragua and Kenya will engender questions about more broad, scholarly approaches to indigenous women globally. We hope that, in perusing Sharon A. Bong's theoretical approach to faith-rights feminists in Malaysia, readers will be moved to consider femininity across hyphenated experiences outside of the bounds of gender theory. Upon reading Valsala Kumari K.B.'s argument concerning the effects of microcredit on women in Kerala, India, the editors hope that the heightened importance of the discussions of economy and sustainable growth in relation to femininity will become evident to the reader, and incite further consideration of this multi-faceted topic. The editors encourage this type of reading and counter-reading to enrich the interpretation of knowledge in and effects of these chapters on the discourse of gender and violence—for it is because of and through such gaps that we can conceive of critical cultural studies and scholarship concerning femininity and violence as an ever-expanding spectrum of the present and evolving thought.

Chapter 1

Indigenous Women's Anti-Violence Strategies

Yifat Susskind

Introduction

In the summer of 1983, a group of women from the National Women's Association of Nicaragua and the Ministry of Health for the Atlantic Coast region of Nicaragua extended an invitation to a small group of women in the United States. The Nicaraguans wanted the women from the US to see for themselves the impact of their government's undeclared war on the women and families of Nicaragua, including indigenous women, whose voices were so rarely heard. Out of that exchange grew MADRE, which is today an international women's human rights organization that works in partnership with indigenous women's groups in Nicaragua, Kenya, Guatemala, Colombia, Peru, Mexico, and numerous other countries, to combat gender-based violence and other human rights abuses.

Among the women on that first MADRE delegation there were activists from the US battered women's movement. Most of these women conceived of "violence against women" mainly in terms of domestic violence. That narrow conception was soon dislodged as they listened to the stories of the indigenous women who were hosting them. The Nicaraguan women spoke of the US -backed militias that targeted civilians with mass killings, rape, torture, abduction, and the destruction of crops and livestock, as well as the bombing of day-care centers, schools, and hospitals all in order to overthrow Nicaragua's left-wing government. They told stories of being discriminated against as indigenous people and of being denied basic services, such as education in their own languages.[1] They spoke of losing their traditional leadership roles within their communities to forces of colonization and religious conversion. All of this they defined as violence against women.

Since that initial exchange, MADRE has stressed the importance of understanding that violence against women occurs *in relation to* facets of women's identity that include, but extend beyond, gender. Indeed, each woman's experience of violence is mediated by the interplay of multiple identities, such as race, class, caste, religion, sexual orientation, geographic situation, and ethnicity. Based on this understanding, MADRE works with indigenous women to develop programs that combat gender-based violence. MADRE articulates a unique indigenous perspective on violence against

---

1 Philip A. Dennis, *The Miskitu People of Awastara* (Austin: University of Texas Press, 2004).

women that both builds on and critiques the insights and strategies of the conventional human rights framework and the mainstream of the global women's movement.

Towards an Integrated Analysis of Indigenous Women's Rights

In recent years, the metaphor of "intersectionality" has been used to communicate inter-relationships between various aspects of identity and the ways that identity is used as a rationale and a vehicle for meting out privilege and oppression.[2] Indeed, much theoretical work has been devoted to elaborating this concept and to applying it in various fields, including that of human rights. Yet, for indigenous women, who have long experienced violence and discrimination on the basis of multiple identities, "intersectionality" is not an arcane academic concept, but a daily lived reality. The theoretical perspective that emerges from the concrete experience of living as an indigenous woman recognizes both the near-universality of violence against women and the specificity of violence perpetrated on the basis of distinct, but overlapping, identities. This approach is not only a theoretical proposition, but also the bedrock of strategies that most effectively combat violence against indigenous women—indeed, against all women—within a human rights framework.

Indigenous women from such places as Nicaragua, Australia, and the US insist that anti-violence strategies must account for the ways that multiple identities and systems of domination interact to construct women's experiences of violence. For, while the *threat* of gender-based violence impacts every woman, certain women are specifically targeted for violence on the basis of other variables that circumscribe their identities, such as ethnicity and language. The multiple forms of discrimination that render these women more likely to be abused also function to deny them access to mechanisms to redress abuse. At a 2005 MADRE anti-violence training in the village of Archer's Post, Kenya, one participant, Margaret Nguko, spoke about the ways that gender discrimination and discrimination against indigenous peoples overlapped to compound indigenous women's subordination: "Because I am a woman, I don't have a voice in my community. Because we are nomadic, we don't have a voice in the government."[3] In light of Nguko's comments, indigenous women must situate their anti-violence work at the intersections of movements for women's human rights *and* indigenous peoples' rights when responding to the multiple forms of discrimination that they face.

The Importance of Collective Rights

For indigenous women, the key to combating gender-based violence lies in the promotion of indigenous peoples' collective rights. For example, Monica Aleman, a young indigenous woman leader from Nicaragua, testifies:

---

2 See, for example, Kimberley Crenshaw, "Mapping the Margins: Intersectionality, Identity Politics, and Violence against Women of Color," *Stanford Law Review* 43, No. 6 (July 1991): 1241–99.

3 Margaret Nguko, interview by the author, Archer's Post, Kenya, 2005.

In our community, like other communities worldwide, violence against women is aggravated by factors such as male unemployment and substance abuse. But for indigenous men, joblessness and the psycho-social crises that lead to substance abuse derive largely from the violation of collective rights. Therefore, collective rights are part of what we must address to combat violence against indigenous women.[4]

This claim has confounded many in the global women's movement who fail to see how collective rights constitute a "women's issue." Yet, the indivisibility of all human rights means that indigenous women do not enjoy their right to a life free from violence while the collective rights of their people are also systematically violated—manifested at the very least in a double layer of violence. Dr Myrna Cunningham is an internationally recognized indigenous leader and a long-time partner of MADRE from the Atlantic Coast of Nicaragua. She explains collective rights and their importance to indigenous women:

Exercising our rights—both as indigenous people and as women—depends on securing [...] our collective rights. [These] include the right to full recognition as peoples with our own worldview and traditions, our own territories, and our own modes of organization within nation-states; the right to self-determination through our own systems of autonomy or self-government based on a communal property framework; and the right to control, develop, and utilize our own natural resources.[5]

Cunningham emphasizes that collective rights (of the sort that indigenous peoples are demanding) and individual human rights (of the sort that have upheld the legal basis for opposing violence against women) are complementary. In other words, indigenous peoples are entitled to collective rights in addition to the rights guaranteed to all people by the full body of human rights instruments and standards.

Indigenous Women and the Global Women's Movement

Indigenous women have been part of the global women's movement since its inception and were active in the international processes that yielded critical instruments for combating violence against women, such as the Convention for the Elimination of All Forms of Discrimination Against Women, the optional Protocol of Belem do Para, and the 1995 Beijing Platform for Action. Yet their commitment to the elimination of violence, and the priorities and perspectives they bring to this work, have often been disregarded or misunderstood within the mainstream women's movement. Indeed, the global women's movement has at times reproduced the very types of hierarchies and exclusions that it has challenged in pursuit of its goals. Cunningham further explains:

Like other women from historically marginalized groups, indigenous women have had to fight to be heard in a movement where the only ostensible criteria for participation are to show up and be a woman. Even now, after decades of international conferences,

---

4 Monica Aleman, interview by the author, June 18, 2007.

5 Myrna Cunningham, "Indigenous Women's Visions of an Inclusive Feminism" *Development* 49, No. 1 (2006): 55–6.

discussions, publications, and much hard work, issues that are a matter of life and death for indigenous women—racism, for example, or the exploitation of the earth's resources—are relegated to a tagged-on conceptual category called "diversity," in the dominant feminist paradigm.[6]

Despite their frustration with these dynamics, many indigenous women recognize the importance of the global women's movement in their work against gender-based violence and are committed to generating change from within the movement. For example, indigenous women have partnered with MADRE to create leadership development and skills-training programs to maximize their effective participation in international processes, such as the United Nations World Conferences on women and other international forums. Since 1999, MADRE has supported the creation and development of the International Indigenous Women's Forum (known by its Spanish acronym, FIMI). This network of indigenous women leaders from Asia, Africa, Europe, and the Americas defines combating violence against women as one of its primary goals.

Most of MADRE's partnerships with indigenous women have been at the community level. For example, MADRE has worked to support women in Ayacucho, Peru, working to produce and broadcast indigenous women's radio programming. Through the project, indigenous women gain media skills and disseminate critical information on reproductive health and violence against women to their communities. MADRE has also worked with indigenous women to bridge the gap between their work at the community level and the initiatives of the global women's movement that occur in the international arena. Through MADRE, indigenous women have pressed the women's movement to provide translation services, scholarships, child-care, and other measures to help offset the lack of income, family obligations, and work burdens that often hinder indigenous women's participation in the global women's movement.

When Flawed Assumptions Yield Flawed Strategies

Indigenous women's critiques of the mainstream women's movement center around the movement's tendency to stress the universality of women's oppression at the expense of recognizing differences in the forms and subjective experiences of that oppression. That tendency has produced conceptual approaches to violence and anti-violence strategies that fail to address the specific needs and realities of indigenous women. These include:

- Restricted conceptualizations of "domestic violence."
- An uncritical emphasis on separation from abusive partners.
- The privileging of criminalization strategies in anti-violence work.
- The notion that gender-based violence is rooted in "culture."

---

6 *Ibid.*, 56.

An Indigenous Critique of "Domestic Violence"

It has been widely recognized that "domestic violence" occurs in every country of the world and in every social sector. It is also well known that such violence increases when communities, families, and couples are subjected to poverty, armed conflict, or social upheaval. This correlation between gender-based violence and other human rights violations, such as poverty, puts indigenous women at particular risk for experiencing battering, rape, and other abuses by male partners and family members. For example, in Australia, indigenous women are 45 times more likely to endure violence within their families than are other Australians.[7] The alarming degree of violence among indigenous peoples in Australia is part of the legacy of racist subjugation, including the forced removal of tens of thousands of children from their families between 1900 and 1970 in order to "'breed out' aborigine blood" (the so-called "Stolen Generation").[8] Today, institutionalized racism is manifested mainly in governmental neglect, which denies aboriginal communities health education programs, meaningful employment, and decent living conditions. According to James Ensor, director of the Oxfam aid agency in Australia, "chronic under-funding of basic services that ordinary Australians take for granted, has contributed to this crisis."[9]

Like their counterparts in the mainstream women's movement, indigenous women anti-violence activists place a premium on safety and justice for survivors of violence. But their concern extends beyond the welfare of individual survivors. Indigenous women view gender-based violence, not only as an assault on individuals, but as a symptom of crisis within the broader collective of their people. This crisis stems largely from violations of collective indigenous rights. For indigenous men, these violations have meant the loss of territories, traditions, livelihoods, social networks, and other elements that support emotional health and a positive masculine identity. A 2006 FIMI report notes:

> Violations of collective rights have subjected indigenous men to armed conflicts, environmental destruction, displacement, migration, urbanization, racism, unemployment, and poverty; and have exposed indigenous men to drugs, alcohol, models of masculinity predicated on domination, and religious doctrines that sanction male violence.[10]

All these factors contribute to indigenous men's violence against indigenous women, rendering the term "domestic violence" both inadequate and ahistorical. Positing the

---

7 Neena Bhandari, "Australia: Ignoring Abuses of Aboriginal Women, Children" *Inter Press Service News Agency*, May 22, 2006, <http://ipsnews.net/news.asp?idnews=33317> (accessed September 13, 2006).

8 To view a digitized version of the Aborigines Act of 1905 <http://nla.gov.au/nla.aus-vn672744-2x>. For a summary of the law, its consequences, and subsequent actions taken to reverse the effects of the Aborigines Act of 1905, see <http://www.eniar.org/stolengenerations.html>.

9 Bhandari, *op. cit.*

10 International Indigenous Women's Forum (FIMI), "*Mairin Iwanka Raya*: Indigenous Women Stand against Violence: A Companion Report to the United Nations Secretary-General's Study on Violence against Women" (New York: FIMI, 2006).

collective as its referent, FIMI has offered the term *internalized violence* to describe the range of abuses perpetrated against indigenous women by indigenous men. That term underscores the need for anti-violence strategies that treat individual cases of abuse as problems of the collective and that address gender-based violence as part of the matrix of threats to indigenous communities.

Rose Cunningham is a Miskitu educator and anti-violence advocate who has worked with MADRE since its founding to develop strategies to combat gender-based violence. She is the director of Wangky Tangni ("Flower of the River" in Miskitu), a community development organization on Nicaragua's Atlantic Coast, which addresses violence against women in the context of the restoration of indigenous rights and of defending the human rights of both women and men in the community. Wangky Tangni offers women leadership development programs that address violence against women. The organization also promotes women's political participation and gender equity through sustainable development projects, human rights trainings, and health care programs that incorporate indigenous and Western perspectives on medicine. The organization's income-generating projects for women help reduce women's economic dependence on abusive partners, while discussion groups enable survivors of abuse to support one another.

Wangky Tangni recognizes that many indigenous women derive identity and power from their traditional roles as midwives, advisors, spiritual guides, and leaders who are principally responsible for transmitting knowledge, cultural values, and agricultural technology in their communities. Hence, Wangky Tangni works to preserve and develop these roles for women, thereby strengthening women's social status and confidence; this, in turn, fortifies women's capacity to confront gender-based violence. All of Wangky Tangni's programs—including a food security project and a women's income-generating program—serve simultaneously to promote women's human rights and the collective rights of the Miskitu people. Indeed, as Rose Cunningham says: "[W]hat would it mean in practice to separate the part of me that is a woman and demands freedom from violence from the part of me that is Miskitu and demands indigenous rights?"[11]

What It Means to Leave

Many advocates of battered women place a premium on women's capacity to end abusive relationships—clearly a necessary strategy in many cases. However, the mainstream feminist view of women who do not leave abusive relationships as helpless or pathological fails to recognize that, for indigenous women, separation may entail a different set of threats—including threats of violence—that non-indigenous women may not face.[12] For example, in a context where escaping an abusive partner requires an indigenous woman to relocate outside of her community, she may face a loss of cultural identity in a social context that amounts to forced assimilation, as well as discrimination and racist violence directed at her because

11 Rose Cunningham, interview by the author, March 2006.

12 Donna Coker, "Race, Poverty and the Crime-Centered Response to Domestic Violence," *Violence Against Women* 10, No. 11 (2004): 1331–53.

she is indigenous. At a 2004 MADRE anti-violence training with indigenous women in Chiapas, Mexico, one participant who did not wish to have her name published commented: "I stayed because the only other thing I could do was go north to the *maquilas*. I have heard of the killings of young girls on the border. I was too afraid to go there."[13]

Rebecca Lolosoli, a MADRE partner and indigenous Samburu woman from Kenya, developed a bold strategy to meet the needs of indigenous women forced to flee their communities because of gender-based violence: she founded an independent, women-run village for survivors. In 1990, Rebecca and 15 other women established Umoja, which means "unity" in Swahili. The women were survivors of rape by British soldiers stationed for training on the women's ancestral lands.[14] Because of the rapes, the women were ostracized by their husbands. Many of them were forced from their homes for having "shamed" their families. Under Lolosoli's leadership, the women joined together and appealed to the local District Council, which governs land use. They were granted a neglected field of dry grassland, where they have worked hard to create a unique and flourishing community. One of the women's first collective acts was to file a lawsuit against the British military for the rapes of over 1,400 Samburu women during the 1980s and 1990s.[15]

The Problem of Due Diligence and Alternatives to Criminalization Strategies

Through instruments such as the Convention on the Elimination of All Forms of Discrimination Against Women (CEDAW), the Beijing Platform for Action, and the outcome document of the Beijing Plus Five Review Process, the global women's movement has demanded that states criminalize and punish acts of violence against women. Yet, these same states continue to wage a concerted campaign of violence against indigenous women. Indeed, in some states, entire sectors of women, such as undocumented immigrants, are themselves criminalized by the state. In that context, the question arises: How can states be held accountable to uphold the human rights of these women?

The criminalization of domestic violence is a potentially effective strategy. Yet such strategies must be undertaken with critical regard for the physical and structural violence perpetrated by states themselves against indigenous and other women on the basis of group membership. For example, in the United States, mandatory arrest policies in domestic violence cases have increased state intervention in and control over the lives of indigenous women and their families (along with other women

---

13 Training participant, interview by Monica Aleman, MADRE Reproductive Rights and Community Mental Health Project, Chiapas, Mexico, March 2004.

14 "United Kingdom: Decades of Impunity: Serious Allegations of Rape of Kenyan Women by UK Army Personnel," *Amnesty International*, <http://web.amnesty.org/library/index/ENGEUR450142003> (accessed June 18, 2007).

15 The investigation eventually rejected the Kenyan women's claims, and the British army was absolved of all responsibility for the alleged rapes (Press Association, "British Military Inquiry Rejects Kenya Rape Claims," *The Guardian*, December 14, 2006).

of color, immigrants, and poor women).[16] These women and families are already disproportionately incarcerated and scrutinized by the US systems of child welfare, criminal justice, and immigration. Meanwhile, mandatory arrest policies have greatly increased the number of women arrested (most of them for acting in self-defense). Immigrant women—including many indigenous women who lack immigration documents—are threatened with deportation when arrested.[17]

The problem is not merely that indigenous women do not enjoy their right to equality before the law, but that laws are written and interpreted in ways that discriminate against and endanger them. In other words, for women who are under attack by the state, the laws themselves often become a source of violence against women. This dynamics is not adequately accounted for in the strategies to criminalize domestic violence. For example, in the United States, the mainstream of the battered women's movement has at times endorsed a right-wing tendency to address symptoms of social crisis (such as substance abuse and male battering) by enhancing the state's power to incarcerate and control. Donna Coker, Associate Dean and Professor of Law at the University of Miami, School of Law, writes: "It is no accident that the Violence Against Women Act, the most comprehensive piece of US domestic violence federal legislation ever enacted, was part of the 1994 crime bill."[18] The bill was an expression of the Clinton-era, a tough-on-crime trend that criminalized people on the basis of race and class.

Indigenous women have developed anti-violence initiatives that both enforce states' due diligence obligations towards women and defend women whom the state itself oppresses. These initiatives include efforts to complement criminalization strategies, such as restorative justice processes, and to establish alternatives to criminalization, such as political mobilizations. For example, in the US, the Navajo Peacemaking Court has ruled on domestic violence cases, while similar processes have been undertaken in Australia, Canada, and elsewhere. Proponents of restorative justice such as John Braithwaite, Professor in the Law Program, Research School of Social Sciences at Australian National University (ANU), and a member of ANU's Center for Restorative Justice, argue that offenders are more likely to be held accountable by such processes than by the criminal justice system.[19] This enhanced accountability stems from the fact that restorative justice often requires offenders to apologize publicly to survivors, agree to be monitored by family and friends, and provide material compensation to the survivor. Survivors, meanwhile, may benefit from mechanisms that enable them to mobilize family and friends in confronting their abuser and from building support networks that combat isolation and the degradation of families and communities, which commonly result from incarceration, and state surveillance and control. Currently, indigenous women are working to strengthen restorative justice processes by improving norms for due process and standards

---

16 Donna Coker, "Crime Control and Feminist Law Reform in Domestic Violence Law: A Critical Review," *Buffalo Criminal Law Review*, Vol. 4 (2001): 850–51.

17 *Ibid.*, 1334.

18 *Ibid.*, 1337.

19 See John Braithwaithe, *Crime, Shame and Reintegration* (Cambridge: Cambridge University Press, 1989).

based on gender equality. In essence, this is a project that entails bridging traditional judicial practices and international human rights standards.

Rose Cunningham's work offers a model of restorative justice that infuses traditional practices with the benefits of international human rights norms. As noted earlier, the organization that she runs, Wangky Tangni, is a community-based conflict mediation program that offers recourse to survivors of gender-based violence. For most of these women, the state's legal system is neither accessible (the Nicaraguan government does not provide translation services, and many indigenous women are not fluent in Spanish) nor accountable (facilities are located far from communities, and there are no reliable or affordable transportation or communication services). Working with MADRE, Wangky Tangni has conducted dozens of trainings in human rights for community members, combining traditional indigenous justice processes and international human rights instruments to defend women's right to a life free of violence.

Restorative justice processes are generally viewed as complementary to criminal proceedings. As such, they remain linked to states and the attendant problems of due diligence.[20] In many communities, political mobilization may be a better strategy than relying on the state as an effective arbiter or as a resource for social services that can help redress and reduce violence, such as health care, education, and affordable housing. Organizing efforts that empower survivors of violence to view themselves as activists demanding rights, rather than as victims awaiting social services, can work simultaneously to challenge violence perpetrated within the community and violence perpetrated by the state.

Like Rose Cunningham, Rebecca Lolosoli has worked with MADRE to bring human rights trainings to the women in Umoja, Kenya. She was active in MADRE's 2005 series of trainings for women in Umoja on preventing the spread of HIV/AIDS. The workshops situated HIV/AIDS prevention within a framework of advocating for women's human rights. Such trainings have fortified women's political mobilizations against gender-based violence by linking the right to a life free of violence with other imperatives, such as the need to combat HIV/AIDS. Referring to the Beijing Platform for Action, introduced to local women in one of these trainings, Lolosoli commented:

---

20 Due diligence is a measure of states' efforts and political will in fulfilling their commitments to human rights standards ("Respect, protect, fulfil [*sic*]—Women's human rights: State responsibility for abuses by 'non-state actors'," *Amnesty International*, <http://web.amnesty.org/library/Index/engIOR500012000> [accessed June 22, 2007]). The standard of due diligence requires states to prevent, investigate and punish internationally recognized human rights. As such, it places responsibility on governments to address human rights abuses even when the perpetrators are not state actors. For example, the UN Declaration on the Elimination of Violence against Women says that states should "exercise due diligence to prevent, investigate and, in accordance with national legislation, punish acts of violence against women, whether those acts are perpetrated by the state or by private persons" (DEVAW, December 20, 1993; <http://www.ohchr.org/english/law/eliminationvaw.htm>).

Now that we have seen it in writing—and seen that even our own Kenyan government has signed this—we know that we are not asking for pity or kindness but for our basic rights when we demand an end to our husbands' beatings.[21]

In 1999, when the women of Umoja participated in their first human rights training, none of them had ever spoken in public. Today, they are active participants in local government and are recognized as leaders in their district. The women of Umoja are currently organizing to demand that an anti-violence unit be added to the local police force and that trainings for women police officers be capacitated to address gender-based violence. These anti-violence strategies are part of the Umoja women's broader efforts to create a better life for themselves and their community—in other words, to defend the full range of their human rights. To that aim, the women have developed a system of resource sharing, a communal sickness/disability fund, and a modest, but successful, cooperative cottage industry selling traditional Samburu beadwork to tourists. In cooperation with MADRE and the Indigenous Information Network, the women work to defend Samburu rights to land, water, and health and education services. Through their political mobilizations, they have gained a measure of confidence and hopefulness that facilitates their work against gender-based violence and fuels their conviction that eradicating violence against women is indeed possible.

Like women everywhere, the women of Umoja see economic autonomy as a key to avoiding dependence on abusive men. Although they remain deeply impoverished by most people's standards, the women have succeeded in making sure that their daughters (as well as their sons) attend school. And they have freed themselves of the economic pressure to circumcise and marry off their daughters at a young age. In fact, Lolosoli's 12-year-old daughter, Sylvia, openly declares her refusal of circumcision and has every intention of going to university after high school.

Negotiating Tensions between Culture and Human Rights

While indigenous women conceive of women's human rights and collective rights as two parts of a coherent whole, conventional interpretations and applications of human rights often compartmentalize sets of rights, sometimes even setting them in opposition to one another. Since the 1990s, narrow conceptions of "cultural rights" have been used to justify violations of women's human rights, particularly rights pertaining to sexuality, reproduction, marriage, divorce, inheritance, education, physical abuse, and property. Proponents of cultural relativity designate abuses of women's rights in these areas as "cultural," and therefore beyond the legitimate reach of human rights reforms. Much of the global women's movement has railed against such interpretations, claiming the universality of human rights to mean that every woman is entitled to exercise the full range of her rights without exceptions based on culture, tradition, or religion. Indigenous women commonly share this understanding of the universality of rights but articulate positions outside of the relativist/universality dichotomy. Committed to defending both cultural rights and

---

21 Rebecca Lolosoli, interview by the author, March 2006.

women's human rights, indigenous women reject the underlying premise of both sides in this debate, namely, that women are the victims of culture.

Celestine I. Nyamu-Musembi, a fellow of the Institute of Development Studies at the University of Sussex, Sally Engle Merry, Marion Butler McLean Professor in the History of Ideas and Professor of Anthropology at Wellesley College and Professor of Anthropology and Law and Society at New York University, and others have pointed out that, while culture can be used as an excuse to violate human rights, it can also be used to promote rights, for example, by emphasizing the cultural values of fairness, egalitarianism, and the sanctity of human life that underpin both the human rights framework and many of the world's cultures.[22] This project positions human rights in dialogue with—not in opposition to—local cultures. Thus, indigenous women see the criminalization of rights violations (as enshrined, for example in Articles 2[f] and 5[a] of CEDAW, which require states to abolish customs and practices that violate women's human rights) as a necessary, but only partial, step in securing human rights. Building on CEDAW, indigenous women seek to find points of alignment between international human rights instruments and local values and practices that uphold women's rights. This approach promotes both gender equality and cultural identity as crucial bases for the full enjoyment of human rights and also enables women to utilize (rather than attempt to circumvent) culture in anti-violence strategies.

The anti-violence strategies that Lolosoli and Cunningham have developed with the women in their communities draw heavily on their own cultures as sources of resistance to violence. Both women share a critical conception of culture as a dynamic, versatile force that is shaped by people's choices, even as it is used to limit those choices. Lolosoli says:

> The men say that if we are against FGM (female genital mutilation) we are against our culture, but that is not true. We are not against our culture; only bad parts that hurt us [...]. FGM is part of our culture, but so is our music, which gives us strength and happiness.[23]

The women of Umoja use traditional Samburu group singing to greet visitors, mark holidays, and celebrate their collective achievements. By singing together, the women generate joy, express a range of emotions, and reinforce their relationships to one another. Each of these effects supports women's capacities to heal from gender-based violence and to continue the challenging work of maintaining Umoja as a women-run village dedicated to eradicating violence. Lolosoli notes: "Samburu women have always sung together. When we do this, we are powerful."[24]

---

22 Celestine Nyamu-Musembi, "How Should Human Rights and Development Respond to Cultural Legitimization of Gender Hierarchy in Developing Countries?" *Harvard International Law Journal* 41, No. 2 (2000): 381–418; Sally Engle Merry, "Changing Rights, Changing Culture," in *Culture and Rights: Anthropological Perspectives* (ed.), by Jane K. Cowan, Marie-Benedicte Dembour, and Richard A. Wilson (London: Cambridge University Press, 2001), 31–55. See, also, Carole Nagengast and Terrence Turner, "Introduction: Universal Human Rights versus Cultural Relativity," *Journal of Anthropological Research* 53 (1997): 269–72.

23 Lolosoli, *op. cit.*

24 *Ibid.*

Cunningham's anti-violence strategies draw even more directly from her indigenous culture. The Miskitu cosmology, like that of many indigenous peoples, posits an egalitarian duality between the masculine and feminine realms. In Miskitu tradition, women are revered and violence against them is considered deviant. This worldview offers a very different starting point for combating violence than worldviews in which religion or custom is used to sanction male violence. Cunningham notes: "For us, our traditional culture holds the seeds for condemning violence against women."[25] Colonization, Christianity, and assimilation have eroded egalitarian indigenous traditions, yet the latter continue to shape the identity and worldview of some indigenous peoples and to provide a foundation for indigenous anti-violence strategies.

This is evidenced in how Wangky Tangni organizes inter-generational community dialogues in which elders share traditional stories of women's power and reinforce an understanding of violence against women as inherently dysfunctional. Cunningham notes: "The dialogues help us to fight violence against women and to preserve our traditional stories and the role of our elders as transmitters of Miskitu culture and wisdom."[26] As in Umoja, Wangky Tangni's programs mobilize culture in opposition to gender-based violence, and thereby link strategies against violence with strategies to maintain indigenous identity and cultural rights.

Conclusion

Since it emerged onto the global stage at the World Conference on Human Rights in Vienna in 1993, the global women's movement has succeeded in shifting the traditional human rights framework by displacing the dichotomy between the private and public spheres. By insisting on the state's responsibility for rights violations committed by non-state actors, the women's movement has won important gains in fighting violence against women, particularly within the family. But the central demand of indigenous women goes even farther in extending the human rights paradigm, for theirs is more than a claim for inclusion within the existing framework. Rather, by linking women's human rights to collective rights, indigenous women call for a fundamental overhaul of the human rights framework, including its application by the global women's movement—for, both the mainstream human rights and women's movements posit the individual as the subject of rights.

This privileging of individual over collective rights, which is perpetuated, largely unnoticed, within the mainstream women's movement, is the primary reason that the movement has failed to meet the needs of the world's indigenous women, including their dire need for effective strategies against gender-based violence. As FIMI notes in its 2006 report:

> [T]he tendency towards exclusion within the global women's movement [...] results from mainstream feminists' failure to recognize and critique the intellectual foundations of

---

25 Cunningham, interview.
26 *Ibid.*

their politics and to see their assumptions as philosophical choices that select for certain political positions and exclude others.[27]

Indigenous women, including the leaders of MADRE's sister organizations in Nicaragua, Kenya, and elsewhere, stress the need for the global women's movement to adopt anti-violence strategies that reflect the realities of indigenous women's lives. These indigenous women call for recognition of the centrality of collective rights to defending the full range of indigenous women's human rights, including their right to a life free from violence.

Bibliography

Aleman, Monica. Interview by the author. June 18, 2007.

Amnesty International. "Respect, protect, fulfil [*sic*]—Women's human rights: State responsibility for abuses by 'non-state actors.'" *Amnesty International*. <http://web.amnesty.org/library/Index/engIOR500012000>.

—— "United Kingdom: Decades of Impunity: Serious Allegations of Rape of Kenyan Women by UK Army Personnel." *Amnesty International*. <http://web.amnesty.org/library/index/ENGEUR450142003>.

Bhandari, Neena. "Australia: Ignoring Abuses of Aboriginal Women, Children." *Inter Press Service News Agency*. May 22, 2006. <http://ipsnews.net/news.asp?idnews=33317>.

Braithwaithe, John. *Crime, Shame and Reintegration*. Cambridge: Cambridge University Press, 1989.

Coker, Donna. "Crime Control and Feminist Law Reform in Domestic Violence Law: A Critical Review." *Buffalo Criminal Law Review*. Vol. 4 (2001): 850–51.

—— "Race, Poverty and the Crime-Centered Response to Domestic Violence." *Violence Against Women* 10, No. 11 (2004): 1331–53.

Crenshaw, Kimberley. "Mapping the Margins: Intersectionality, Identity Politics, and Violence against Women of Color." *Stanford Law Review* 43, No. 6 (July 1991): 1241–99.

Cunningham, Myrna. "Indigenous Women's Visions of an Inclusive Feminism." *Development* 49, No. 1 (2006): 55–9.

Cunningham, Rose. Interview by the author. March 2006.

Dennis, Philip A. *The Miskitu People of Awastara*. Austin: University of Texas Press, 2004.

European Network for Indigenous Australian Rights. "The Stolen Generations." <http://www.eniar.org/stolengenerations.html>.

International Indigenous Women's Forum (FIMI). "*Mairin Iwanka Raya*: Indigenous Women Stand against Violence: A Companion Report to the United Nations Secretary-General's Study on Violence against Women." New York: FIMI, 2006.

Lolosoli, Rebecca. Interview by the author. March 2006.

---

27 International Indigenous Women's Forum, *op. cit.*, 15.

Merry, Sally Engle. "Changing Rights, Changing Culture." In *Culture and Rights: Anthropological Perspectives*. Edited by Jane K. Cowan, Marie-Benedicte Dembour, and Richard A. Wilson. 31–55. London: Cambridge University Press, 2001.

Nagengast, Carole, and Terrence Turner. "Introduction: Universal Human Rights versus Cultural Relativity." *Journal of Anthropological Research*, No. 53 (1997): 269–72.

Nguko, Margaret. Interview by the author. Archer's Post. Kenya. 2005.

Nyamu-Musembi, Celestine. "How Should Human Rights and Development Respond to Cultural Legitimization of Gender Hierarchy in Developing Countries?" *Harvard International Law Journal* 41, No. 2 (2000): 381–418.

Press Association. "British Military Inquiry Rejects Kenya Rape Claims." *The Guardian*. December 14, 2006.

The National Library of Australia. "The Acts of Parliament of Western Australia: The Aborigines Act of 1905." <http://nla.gov.au/nla.aus-vn672744-2x>.

Training participant. Interview by Monica Aleman. MADRE Reproductive Rights and Community Mental Health Project, Chiapas, Mexico. March 2004.

Chapter 2

Going Beyond the Universal-versus-Relativist Rights Discourse and Practice: The Case of Malaysia

Sharon A. Bong

Introduction

As a women's rights activist and Christian feminist, how would I begin to respond to women and men who are conditioned to believe that inequitable, and often violent, gender relationships are a way of life that God intended? To what extent are cultures and religions sources of affirmation of the rights of women as much as they are impediments? Having been involved in the women's movement in Malaysia with regional and international exposure since the 1990s, I was convinced that one had to look towards religion to advance women's rights in the context of Malaysia, where life decisions are significantly impacted not only by religious teachings but also by cultural practices. In this chapter, I attempt to show how and why it is imperative to negotiate the tensions between rights and religions in global and local contexts. From the standpoint of the faith-rights-based activists I interviewed—those whose activism is informed by a rights framework and imbued with a spiritual ethos—I argue that foreclosing the universal-versus-relativist debate in gender studies as a deadlock is an act of epistemological violence.

It is vital to revisit the universal-versus-relativist impasse[1] and acknowledge that rights and religions matter because there is a need to live out the tensions of universality and relativism and secularity and religiosity (faith perspective) if one is committed to contextualizing women's rights in material, temporal, and spatial particularities. Contrary to this living out of the tension of rights and religions is a political or religious fundamentalist position: one that is essentially intolerant of the fluidity of hyphenating knowledge and practices that are oppositional, or of acknowledging the cross-currents inherent in these discourses. Working out

---

1 A universal-versus-relativist impasse is the contestation between the ascendancy of universalism (that is, values such as human rights that are deemed applicable to all and at all times) and the ascendancy of cultural relativism (that is, values such as human rights are not deemed applicable to all and at all times). One redresses this deadlock by "complicating rights talk with religion." I borrow this phrase from Martin Marty ("Religious Dimension of Human Rights," in *Religious Human Rights in Global Perspective: Religious Perspectives* (ed.), by John Witte and Johan D. van der Vyver [The Hague; Boston; London: Martinus Nijhoff Publishers, 1996], 6).

these hyphens of universality–relativism and secularity–religiosity is unsettling because one does not quite arrive at closures (an either/or positioning), but straddles "both-and" options of knowing and doing women's rights as universalized *and* particularized. Positioning rights as both universal and particularized, however, disrupts epistemological violence, and, hence, by breaking down this impasse, offers a paradoxical breakthrough. I show this through textual analysis of data generated through in-depth interviews with 27 faith-rights-based activists in Malaysia.

These boundary crossings are symbolized through the inter-connectedness of the intimate and the extimate.[2] The intimate as the subject is the hegemonic positioning of women's rights as universal and by extension, secular. The impulse to secularize the rhetoric and practice of women's rights stems in part from most activists' disenchantment with religion—particularly, with the abuse of religion in rights discourse that they often witness. The "vertigo of secularization" is an indefatigable refusal to complicate, convolute, and contaminate rights talk with religion.[3] As such, the intimate is positioned as antithetical to the extimate: that which we relegate as alien or disembodied from the subject. The extimate finds its parallel in disavowing the particularization of rights within multi-ethnic, multi-cultural, and multi-religious local spaces in bringing global conventions home.

By inference, to recognize that the subject is paradoxically constituted by disavowing *and* desiring the extimate is to contend that rights are culturally and religiously contingent. To do so is to hold in abeyance the safeguard of an either/or approach that privileges either the "*fundamentalism* of rights"[4] or religious fundamentalism, and by extension, cultural relativism, I show this through the selected narratives of faith-rights-based activists: those who work within a rights framework that is imbued with a spiritual ethos for social justice. Through these embodied experiences of knowing and doing women's rights, faith-rights-based activists show how women's rights are operationalized in local contexts by demystifying texts that are both secular (women's rights conventions) and religious (in particular the Qur'an and the Bible). These women inhabit this liminal space for negotiating the hyphens of universality–particularity (or relativism) and secularity–religiosity. They embody what it means to live out these tensions in their vocational and personal lives, and show the implications and costs of not negotiating these hyphens.

This exploration outlines the discussion through the following paradigms: 1) the intimate: the global vision of women's rights that is universalized and secularized; and 2) the extimate: the local practice of women's rights that reconstitutes cultural relativism as particularizing women's rights in order to ground it in local contexts. The local vision that potentially impacts the global practice of women's rights

---

2 Joan Copjec, "Vampires, Breast-feeding, and Anxiety," in *The Horror Reader* (ed.), by Ken Gelder (London and New York: Routledge, 2000), 59.

3 Maria Pia Lara, "In and Out of Terror: The Vertigo of Secularization," *Hypatia* 18, No. 1 (2003): 184–5.

4 Marek Piechowiak, "What Are Human Rights? The Concept of Human Rights and Their Extra-Legal Justification," in *An Introduction to the International Protection of Human Rights* (ed.), by Raija Hanski and Markku Suksi (Turko/Abo: Institute for Human Rights, Abo Akademi University, 1999), 11.

suggests possibilities of moving forward beyond the deadlock of the universal-versus-relativist debate. In doing so, Malaysian faith-rights-based activists deconstruct competing claims of ascendancy arising from the "truth" of religious texts versus the "universality" of rights discourses. The return to texts and treatises is fundamental in demystifying the underlying causes of gender-based violence.

Method and Methodology

This chapter is premised on the provisional link between the categories of rights and religion within the context of faith-rights-based activism in Malaysia. In grounded theory methodology, this constitutes a "hypothesis." Employing a grounded theory methodology that is inductive, my theory is built from data. The latter is generated by in-depth, semi-structured, and audio-recorded interviews with 27 faith-rights-based activists in Malaysia, two of whom are men; the interviews were conducted from July to December 2000. The criteria for sampling or selection of interviewees is heterogeneous in terms of their multi-religious, multi-cultural, and multi-ethnic backgrounds[5] yet homogenous in terms of their being activists (or doers) engaged in the practice of women's rights.

All interviewees are Malaysian citizens. The basis of my sampling similarly approximates (if not fully represents) a cross-section of this heterogeneity that is the hallmark of being Malaysian. The proliferation of identity markers in relation to ethnicity (understood as synonymous with cultures in the context of Malaysia) and religions among the 27 interviewees are: Malay-Muslim (seven), Indian-Christian (or Protestant) (seven), indigenous-Catholic (three), other (Eurasian)-Catholic (two), and one interviewee each as Chinese-Muslim, Chinese-Buddhist, Chinese-Catholic, Chinese-non-believer, Malay-Indian-Muslim, Indian-Hindu, Chinese-Indian-Catholic and other-Muslim. They have hands-on experience in serving disenfranchised communities, such as survivors of gender-based violence through counseling services, advocacy campaigns for policy change, law reforms, action-based research, and consciousness-raising workshops.

The 27 interviewees were asked: a) to give an account of how their faith-right-based activism began; b) to consider the cultural and religious factors impacting their activism; and c) to assess the link (if any) between their faith and their political activism. Their responses to those questions are the bases upon which I have accorded epistemic privilege to these gatekeepers of local knowledge, who know and do rights. The theory that I have generated from the data provided by them culminates in the thesis of *critical relativism*, which I theorize as a reconstruction

---

5 According to the most recent Population Census, the ethnic composition of Malaysian citizens of the total of 23 million is: 65 percent Malay, 26 percent Chinese, and 7 percent Indian. In Malaysia, ethnicity is highly correlated with religion as all Malays are Muslims. Muslims account for 65 percent of the population followed by Buddhists (19 percent), Christians (9 percent), Hindus (6 percent), traditional Chinese religions including Taoism and Confucianism (2 percent), and indigenous spiritualities. See, *Population Distribution and Basic Demographic Characteristics Report: Population and Housing Census 2000*. Putrajaya, November 6, 2001. <http://www.statistics.gov.my/English/page2.html> (accessed March 30, 2007).

of cultural relativism that advances, and not impedes, women's rights. Through the local practice of women's rights, faith-rights-based activists in Malaysia show the ways in which the demystification of secular treatises and religious texts identifies and dis-identifies with the global vision of women's rights.

As the integration of women's rights into Malaysian cultures and religions is a sensitive topic, ensuring the privacy and confidentiality of interviewees has been deemed paramount (that is, identifiable particulars will not be disclosed). In compliance with human ethics, interviewees were invited to choose pseudonyms for themselves. In this chapter (which is part of a larger project),[6] I have quoted extracts from interview transcripts of "Inai Init," "AA," "Ash," "Rais," "Jothy," "Ayesha," and "Mariah." As a feminist researcher, it is important to approximate collaborative theorizing with interviewees as many of them are my peers. Such self-reflexivity precipitates active listening to their voices in the text (interview transcript) and in the interpretation of data or data analysis (else this might constitute an epistemological violence in forcing data to fit theory).

I am the sole interpreter of the data generated from these interviews. Data analyses was facilitated by ATLAS.ti (version 4.2), a Computer-Assisted Qualitative Data Analysis Software (CAQDAS) through coding. In this chapter, the theory generated shows how the research draws from the sound principles and practice of grounded theory methodology to satisfy the criteria of expert quality qualitative researching, which grounds the validity of the data, reliability of the methodology, and generalizability of analyses.[7]

The Intimate: A Global Vision of Women's Rights

The global vision of women's rights is revolutionary in its insistence on the principles of universality and indivisibility. The fruits of labor of the global women's movement punctuate the trajectory of human rights with the assertion that "women's rights are human rights." As affirmed in the *Beijing Declaration and the Platform for Action* (PFA) of the 1995 Fourth UN World Conference on Women, "the human rights of women and of the girl child are an inalienable, integral and indivisible part of universal human rights."[8]

Women's rights as indivisible rights pertain to the recognition that first- and second-generation rights—civil and political as well as economic, social and cultural rights—are interdependent. Women can only be empowered if they have full and equal access to these fundamental liberties and freedoms, which are inalienable to

---

6 See, Sharon A. Bong, *The Tension between Women's Rights and Religions: The Case of Malaysia* (Lewiston, Queenston, Lampeter: The Edwin Mellen Press, 2006).

7 Generalizability of analyses refers to the extent to which one's research findings, based on a relatively small sample, has the potential to resonate with the lived experiences of a larger group. This is possible in qualitative researching when the researcher is able to account for validity of data (that is, procured through ethics in researching) and reliability of method (that is, in-depth interviewing). See Jennifer Mason, *Qualitative Researching* (London: Sage, 1996).

8 United Nations, *The Beijing Declaration and the Platform for Action: Fourth World Conference on Women* (New York: UN Department of Public Information, 1996), 17.

women by virtue of their inherent dignity and value as human persons. These are not privileges that are to be arbitrarily dispensed to them. The correlation of first/second-generation rights by global feminisms is, thus, reflected in the 12 critical areas of concern outlined in 1995 Beijing PFA.[9] The consideration of "third-generation rights" or the collective rights of economically, socially, and culturally disenfranchised groups, enhances the inclusiveness of the PFA as a global consensual document. For instance, the five-year review and subsequent ten-year review of the 1995 Beijing conference (Beijing +5, +10) deliberate on the rights pertaining to marginalized populaces, such as disabilities, refugees and migrants, sexual orientation, indigenous rights, women and aging, and young women.[10]

In addition, the positioning of women's rights as indivisible foregrounds endemic and systemic discrimination, as well as gender-based violence perpetrated by state and non-state actors against women in both public and private spaces. The hallmark of the global women's movement is, thus, its commitment to minimizing the disparity between the rhetoric and reality of women's rights as experienced by women particularly at the grassroots (the latter should not be understood as a monolithic category).[11] Hence, to politicize women's rights is to strive for a substantive "gender justice," which is the sum of "gender equality" and "gender equity."[12] Women, in principle, are accorded the right to political participation, legal redress, economic and social resources, and personal development. But in practice, women's realization of these rights, as stated in the PFA, is curtailed by "their race, age, language, ethnicity, culture, religion, or disability, or because they are indigenous people[s]," which may deny women their full humanity and partnership with men in gender equitable relations.[13]

Re-aligning the imbalance of gender inequalities and inequities is considerably aided by gender-disaggregated data, which affirm the disproportionate and different impacts of development policies on women and the ranking of nation-states, not only through a human development index (HDI) but also through a gender development index (GDI).[14] The indivisibility of women's rights as such radicalizes

---

9 UN, *op. cit.*

10 IWTC, *Preview 2000: February* (New York: International Women's Tribune Centre, 1999), 9.

11 By "grassroots," I mean communities who are politically, economically and socially disenfranchised, such as survivors of gender-based violence, plantation workers, persons living with HIV/AIDS, migrant workers, sex workers, and indigenous persons.

12 HERA, "'A Call to Action'—Confounding the Critics: Cairo Five Years On," Cocoyoc, Morelos, Mexico, November 15–18, 1998.

13 UN, 1996, *op. cit.*, 10.

14 The HDI provides three indicators of human development that comprise life expectancy; education attainment, including literacy; and standard of living measured by income. The GDI adjusts the HDI from a gendered lens in recognition that these indicators of the good life are tempered by gender inequities. The GDI inadvertently down-sizes the HDI. According to the United Nations Development Programme's *Human Development Report 2006*, Malaysia's GDI value in 2006 was 0.795 and the country's HDI value in the same year was 0.805. <http://hdr.undp.org/hdr2006/statistics/countries/country_fact_sheets/cty_fs_MYS.html> (accessed October 1, 2007).

the conceptualization of rights and development: there can be no human rights without women's rights, as there can be no human development without women's development. Hence, women's rights as asserted in the PFA are "fundamental for the achievement of equality, development and peace."[15]

Women's rights are universal in that they are applicable to all and are equally applicable to all—this is not contested. It is the hegemonic positioning of women's rights as universal, and by extension, *secular* that is contestable. The premise of the "universal-versus-relativist" debate underscoring women's rights is essentially the competing claims of ascendancy, wherein the "'*fundamentalism*' of human rights [*sic!*]" that is inherently secular, and hence universal,[16] is pitted against religious fundamentalism which is "secularization-resistant," and hence transcendent.[17] On the one hand, religious fundamentalism is broadly defined as "a given faith [that is] upheld firmly in its full and literal form, free of compromise, softening, re-interpretation or diminution [...] [it] repudiates [any] kind of watering down of the religious claims."[18] On the other hand, the assertion that fundamental human rights principles, by virtue of their entry into international law, have become "hegemonic and therefore universal by fiat [thus overriding relativist arguments]" is no less problematic.[19] An impasse ensues: How does one begin to disrupt the epistemological violence that ensues in the battle for ascendancy between religious fundamentalism and the fundamentalism of rights?

In considering the merits of grounding globally ratified documents, such as the Platform for Action and CEDAW, in local contexts, it is worthwhile to pause and reflect on what they contain with respect to the question of women's rights, cultures, and religions. Firstly, cultures and religions are not vilified within the secularist framework of women's rights. Article 5 of CEDAW qualifies that it is only discriminatory aspects of cultures and religions "based on the idea of the inferiority or the superiority of either of the sexes or on stereotyped roles for men and women" that should be modified by state parties.[20] Rather, it is also that global feminisms are expressly intolerant of "cultural relativism"—that cultural or religious grounds are "morally equal or valid" because proponents of cultural relativism often deploy it as a justification for human rights abuses, particularly against women.[21]

Secondly, the PFA states that the "right to freedom of thought, conscience and religion is inalienable and must be universally enjoyed [...] [in] order to realize equality, development and peace, there is a need to respect these rights and freedoms fully."[22] The draftswomen of this blueprint for women's rights thus not only assert

---

15 UN, 1996, *op. cit.*, 8.

16 Piechowiak, *op. cit.*, 11.

17 Ernest Gellner, *Postmodernism, Reason and Religion* (London and New York: Routledge, 1992), 6.

18 *Ibid.*, 2–4.

19 Jerome Shestack, "The Philosophical Foundations of Human Rights," in *Human Rights: Concepts and Standards* (ed.), by Janusz Symonides (Aldershot: Ashgate, 2000), 60.

20 Center for the Study of Human Rights, *Women and Human Rights: The Basic Documents* (New York: Center for the Study of Human Rights, Columbia University), 1996, 61.

21 Shestack, *op. cit.*, 56.

22 UN, 1996, *op. cit.*, 25.

that women's rights are universal (inalienable, integral, and indivisible), but they also affirm the integrity of diverse cultures and religions. It is from this overlaying of discourses that I discern that, firstly, universality is not necessarily synonymous with secularity, and secondly, that secularity is not necessarily antithetical to religiosity. My exploration further posits these questions: who decides this and for whom within the highly contested arena of women's rights? It seems that some are more equal than others in this non-level playing field.

In addition, when complicating rights talk with religion becomes too problematic, the universality and secularity of women's rights take precedence. Thus the PFA adds that "it is acknowledged that any form of extremism [such as religious fundamentalism] may have a negative impact on women and can lead to violence and discrimination."[23] In light of well-documented, gender-based discrimination and violence, the Platform recommends that:

> [while] the significance of national and regional particularities and various historical, cultural and religious backgrounds must be borne in mind, it is the duty of States, regardless of their political, economic and cultural systems, to promote and protect all human rights and fundamental freedoms.[24]

The primacy of the universal and secular are thus privileged over and above the particular and contextual.

To recapitulate, the trajectory of women's rights as a global re-visioning of human rights hyphenates certain categories to symbolize their distinctiveness yet inter-connectedness. Those categories include first- and second-generation rights (civil and political as well as economic, social, and cultural rights); and more problematically, the universality–relativity of rights discourse and practice. The conundrum of the universal-versus-relativist impasse poses the following "local" question: in what ways does the local practice of women's rights in a Malaysian context identify and dis-identify with this global vision of women's rights through the demystification of secular treatises and religious texts?

The Extimate: Local Practices in Women's Rights

Spiritualizing Rights

The local practice of women's rights is revolutionary in its insistence on the principles of universality and indivisibility, not only from a gendered lens, but also from a postcolonial one through spiritualizing rights and politicizing religion.[25] The pragmatic tension between universality and cultural relativism in terms of a committed and effective translation of women's rights in local contexts is inherent in global treaties on women's rights, such as the 1995 Beijing PFA, the 1994 Cairo

---

23 *Ibid.*

24 UN, 1996, *op. cit.*, 21–2.

25 The allusion here is to the Asian values debate that legitimizes cultural specificity within the milieu of multiculturalism and multi-religiosity of Malaysia.

Programme of Action, and the 1979 Convention on the Elimination of all Forms of Discrimination Against Women (CEDAW). The Platform for Action, for instance, reaffirms the "universality, objectivity and non-selectivity" of women's rights and asserts that "the universal nature of these rights and freedoms is beyond question."[26] Its persuasive rhetoric is also cognizant of the contingencies of "national and regional particularities," particularly state sovereignty which may impinge upon the implementation of the PFA.

Non-Western readings of these texts partly distance the practice of women's rights from its rhetoric. Taking into account the discrepancy between the Western rhetoric and the non-Western practice of rights that threatens the seamless hegemony of the interpretation of rights, effects, "a process of displacement that, paradoxically, makes the presence of the book wondrous to the extent to which it is repeated, translated, misread, displaced."[27] "Inai Init," an indigenous person from East Malaysia who works with her community on land rights and the right to self-determination, brings the point home by asserting the necessity of situating rights from the standpoint of indigenous spiritualities and traditions. She notes:

> [At] the beginning I remember we used to [...] base our discussions on the human rights declaration, where everyone should have the right to shelter, right to life, and when you talk about justice [...] fairness and democracy, people did not understand [...] [but] when I started to talk to people about their culture, people's *adat* (tradition), people's belief [...] [they] understood me. And it was closer to our heart, it was easier to understand and identify [with] [...]. So I realized then that [...] to reach people, it must touch them. (Interview transcript, 25)

The local translation of internationally endorsed covenants evinces a textual multi-layering which facilitates a basic understanding of covenantal concepts and precepts. Multiple and indigenous narratives are then interwoven with global conventions to make sense of and to add to the vocabulary of international human rights conventions what is considered "right conduct" and "right thought." Subsequent critical readings reflect a heightened awareness of the extent of the validity and applicability of global conventions—especially as to whether or not translations (that is, interpretations) of texts speak to the hearts of the people. This process as described by "Inai Init" is iterative: covenantal rights become intelligible and acceptable to some degree when read against the canon or oral weight of tradition and belief. These are, in turn, measured against the comparative value of a universalized doctrine.

The applicability of women's rights documents is even more problematically challenged in relation to the practice of polygamy in the context of Malaysia. According to "AA," a Muslim feminist who works with survivors of gender-based violence in Islamic culture, the campaign against sexual harassment draws on "a human rights language" that entails "the concept of discrimination, equal opportunities" (interview transcript, 10). In contrast, the interpretive authority of Sha'riah laws on the marriage contract that governs Muslim women has to be sensitively and

---

26 UN, 1996, *op. cit.*, 121.

27 Homi Bhabha, *The Location of Culture* (London and New York: Routledge, 1994), 102.

strategically approached as this may constitute a potentially transgressive act (in interweaving rights into the practice of one's faith), as "AA" notes:

> [In] the context of polygamy [...] I would not use the Women's Convention. I would actually use a *Qur'anic* verse. But I would use [the Convention] if I were talking [...] to a non-Muslim about law reforms, civil rights where for this particular example, it's more equal OK, where a [non-Muslim] person can only marry once [...]. You have equal rights to form partnerships. But it's different for the Muslim woman [...] it doesn't matter if there is a Women's Convention on that [...] what they have to grapple with is their faith. (Interview transcript, 10)

In effect, it is not only the applicability, but the universality, of rights that is tested and challenged in multi-racial, multi-cultural, and multi-religious sites. As illustrated by "AA," consciousness-raising by activists of communities with which they work, sustained by covenantal rights, potentially displaces interpretation of religious texts through each repetition, translation, and non-reading (by those who privilege religious texts over and above rights treatises). The failure to bridge the universalization and particularization of women's rights can be avoided through an innovative use of international conventions to complement, but not override, tradition and belief. "AA"'s ways of knowing and doing rights as universalized and particularized disrupts the epistemological violence of not doing so.

As such, a "colonial text" (such as the Bible and rights treatises in Malaysian context) "can neither be 'original'—by virtue of the act of repetition that constructs it—nor 'identical'—by virtue of the difference that defines it."[28] Women's rights conventions eschew the position of the "colonial text" and facilitate fluidity and plurality of meanings, as the text's applicability is impinged and made relevant by the living cultures of the Other or extimate. Another interviewee, "Ash," a Muslim feminist in Malaysia who is involved in women's reproductive health and rights, asserts:

> Some people argue that maybe when you want to take the documents forward, this rights perspective, that you must never bring in the religion on board [...] that you should [...] leave the religion aside. I don't know in reality, [...] whether that is possible." (Interview transcript, 21)

From the extract above, the secularity of rights enshrined in UN conventions is challenged paradoxically to concretize secularism in the grassroots work by bringing global human rights conventions home. Secularism is relativized through interweaving rights and religions, to effect a translation of rights within cultural and religious frameworks. In light of that logic, "Ash" adds:

---

28 *Ibid.*, 107. Malaya, as Malaysia was known in its early history, was colonized by the Portuguese (1511–1641), the Dutch (1641–1874), and the British (1874–1957). It achieved independence in 1957. The "colonial text" refers not only to the Bible, which many Malaysians still regard as a Western import, but also to global treatises on human rights and women's rights that are perceived as "Western" hegemonic discourses.

> The spirit of the document, what is spelt out is indeed very relevant [...] the challenge is how to operationalize these documents into something that will be relevant to the people [...]. At the end of the day [...] it's not important that [people at the grassroots] know this is Beijing or Cairo. [...] In fact you have to make so that these issues are local issues not [laughs] Cairo's issues or Beijing's issues, not issues of women who are fighting at international level but it is issues of daily lives as relevant as eating rice [both laugh]. That to me is the challenge. (Interview transcript, 21)

In being read, deciphered, translated, and interpreted in different contexts by various factions, texts such as the Beijing Platform for Action and the Cairo Programme of Action are subject to displacement as blueprints for the global advancement of women's rights. Consuming these ethical tracts by integrating them into one's own life is tantamount to "eating"—an apt metaphor for internalizing the flavor of the values of rights treatises which may or may not complement traditional platters and cultivated palates. "Ash" observes that "the right to eat may be universal [...] [but] what you eat is not [...] [it's] going to be contextualized" (Interview transcript, 21), thus arguing for the particularization of rights in local contexts. Operationalizing texts (in implementing rights) that are rendered "colonial" by virtue of their hegemonic logic of universality is thus a transgression because it goes against the grain of Western feminists' positioning of rights as universalized without regard for cultural specificities. This is so because one has the temerity—amid international and civilizational pressure to conform—to pause to weigh the legitimacy and relevance of global conventions when transported for local consumption.

Thus, the actualization of internationally ratified conventions paradoxically entails their displacement. To decipher, translate, and mainstream their central tenets into state policies and enabling legislation is to particularize the universal. The interviewed activists consider both the concrete application as well as the fluid interpretation of internationally ratified conventions as impacted by the contingencies of cultures and religions. Re-writing the center (that is, dominant positing of rights as universal and secular) through a hermeneutical engagement is a corollary of negotiating rights within cultural and religious frameworks. "Rais" who works on sexuality rights, thus asserts:

> In terms of religion, it is very difficult [...]. For a long time I thought the Bible was actually silent about women who loved other women. But, in fact, it's not; [it's there] in Romans Chapter One, verse 24, and for a long time I used to say, "Oh well, they're talking about men and not talking about women you know." We could just proceed but of course you can't do that [...]. Whatever opinions people have about male homosexual relations, it's doubly intensified when they come to analyzing women because, of course, women are not considered as equals of men in the first place. (Interview transcript, 20)

Redressing state prosecution and the societal persecution of disinherited bodies by virtue of their alternative sexual orientations calls for a de-privileging of one text (that is, rights treatises and religious texts) over and above another. Grounding sexual rights in this instance entails deciphering, translating, and interpreting the Bible in tandem with international conventions as secularized covenants. The latter, in the form of the Beijing PFA, affirms the bodily integrity of all women in having control over their reproductive and sexuality health and rights, "free of coercion, discrimination and violence."[29] Such re-interpretation invites questions such as: How does one reconcile a religious sanction of heterosexuality (even hetero-sexism) with covenantal rights that affirm one's sexual autonomy and responsibility, health, and pleasure? And is there a need to do so? Or is it more politically expedient (or perhaps viable) to gloss over or exploit slippages on lesbianism, such as the absence of overt religious injunctions, as initially perceived by Rais? To what extent would these readings of religious texts demystify the institutionalized discrimination of sexually marginalized communities?

The spiritual grounding of secularized texts avoids "the violence of abstraction" or epistemological violence.[30] This means that texts are no longer alienated from lived realities of communities that are impinged by cultural and religious prescriptions. "Jothy," a feminist member of a Christian religious order, explains that gender-based violence is "symptomatic of a much deeper ailment of the male–female relationships within the domestic sphere," and needs to be dealt with as a "spiritual, theological issue, not just as a social one" (Interview transcript, 16). There are lessons to be learned from conducting consciousness-raising workshops that reach out to the Tamil-speaking Christian women in Malaysia, women who are triply marginalized due to their status as ethnic minorities, oppressive socio-economic position (often accompanied by illiteracy), and gendered identity within the nations.[31] Speaking about her work with Tamil Christian women, "Jothy" states:

> We begin to look at the social issues which these Indian women are unaware of and present it to them in Tamil […] because [previous work done] has been very much middle class […]. It's always been in English. And we feel that we ought to bring it to them in the context of the Bible and what Jesus is doing and then see their own lives and what they can do. (Interview transcript, 16)

Jothy, in eschewing the epistemic and hermeneutical "violence of abstraction" makes the translations of texts accessible to women's grassroots movements and situates the knowledge of those who inhabit and negotiate their bodies and sexualities within the intersection of gender, race, caste, class, cultures and religions. On the one hand, "Jothy's" exhortation to these Christian women, that they should "claim their right, claim their inheritance to speak again about [domestic] violence, to resist it and to stand up for their rights, to the money that is earned," draws from Biblical and human rights imperatives of upholding the dignity of women. On the other hand, the mediators of this knowledge and translators of text and experience—the NGO activists—hold themselves accountable for the imposition of their middle class values and (Western-informed) feminist readings onto women at the grassroots. For, those who know and do rights as faith-rights-based activists coming mostly from middle-class background are humbled when women at the grassroots sometimes

---

29 UN, 1996, *op. cit.*, 59.

30 Chung Hyun Kyung, *Struggle to Be the Sun Again: Introducing Asian Women's Theology* (Maryknoll: Orbis Books, 1990), 101.

31 Tamil women are of Indian ethnicity and they may be Muslim, Christian, Hindu, or Buddhist. Cumulatively, they are considered a minority group in the context of Malaysia.

respond: "[We're] not beaten. We're not treated badly. So why do you have to bring all this [consciousness-raising] up?" (Interview transcript, 16).

Politicizing Religion

A corollary to the spiritual grounding of rights treatises is the politicization of religious texts. The PFA promotes the "girl-child's awareness of and participation in social, economic and political life" and ensures women's equal access to and full participation in power structures and decision-making and leadership.[32] According to "Jothy," the PFA tenet quoted above has its parallel in the scriptural basis of a priestly vocation. Jothy thus asserts:

> That's why I see this issue of ordination as a political issue of addressing power, control and authority. And the need to define it I think in a more genuine and truthful way is to see how Scriptures see "calling," a religious calling […] this whole question of thrones that are lifted up is a peculiarly Christian thing. And it's important for women because it deliberately excludes them, reduces them to base level […]. It's all right to have thrones but when women are prohibited from entering those spaces and it's God's space after all […] it's a space of power. (Interview transcript, 20)

"Jothy's" theologizing conflates political space and "God's space" as essentially "[spaces] of power" (Interview transcript, 20). In doing so, Jothy realigns the boundaries of exclusion/inclusion with regard to women's ordination to the priesthood. She re-constitutes one's vocational "calling" premised on a scriptural affirmation of the inherent worth of women (and men) as created in God's image. Thereby she strategically validates and potentially authorizes women's access to "power, control and authority" within public/private and secular/sacred realms. "Jothy" contends that this is a more "genuine and truthful way [of seeing]" (Interview transcript, 20). Her views reveal the contingency of scriptural interpretations on the reading, translation, and practice of human rights discourses.

Therefore faith-rights-based activists show that it is not despite of, but because of, the complexity and proliferation of meanings evinced from the translation of religious texts that religious texts may be posited as invaluable resources for feminist theorizing and practice. Thus, faith-rights-based activists work towards knowing that is contextualized with the cognizance that they do not permanently arrive at closures of thoughts and expressions. This is also why they insist on disruptions that challenge the biased interpretations of the Qu'ran. Ayesha, a Muslim feminist in Malaysia, testifies:

> [W]hen we decided to go back to the source of the religion, to the text of the religion, we were really surprised to find that this is not what the religion teaches […] [And that] it was for us all […] a very liberating and spiritually uplifting experience to actually read the *Qur'an* and find out how the *Qur'an* insistently talks about justice, about equality, about compassion. (Interview transcript, 8)

---

32 UN, 1996, *op. cit.*, 109–15, 154–5.

In her statement, "Ayesha" refutes Islamic cultural biases suggesting that women's value is half that of men, that women are inferior to men and that women must be obedient to men according to divine sanctions. Her conviction is premised on interpretations of the Qur'anic verses that liken the relationship between men and women to that of "each other's garments" (2:187), the lines which emphasize their reciprocity as "members of one another" (3:195) and "protectors, one of another" (9:71) and which affirm that love and mercy are the foundations of male/female relationships (30:21).[33]

That return to the source of knowledge deemed as the "truth" in conservative interpretations of the Qur'anic text dissuades alternative interpretations of "truth" which can be detected in internationally ratified conventions on women's rights. There are women who are privileged to be able to read the Qur'an from a feminist perspective, such as the Sisters in Islam. They rebuke flawed readings and interpretations of the Qur'an but not the divine text itself in addressing theological issues of wife beating and gender equality. Their profound desire for the recognition of an absolute, uncontested, and explicit affirmation of women's inherent dignity in the Qur'an does not detract from, but rather concretizes, the universality of rights covenants through convergent and complementary readings.[34]

According to "Mariah" and "AA," who are Muslim feminists and whose activism centers on survivors of gender-based violence, it is the issue of domestic violence that most profoundly problematizes social activism that is premised on the battle for primacy between secularized and religious texts. On the point of semantics, Mariah invokes the Islamic feminist scholar, Riffat Hassan and asserts that, in the Arab language, the term beating can mean many things. Essentially, "[the Qu'ran] does allow for beating," she says, "[although] you can argue [what] the more liberal Islamists would say, that [the beating of the wife] shouldn't be practiced since [...] there] are other methods to so-call discipline the wife." "AA" echoes Mariah's critical reservation when she says:

> But there is still that underlined, "OK, you can't beat your wife, but you can discipline her." There's still that underlined bit [and] it's all very arbitrary [...] there is no unequivocal statement. It's a compromise. You cannot eradicate this idea [of] violence. You cannot pass down that idea or you can't pass down the idea of equality. It has to be, "equality, yes but" [...] and the "yes but" is very arbitrary. (Interview transcript, 10)

On the one hand, slippages in the Qu'ran such as the semantics of "beating" and provisional "equality, yes but," as articulated by "Mariah" and "AA," respectively, feed into theological and juridical counter-arguments on "striking-wives-but-not-quite." Such concerns affect directly the differentiated standards of justice and, by extension gender equality, that are accessible to Muslim and non-Muslim women in Malaysia.

---

33 Sisters in Islam, *Are Muslim Men Allowed to Beat Their Wives?* (Petaling Jaya, Malaysia: SIS Forum), 1991(a) and *Are Women and Men Equal Before Allah?* (Petaling Jaya, Malaysia: SIS Forum), 1991(b): 2. Further details available at <www.sistersinislam. org.my>.

34 Sisters in Islam, (1991a,b), *op. cit.*

Malaysian Muslim women who are subjected to Sha'riah laws and courts, risk being subject to an orthodox interpretation of verse 4:34 of the Qu'ran, which tolerates a "single strike" or "*daraba*" in disciplining wives who are *nushuz*, or whose disobedience disrupts marital harmony (this term is applicable to both sexes).[35] In contrast, non-Muslim women are able to seek legal redress through civil law and courts that legislate a zero-tolerance of harm and violence (at least within the rule of law) because they are not subject to the laws of the Qu'ran. "Mariah" remarks:

> Whereas in the civil law [...] there's no excuse for whatever reasons OK. But in Islamic law, yes—no matter how liberally one [treats] [...] that particular passage (4:34) [...] ultimately when it comes to the [Sha'riah] courts, I think they will still have to abide by the provision of that passage [...] [that] if the husband says to the *kadi* (religious leader) in court that, "I've beaten my wife because she was disobedient," [...] that will be taken into consideration. (Interview transcript, 11)

From "Mariah's" remark, the dialectical tension between the absolutism of religious texts and the universality of secularized texts, such as the human rights documents, results in a contested fidelity to either one or the other as resources and dispensers of political, economic, social, and cultural justice. Negotiating the hyphen of faith-rights-based activism points to the limits of strategizing within an either/or positioning in negotiating a both-and positioning of activism that is both rights-based and faith-based.

Therefore, to interpret religious texts from a feminist standpoint is to demystify "the same book" in shifting the centered margins and the margined center. In doing so, one politicizes spirituality by agitating for social justice in fidelity to the eternal and ultimate message of the Qur'an. Faith-rights-based activists spiritualize politics in an effort to standardize and to reform contemporary and local *Sha'riah* courts and laws. They act also as the custodian and dispenser of social justice towards the transformation of faith communities.

Conclusion

To recapitulate, I have delineated the ways in which faith-rights-based activists draw from religious texts, in particular from the Qur'an and the Bible, in tandem with women's rights documents such as the PFA and CEDAW. In doing so, activists demonstrate how these texts serve as shared resources in affirming the right of women and the girl-child, and by extension, gender-equitable relationships. The relevance of returning to texts to negotiate women's rights is significant in light of the debilitating mindsets that are formed when women and men have internalized power relations of domination/subjugation enforced through biased cultural practices and conservative interpretations of religious texts. As such, religious and secular texts are the foundational premise of demystifying gender-based violence that is an extension of gender inequitable relations.

---

35 Sisters in Islam, 1991(a), *op. cit.*, 6.

Faith-rights-based activists who bring these texts to life in their work also disrupt epistemological violence: they deconstruct the competing claims of ascendancy between the divinity of religious texts and the universality of women's rights conventions. Thereby, they further destabilize the false dichotomy of the universal-versus-relativism ideology circumscribing the discourse of women's rights. They show that feminist re-interpretations of religious texts are commensurate with the central tenets of secularized documents that enshrine women's rights as human rights. The insistence of faith-rights-based activists to open-up rather than foreclose ways of being, knowing, and doing rights, shows us why it is a moral and political imperative to ground rights with cultures and religions. Their work demonstrates a fidelity to what I term critical relativism, which is a standpoint that argues for cultural specificity to advance rather than impede the rhetoric and practice of women's rights.

Bibliography

Bhabha, Homi. *The Location of Culture*. London and New York: Routledge, 1994.

Bong, Sharon A. *The Tension Between Women's Rights and Religions*: *The Case of Malaysia*. Lewiston, Queenston, Lampeter: The Edwin Mellen Press, 2006.

Center for the Study of Human Rights. *Twenty-Five Human Rights Documents*. New York: Center for the Study of Human Rights, Columbia University, 1994.

—— *Women and Human Rights*: *The Basic Documents*. New York: Center for the Study of Human Rights, Columbia University, 1996.

Copjec, Joan. "Vampires, Breast-feeding, and Anxiety." In *The Horror Reader*. Edited by Ken Gelder. 52–63. London and New York: Routledge, 2000.

Freedman, Lynn P. "The Challenge of Fundamentalisms." *Reproductive Health Matters* 8 (November, 1996): 55–69.

Gaer, Felice D. "And Never the Twain Shall Meet? The Struggle to Establish Women's Rights as International Human Rights." In *The International Human Rights of Women: Instruments of Change*. Edited by Carol Elizabeth Lockwood *et al*. 1–89. American Bar Association, 1998.

Gallagher, Anne. "Ending the Marginalization: Strategies for Incorporating Women into the United Nations Human Rights System." *Human Rights Quarterly* 19 (1997): 283–309.

Gellner, Ernest. *Postmodernism, Reason and Religion*. London and New York: Routledge, 1992.

HERA. "'A Call to Action'—Confounding the Critics: Cairo Five Years On." Cocoyoc, Morelos, Mexico (November 15–18, 1998).

IWTC. *Preview 2000: February*. New York: International Women's Tribune Centre, 1999.

Kyung, Chung Hyun. *Struggle to Be the Sun Again*: *Introducing Asian Women's Theology*. Maryknoll: Orbis Books, 1990.

Lara, Maria Pia. "In and Out of Terror: The Vertigo of Secularization." *Hypatia* 18, No. 1 (2003): 183–96.

Marty, Martin E. "Religious Dimension of Human Rights." In *Religious Human Rights in Global Perspective: Religious Perspectives*. Edited by John Witte and Johan D. van der Vyver. 1–14. The Hague; Boston; London: Martinus Nijhoff Publishers, 1996.

Mason, Jennifer. *Qualitative Researching*. London: Sage, 1996.

Mohanty, Chandra Talpade. "Under Western Eyes: Feminist Scholarship and Colonial Discourses." In *Third World Women and the Politics of Feminism*. Edited by Chandra Talpade Mohanty, Ann Russo, and Lourdes Torres. Bloomington and Indianapolis: Indiana University Press, 1991, 51–80.

Piechowiak, Marek. "What are Human Rights? The Concept of Human Rights and Their Extra-Legal Justification." In *An Introduction to the International Protection of Human Rights*. Edited by Raija Hanski and Markku Suksi. 3–14. Turko/Abo: Institute for Human Rights, Abo Akademi University, Finland, 1999.

Population Distribution and Basic Demographic Characteristics Report, Population and Housing Census 2000. Putrajaya, November 6, 2001. <www.statistics.gov. my/English/page2.html>.

Shestack, Jerome. "The Philosophical Foundations of Human Rights." In *Human Rights: Concepts and Standards*. Edited by Janusz Symonides. 31–66. Aldershot: Ashgate, 2000.

Sisters in Islam. *Are Muslim Men Allowed to Beat Their Wives?* Petaling Jaya, Malaysia: SIS Forum, 1991(a).

—— *Are Women and Men Equal Before Allah?* Petaling Jaya, Malaysia: SIS Forum, 1991(b).

Tergel, Alf. *Human Rights in Cultural and Religious Traditions*. Uppsala, Sweden: Acta universitatis Upsaliensis, 1998.

United Nations. *The Beijing Declaration and the Platform for Action: Fourth World Conference on Women*. New York: UN Department of Public Information, 1996.

United Nations Development Programme. *Human Development Report 2006*. <http://hdr.undp.org/hdr2006/statistics/countries/country_fact_sheets/cty_fs_MYS.html> (2006).

Chapter 3

Microcredit and Violence:
A Snapshot of Kerala, India

Valsala Kumari K.B.

Introduction

The term "microcredit" refers to small loans usually given to poor and unemployed people to enable them to meet their immediate needs, such as a medical emergency or capital for starting/expanding micro enterprises, or for meeting the educational expenses of their children. The recipients of microcredit are people with few resources, who lack collateral security to borrow money from the formal banking system, and who normally do not have an assured source of income through a stable job. Their main source of credit otherwise would be the village/town lenders, loan sharks who charge exorbitant rates of interest as opposed to normal commercial banking rates.

Although small loans have been given to men and women in different parts of India under different schemes by governmental and non-governmental agencies, the preferred clients of microcredit are poor women. Women are chosen specifically for the following reasons: 1) the impact of poverty is harsher on women than on men; 2) money given to women is likely to be utilized for the common good of the family; and 3) women are better repayers of loans than men. Although microcredit has been widely acclaimed for its positive benefits, some questions remain: Does poor women's access to small capital engender or reduce violence against them? And, does small capital empower women to challenge violence within the family and in society? These critical questions assume significance, not just for feminist interventions, but also for policy makers.

A cursory glance at the landscape of violence will facilitate contextualizing my topic. The State Crime Records of the government of Kerala, India, reveal that violence against women is on the increase: in 2003 there were 394 recorded cases of rape, in 2005 there were 478; the cases of abduction rose steadily from 102 cases recorded in 2003, to 142 in 2004, to 175 in 2005; and, the category defined as "cruelty by husbands and relatives" saw the rise from 2,930 cases recorded in 2003, to 3,222 in 2004, to 3,283 in 2005.[1] If these are the reported figures, it can be inferred that the number of unreported violent crimes against women would be much larger.

---

1 For the data and further information and analysis, see: National Crime Records Bureau, *Crime in India 2005*, <http://ncrb.nic.in/crime2005/home.htm>, in particular <http://ncrb.nic.

It is distressing to note that the state of Kerala, which has the highest literacy rate and the highest female literacy rate in India and which has a quality of life that can be approximated to that of countries in the "developed" world, should have a high rate of violence against women. Dowry murder, which was unheard of in the 1970s, has now become rampant in the state, and segments of society that used to be untouched by such forms of violence have acquired it too quickly. The increase in violence against women led the national government to pass the Domestic Violence Act of 2005, which became applicable in Kerala in October 2006. Purporting a broad definition of "domestic violence," the Act provides civil remedies for women by way of protection orders, residence orders, and monetary relief. It has yet to be implemented in a fully-fledged manner.

It is against this backdrop that I inquire whether microcredit loans exacerbate or diminish violence against women in Kerala. Prior to such an analysis, it is necessary to understand the neoliberal logic of the discourse of microcredit in the context of a quickly globalizing world. In this chapter, I draw on my experiences of having lived in a microcredit neighborhood in the Indian state of Kerala for approximately one year. The neighborhood is an urban slum area, and the microcredit program instituted there is sponsored by Gandhi Smarak Grama Seva Kendram, a non-governmental organization.

The first portion of my analysis deals with the discourse on microcredit in the context of globalization. I proceed to explore relations between the practice of microcredit and violence against women, and I conclude with the presentation of three case studies to show the impact of microcredit on violence in family and society and to suggest that microcredit has a specifically complicated relation to violence against women.

The Discourse of Microcredit and Globalization

One of the first things that should be taken into consideration when contextualizing microcredit in any given cultural setting is the enduring reality of globalization. Whether embraced or not for its potential benefits or damages to communities, globalization has become a fact in today's world. Feminist scholars like Mary E. Hawkesworth have shown that the gendered dynamics in the process of globalization spreads across several different geopolitical and cultural contexts.[2] The gendered aspects of this dynamics include: 1) the feminization of labor (labor force becoming peopled predominantly by women; informalization and flexibilization of labor implying working under insecure, substandard, and unhealthy conditions as temporary/part time workers; and the phenomenal increase of female microentrepreneurs and

---

in/crime2005/cii-2005/CHAP5.pdf>; and, the crime statistics of Kerala police <http://www.keralapolice.org/crimestat.html state>.

2 Mary E. Hawkesworth, "Engendering Globalization," in *Globalization and Feminist Activism* (Lanham and New York: Rowman & Littlefield Publishers, 2006), 1–28. See especially 11–22.

home-based workers[3]; 2) the feminization of migration, characterized by the long-distance journeys undertaken by women unaccompanied by their families to provide transnational child care and characterized by the increase in international sex trafficking of women; and 3) privatization leading to the erosion of state sovereignty and the withdrawal of the state from the social sector, which shifts the burden of care-giving on women while making health and education increasingly unaffordable to the poor segments of population.

On the other side of the debate are staunch supporters of globalization, like Jagdish Bhagwati, whose tremendous faith in the plenipotentiary powers of globalization and especially free trade as an antidote to poverty, makes him seem oblivious to the immiserization of the marginalized, resourceless people and especially their women.[4] According to Bhagwati, the female migrant worker is much better off in the new found home abroad, even if her own children are not with her but are being cared for by relatives at home. In effect, while finding the global care chain liberatory rather than constricting, he endorses what Ernestine Avila and Pierrette Hondagneu-Sotelo characterize as "transnational motherhood"—a motherhood that involves "spatial and temporal separations."[5] Furthermore, his analysis does not account for the fact that the maid's relatives look after her children only for certain hours in a day and that the rest of the day she spends time with her children only when she is in her country, or for the guilt a woman might experience when caring for affluent children while she is unable to care for her own children in order to support her family.[6] While women workers in the electronics and garment industry may assume a semblance of autonomy and self-respect, the extractive and monotonous nature of their jobs is made to appear light, in his writing, by comparing it with alternatives available.

The amount of money involved in global transfers of capital, trade, people, communication, and so on, is large. Against this backdrop, microcredit given to an individual woman is small, and, as such, it elicits several critical questions: When multinational corporations are able to spend billions of dollars to promote their goods, how do indigent women who become micro-entrepreneurs sell their products in the face of global advertisement campaigns? What power differentials separate and subordinate the women? Are governments able to protect them against the onslaughts of the strategies of multinational corporations?

Microcredit is an ambiguous response to these questions. Microcredit without material collaterals has gained worldwide acclaim with the awarding of the 2006 Nobel Peace Prize to Dr Muhammad Yunus and the Grameen Bank he founded. Despite this recent acclaim, microcredit itself is not a new phenomenon. It has existed in different forms and has been referenced through different names

3 Saskia Sassen, "Global Cities and Survival Circuits," in *Global Woman: Nannies, Maids and Sex Workers in the New Economy* (eds), Barbara Ehrenreich and Arlie Russell Hochschild (New York: Metropolitan Books/Henry Holt, 2003), 262.

4 Jagdish Bhagwati, *In Defense of Globalization* (New York and Oxford: Oxford University Press, 2004), 77–8.

5 Pierrette Hondagneu-Sotelo, *Doméstica: Immigrant Workers Cleaning and Caring in the Shadows of Affluence* (Berkeley: University of California Press, 2001), 50.

6 Cf. Rhacel Salazar Parrenas, *Servants of Globalization: Women, Migration, and Domestic Work* (Stanford: Stanford University Press, Stanford, 2001), 116 *et passim*.

in various countries and at different times. But the resurgence of the practice of microcredit and its exponential growth globally from the 1990s onward was enabled by a confluence of interlinked historical processes. The discourse of microcredit can best be contextualized within the larger neoliberal discourse of poverty reduction as championed by the Bretton Woods institutions in the wake of the economic crises of the 1980s and the subsequent restructuring of the economies of developing countries.

Neoliberalism is a structure of belief predicated on the promulgation of the ideals of individual freedom, free market, and uncurbed entrepreneurship. Milton Friedman claims that what is required for the development of underdeveloped countries is the unleashing of the energies of millions of able, active, and vigorous people by creating an enabling environment for this transformation through free capitalistic market.[7] Thus, the scholars and entrepreneurs who favor a neoliberal development policy have been arguing for more "competitive markets" and "innovative entrepreneurs." Neoliberal policies are packaged neatly as a panacea for fixing the problems of "underdevelopment."

The World Bank has also embraced neoliberal ideological underpinnings since 1981. The World Development report of 1981 recommends cuts in public spending and allowing the private sector to provide what governments did earlier as a response to adjustments to fiscal crises in various economies. The commitment of various international financial institutions at the time of the First World level microcredit summit held in Washington, DC, in 1997 to raise $21.6 billion to help 100 million poor families by 2005 bears testimony to their endorsement of the neoliberal principles. It is interesting to note that, hitherto, banks had regarded women as non-bankable because women could not produce sufficient collateral securities for the money they hoped to borrow. But the neoliberal ideology of the global financial institutions made it appealing to target their funds and poverty reduction strategy to a new class of gendered clientele—poor women who are hard working, entrepreneurial, and willing to repay loans at market rates, particularly in the Global South. Thus microcredit became a leading lending strategy of the World Bank to alleviate poverty around the world. This marks a major shift, not just for the World Bank, but for the normal commercial banks in developing countries as well.

Why did microcredit become an attractive proposition for global lending agencies? Karl Marx's analysis is instructive for an understanding of this phenomenon. For capitalist over-accumulation to sustain itself, it has to penetrate newer spheres and create newer social wants and needs. Credit itself becomes a commodity—a surplus commodity—that needs to be reinvested. Where else can one reinvest than in developing countries, which are the biggest emerging markets of the twenty-first century? For example, within five years of starting a microcredit program in Kerala, the credit borrowed at the prevailing market rate by the NHGs (Neighborhood Groups) of poor women as of October 2004 was Rs.875 crores.[8] One can easily imagine the

---

7 Milton Friedman, "Foreign Economic Aid: Means and Objectives," *The Yale Review* 47, No. 4 (1958): 508–9.

8 One crore rupees is equal to 10 million rupees. One dollar equaled 45.85 Indian rupees in October 2004 <www.currency.com>.

potential scope of the credit market that attracts global players, such as international financial institutions, to invest in the newly emerging markets of the world.

In the 1990s the ideology of a free market was given great impetus by being touted as the most efficient and cost-effective strategy to manage the affairs of both the poor and the less affluent. This condition led to the withdrawal of the state from providing welfare measures and safety nets for its poorest citizens, the privatization of state-owned enterprises, and generally competition in all spheres of life. According to this view, "the state has minimal legitimate functions such as providing for defense and public order, protecting private property, and the right to contract, but neoliberals insist that more expansive initiatives to meet human needs are best left to the market."[9]

This is not to imply that once the state withdrew, the vacuum was left unfilled; rather, the gap was soon filled by voluntary work, which was normally conducted under the umbrella of non-government organizations. The latter proliferated in developing countries in the decades following the 1990s. As Hiroshi Sato opines, during the seventh Five-Year Plan of India (1985–90), a limited governmental co-existence began with NGOs when co-operation was called for in national planning.[10] Now it is estimated that there are over 100,000 NGOs functioning in India, and many international donor agencies now insist on incorporating microcredit for poverty alleviation as a component in their programs. It is also estimated that 10 percent of public aid worldwide, which amounts to $8 million, is distributed through NGOs.

The recent spurt in the growth of NGOs nationwide is partly consequential upon the withdrawal of the government functions. These NGOs discharge a range of functions, such as managing education, health, industries, training, disbursing aid, activism in the field of HIV/AIDS, welfare functions like protection of street children, destitute women, orphans, reforestation, protection of environment, and developmental activities. By virtue of the interest of the NGOs or by virtue of the conditionalities imposed by donor agencies, a major area of operation of many NGOs in India has become microcredit. What is impressive is not just the quantitative increase in voluntary organizations that are lending small amounts of money to the poor, but also the diversity of these organizations, which is based on a variety of considerations such as religion, caste, class, and gender. In Kerala itself, microcredit is being implemented by both NGOs and the government.

Microcredit and Violence against Women

Violence against women covers a very broad spectrum of speech and actions that ranges from vehement feeling or expression, mental cruelty, threat of use of force, to exertion of physical force with or without a weapon causing abuse or injury,

---

9 Mary E. Hawkesworth, *op. cit.*, 18.

10 Hiroshi Sato, "India-NGOs: Intermediary Agents or Institutional Reformers?" in *The State and NGOs Perspective from Asia* (ed.), Shinichi Shigetomi (Singapore: Institute of Southeast Asian Studies, 2002), 57–71.

sometimes fatal, to women.[11] Rebecca and Russell Dobash point out that violence against women "is most likely to occur in intimate relationships and to be inflicted by husbands, partners and lovers. Whether sexual or physical assault, women are most at risk from the men they know rather than from strangers, and there is almost no risk of violence to women from other women."[12]

Along these lines, some feminists regard family as the site of oppression,[13] while others, belonging to working class and subordinated racial and ethnic groups, contest this position and instead link domestic violence to the larger societal issue of violence.[14] In the context of psychology of violent behavior, the studies such as those by Ptacek and Bograd suggest that violence is one response to frustration and is informed by the power differentials between men and women (and children).[15] A related way to explain violence against women is to highlight the social and structural causes that are informed by these power differentials (lifestyle, social control, discrimination supported by gendered institutions, and so on). Among sociological theories, Resource Theory is of particular interest for the present discussion. According to this theory, culture and social institutions invest men with power, financial resources, and access to the public sphere; hence, when men experience a lack of resources, violence is used as a last resort to keep women, especially their wives, under control. This is an important insight if we bear in mind that the help offered by microcredit empowers women precisely by material and symbolic resources. Yet, this theory needs to be nuanced since it fails to explain why men who are already resourceless resort to violence. Finally, working at the crossroads of psychology and sociology, Pradeep Jeganathan usefully detects that violence is to be located in the quotidian practices of masculinity that enable space for the reproduction of violence.[16] Jeganathan argues that the practice of "*baya-nethi*" or fearlessness in the Sri Lankan context constitutes a performance of masculinity that is intimately linked with violence. This performative category will prove useful for our understanding of the link between violence and microcredit.

---

11 Cf., among others, Michael Freeman, *Violence in the Home* (Farnborough: Saxon House, 1979).

12 Dobash, R.E. and Dobash, R.P. "The Politics and the Policies of Responding to Violence against Women," in *Home Truths about Domestic Violence: Feminist Influences on Policy and Practice. A Reader* (ed.), Jalna Hanmer *et al.*, (London and New York: Routledge, 2000), 190.

13 Michele Bograd, "Feminist Perspectives on Wife Abuse: An Introduction," in *Feminist Perspectives on Wife Abuse* (ed.), by Kersti Yllo and Michele Bograd (London: Sage Publications, 1988), 12.

14 See, among others, Rayna Rapp, "Family and Class in Contemporary America: Notes toward an Understanding of Ideology," in *Rethinking the Family: Some Feminist Questions* (ed.), by Barrie Thorne and Marilyn Yalom (New York: Longman, 1982), 179.

15 James Ptacek, "Why Do Men Batter Their Wives?" in Bograd, *op. cit.*, 143; Bograd, *op. cit.*, 17 *et passim.*

16 Pradeep Jeganathan, "A Space for Violence: Anthropology, Politics, and the Location of a Sinhala Practice of Masculinity," in *Community, Gender and Violence* (ed.), by Partha Chatterjee and Pradeep Jeganathan (New York: Columbia University Press, 2000), 52.

The few studies that deal specifically with the influence of microcredit on gender violence in a South Asian context have come to different results.[17] I will take as an example the recent study of the effect of women's participation in two microcredit programs, organized by Grameen Bank and BRAC (Bangladesh Rural Advancement Committee). In their assessment of these programs, Schuler, Hashemi, and Riley have found a positive correlation between participation in microcredit and empowerment, the latter category comprising eight dimensions, one of which is women's freedom from domination by the family.[18] Abdullahel Hadi has shown how microcredit based income-generating programs for the poor have clearly reduced both mental torture and physical assault against women.[19] Conversely, Syed Masud Ahmed has established that membership in the microcredit organization BRAC generated a greater level of domestic violence against female members as opposed to non-members, when they first joined the group.[20] Tellingly, Ahmed's study further reveals that, while the violence peaked immediately after the credit was introduced, there was substantial decrease in the violence after a year or so when skill training leading to employment was imparted to the women. Ahmed attributes this dynamics of violence to women's acquisition of power and autonomy produced by their access to knowledge and the public realm, as well as to their better negotiation skills in conflict situations. Alternatively, he ascribes husbands' appreciation of their wives to the changing familial and societal attitude towards women's greater public visibility. Finally, Koenig *et al.* found the effect of membership in microcredit groups on domestic violence to be highly context-specific.[21]

In the light of the ambiguous position in which women are placed when they become affiliated with microcredit loans, we should also heed Ross Mallick's advice. Mallick, who is of the view that microcredit exacerbates gender tensions, strongly recommends micro-level studies before introducing microcredit to local communities.[22] It is important to calibrate these results well, since there seem to have been some methodological problems that need to be taken into account. Commenting on the differential outcomes of the studies on microcredit and violence, Naila Kabeer states that the conflicting results stem from the different methodologies employed,

---

17 Sydney Ruth Schuler, Syed M. Hashemi, and Shamsul Huda Badal, "Men's Violence against Women in Rural Bangladesh: Undermined or Exacerbated by Microcredit Programmes?" *Development in Practice* 8, No. 2 (1998): 152.

18 Syed M. Hashemi, Sydney Ruth Schuler, and Ann P. Riley, "Rural Credit Programmes and Women's Empowerment in Bangladesh," *World Development* 24, No. 4 (1996): 636.

19 Abdullahel Hadi, "Women's Productive Role and Marital Violence in Bangladesh," *Journal of Family Violence* 20, No. 3 (2005): 181–9.

20 Syed Masud Ahmed, "Intimate Partner Violence against Women: Experiences from a Woman-focused Development Programme in Matlab Bangladesh," *Journal of Health, Population, and Nutrition* 23, No. 1 (2005): 99.

21 Michael A. Koenig *et al.*, "Women's Status and Domestic Violence in Rural Bangladesh: Individual-and-Community-Level Effects," *Demography* 40, No. 2 (2003): 269–88.

22 Ross Mallick, "Implementing and Evaluating Microcredit in Bangladesh" *Development in Practice* 12, No. 2 (2002): 162.

different questions asked, and the different understandings of intra-household power relations on which the studies draw.[23]

Kerala, India: Three Case Studies

What follows is a brief examination of three cases cited by members of microcredit groups, which will help us study the impact of microcredit on violence against women both within the household and in the community. The cases relate to the urban microcredit neighborhood groups in Kerala, and the names used in my account are pseudonyms to assure the anonymity of those interviewed.

Empowering Women, Creating Tension

In the course of my fieldwork during 2006–07, I discussed the question of violence with the members of a Local Development Committee (LDC) in charge of 13 microcredit groups. One of the members explained ambivalent changes in the everyday lives of women who participate in the microcredit groups that she manages. In her account, she underscored the unfortunate timing, for example, of guests, mostly relatives and friends, who wished to pay social visits, and would usually arrive on Sundays; initially those visits created tensions in certain families because that was the day on which the weekly microcredit meetings would be held. "But now," my source continues, "the husbands and other family members [also] ask the woman, 'Don't you have a committee meeting today?' 'Don't you have to go?'"[24]

This member sees a real transformation in the sequestration of women as a consequence of the coming of microcredit. The change, according to her, is occasioned by the benefits that even men see as accompanying microcredit. Among others, these include their women's acquisition of new knowledge, their overcoming of financial problems, their ability to get loans from their own savings, and so on. This attitudinal change among men came about not without a price, for some families witnessed tensions brewing out of conflicting interests between the woman who was a microcredit group member and her husband who wanted her to entertain guests. Hence it may be concluded that the microcredit meetings essentially altered power relations within the family (and by extension, the community) and seriously jeopardized men's exercise of control over women in the private sphere. It is interesting to note that it is only when the men started perceiving the benefit of the microcredit loans to themselves that women were permitted to attend the microcredit meetings regularly. Significantly enough, however, the women's attendance was predicated on their continued buy-in of the gendered division of labor, primarily within their homes.

When I asked the LDC member whether she thought that partaking in a group of women had in any way contributed to those women becoming arrogant as some men had complained, she replied that that was not the case. Pointing out the plethora of

---

23 Naila Kabeer, "Conflicts over Credit: Re-evaluating the Empowerment Potential of Loans to Women in Rural Bangladesh," *World Development* 29, No. 1 (2001): 66–7.

24 Anonymous, interviewed by the author, Alapuzha, Kerala, August 23, 2007.

economic benefits accruing to women and their men from women's membership in microcredit groups, she observed:

> [T]oday, if a man comes back home drunk, the woman is able to interrogate him or advise him not to repeat it. This is because she gains knowledge through microcredit meetings. [...] When she gains knowledge, she acquires the ability to respond. The women have obtained the ability to turn back and respond.[25]

The LDC member highlights the fact that the cause of "microcredit tension" was not generated by women's newly acquired arrogance, but by their acquisition of the ability to "turn back and respond" to violent behavior against them rather than to take it lying down, to which they had been previously habituated. It is interesting here to note the differential perceptions about the causes of the tension between men and women. Microcredit loans have instigated a slow and perceptible shift in power dynamics between men and women. It is understandable that men would feel challenged when their actions are interrogated or when they are called upon to account for their actions. The tension witnessed in families attests to the birth of a new power equilibrium.

The same LDC member narrated another incident, which supports this observation. The story concerns a woman who was married to a man in a neighboring village and who subsequently realized that he had another wife. When she questioned her husband about this, he started battering her. The microcredit group received the news and went to that village, noting:

> We sent word for her husband and he came. He is a local leader of the Congress Party. We told him, we have received a petition and have come to enquire about it. He became furious and asked us, "Do you know who I am? I am the president of the Congress Mandalam Committee. And who are you? Are you the CBI (Central Intelligence Bureau)?" He took out his letter pad and asked us for our names and addresses and started writing our names and addresses in his letterhead stationery. I then took a pen and paper and started asking his mother and sisters for their names and started writing down their names and addresses. I told him that we belong to the group called "Mochitha" ("The Liberated") from Gandhi Smaraka Grama Seva Kendram and gave him our names and addresses. He realized that there are people to question his actions on his wife's behalf. He immediately calmed down and started answering all our questions. We helped her get a divorce and got back the entire dowry, gold and utensils.[26]

This is a good example of women uniting to fight on behalf of a woman who was being battered. What is interesting is the fact that when the abuser reminded the women of his position within the local political hierarchy, the women refused to yield to him and instead embraced the same strategy—they reminded him that they, too, held power by belonging to the group called "The Liberated." By writing down the names and addresses of the people in his house, they threatened surveillance over his domain. The man's discovery of the women's power made him retract his

---

25 *Ibid.*
26 *Ibid.*

original stance and forced him to treat them as his equals, to return all the wealth that his wife brought with her, and to agree for the divorce.

Acquisition of Knowledge and Violence against Women by Women

The same LDC member narrated an interesting example of how this newly acquired power of knowledge manifested itself in the community:

> One group member got into financial problems. She had borrowed 25,000 rupees from a group but failed to repay it. The group took her mother as hostage and kept her under their custody for four days [...]. We went to the house where she was being kept under house arrest and asked them to free the woman [...]. [Since] they did not let the woman free [...], after drafting a petition, we returned to the same house with the police and got the woman released. They belong to the microcredit group of the CDS (Community Development Services). We belong to Gandhi Smaraka Grama Seva Kendram. Certainly we got the courage to do what we did from our experiences in microcredit group.[27]

As we have seen, the scholars have highlighted the variable effects that microcredit programs have on men's violence against women. Yet the last story reveals a hitherto unrecorded scenario where microcredit programs may lead to violence inflicted by women on another woman. To my specific question to the LDC member as to whether the group was not behaving violently by keeping an elderly woman under their custody against her will for four days, she replied:

> Perhaps the women thought that by abducting the mother and keeping her under their custody, the daughter would come in search of her and then they can keep the daughter and release the mother. Although the mother was under the group's custody, they looked after her well giving her meals in time. Most of the women had lent the money to the daughter without their husbands' knowledge and it was only just that they get back the money they lent.[28]

It is interesting that not only did the LDC member quite adroitly dodge my question, but her tone also exuded an element of justification. The loan was pooled by individual members, perhaps without their husbands' knowledge. The mother was made to pay by way of confinement for four days for the daughter's failure to repay the loan. The credit group that abducted the mother was using the collective strength they had gained through the exercise of microcredit in an unlawful activity of violence against another woman. Even though she was involved in freeing the woman, the member seems not to realize the gravity of the situation: this is a violation of one of the most fundamental of human rights, namely, freedom of movement.

The system established through the implementation of microcredit loans within a community becomes a conduit, not just for financial mediation, but also for multiple flows, one of them being transfusion of knowledge. The acquisition of knowledge is a double-edged sword as far as violence is concerned. On the one hand, this newly acquired knowledge may lead to the interrogation of injustices and domination; a

---

27 *Ibid.*
28 *Ibid.*

person equipped with knowledge will be in a better position to diffuse tension by virtue of the fact that they have acquired more power through knowledge and, hence, more bargaining capacity and better skills to navigate the rough waters of negotiation. Through their education in different legal matters, some members of the microcredit group have gained the strength to confront violence inflicted on their group member. Microcredit paved the way, not only for new legal information for the members, but also for a sense of unity forged through networking and a new sense of confidence that propelled them to approach the police for redress of the violence and to accompany the police to the place of house arrest. This is an extraordinary demonstration of courage and solidarity, as normally, women dare not go to a police station. Thus, the knowledge acquired at microcredit meetings has been rightly perceived by the LDC member as empowering. Women felt empowered to challenge violence and to creatively find solutions to problems they faced in their everyday lives. Microcredit gave them a platform from which to speak back against violence; it provided them with a rehearsal stage for breaking their silences and responding to injustices, violations, and violence. It also gave them an opportunity to draw on the social capital created by strong intra-group ties through networking to confront affronts to their dignity, self-respect, and bodily integrity.

However, there is a flip side to this story. As regards the CDS microcredit group, which had confined the woman for four days, an ethos of "righteousness" impelled them to engage in violence against the mother of a member of the other credit group and persuaded them to abandon all legal and democratic avenues of recovery of credit. Their newfound sense of solidarity and confidence generated through microcredit engendered violence against another woman who personally was not responsible for any sin of commission or omission. The self-confidence and sense of solidarity among women is a new phenomenon found in the majority of neighborhoods where microcredit has been implemented and is profoundly changing the attitudes and roles and responsibilities of the members. With the erosion of women's faith in the government institutions' ability to redress grievances without delay, in this case, they took upon themselves the role of the government and thereby posed a threat to the maintenance of law and order.

Alcohol and Violence

The secretary of a microcredit group set in an urban slum area related a few cases where violence against women was generated by excessive drinking.[29] In one of these cases, the group intervened and helped the redress with ease. To tell the truth, in this "success story," the microcredit group did not succeed in weaning the husband away from occasional drinks, but he has acquired greater familial responsibilities. In another case, the situation was far more complicated. Babu (pseudonym) was raised as an only child and, as such, was spoilt by his parents. In particular, his father had initiated him into drinking at a very early age, and as a grown up man Babu could not live without alcohol. This caused marital problems and the separation from his

---

29 Anonymous, interviewed by author, Alapuzha, Kerala, August 25, 2007.

wife and two children. In a drunken state, Babu battered his wife badly, and she attempted suicide but was saved at the last moment. Babu's mother approached her own microcredit group, but the members refrained from mediation and retorted: "It is you and your husband together who spoilt your son!" They explained:

> Let Babu come to us and ask us. We will intervene only after he himself transforms. What if we intervene and something happens in between? They will blame us saying that it is we who intervened and brought back his wife. We had warned him several times. Once he drinks his nature suddenly transforms. It is the question of a woman's life.[30]

The secretary proceeded to assess the problem in more general terms, applicable both to her community and wider sphere: "A man who drinks daily needs a companion. He has to drink even if he does not have money. Someone else will buy him a drink. Somehow or the other he will drink. In the majority of families, all problems arise only from drinks."[31] Indeed, alcoholic beverages are one of the most important causes of violence against women in India. Not only do the poor women have to provide men with money to maintain their drinking habits, they have to bear the brunt of violence of their husbands when they become drunk. Shireen Jejeebhoy notes that not only is wife-beating "deeply entrenched" in India but also "attitudes uniformly justify wife-beating, and few women would opt out of an abusive marriage."[32]

This example was cited as one in which the microcredit group failed to prevent violence against a young member of a neighboring microcredit group. Several times they tried to reason with the husband, but he seemed to be intransigent. The group's excuse for not intervening after the girl's failed suicidal attempt is fear of blame. What if, at their initiative, the wife is brought back to her husband's house and he repeats his violence and she does another attempt at suicide? Prudence dictated that they should wait until he reformed himself before the microcredit group could bring his wife back to him.

Whether it is the newly responsible husband, or Babu, or the local political supremo, what characterizes the relation of these men to women (whether it be their wives or the women of the microcredit group) is the *performance* of their masculinity through violence against them. What microcredit does is to bring this violence under more intense public scrutiny, thereby making the private behavior public and ultimately leading to "*lajja-bhaya*" or shame-fear for the perpetrator of violence.[33] It is only when these men realize that the violence they had perpetrated against their wives had left the private space of their homes and was being subject to the public scrutiny that they had stopped their violent behavior (see, in particular, the case of the local politician's wife). However, in the case of the abducted mother, women with their newly found strength in unity and networking

---

30 *Ibid.*

31 *Ibid.*

32 Shireen Jejeebhoy, "Wife-beating in Rural India: A Husband's Right? Evidence from Survey Data," *Economic and Political Weekly* 33 (1998): 861.

33 Gananath Obeyesekere, *The Cult of the Goddess Pattini* (Chicago: The University of Chicago Press, 1984), 505.

became *publicly violent* against another woman and confined her to the private realm of a guarded house.

Conclusion

My exploration has revealed three instances where microcredit empowered women in different ways. In the first case, the microcredit group was able to collectively and successfully bargain for the return of wealth and a divorce from an abusive husband. In the second case, microcredit empowered one group of women forcefully to confine an elderly woman for four days and another group forcefully to enforce the release of the woman in captivity. In the third case, a young microcredit member was motivated to attempt suicide, and her mother-in-law's microcredit group failed to prevent that self-inflicted violence. If in some instances microcredit empowers women to act collectively to end violence, in some instances it engenders violence, thus rendering its assessment complicated. In light of these examples, it becomes obvious that the effects of microcredit on violence against women are complex and sometimes contradictory. Most importantly, they are context-specific: they depend on the already existing structures of power at different levels. The instances cited go to show that, while the power gained through membership in microcredit groups may help women to counter violence against them, it can also generate new forms of violence against women—by women themselves. Interestingly, no instance of violence against men by women has come to notice.

Finally, these examples should not lead one to overlook the success that microcredit strategy has accomplished in Kerala. The *"Kudumbasree,"* which is the state level mission in charge of implementing poverty alleviation programs mainly through microcredit and allied activities, has several successes to its credit. According to the Kerala State Planning Board's *Economic Review for 2006*, the *Kudumbasree programme* has covered the entire rural area of the state: 163,426 neighborhood groups have been formed; 2,268 group microenterprises of women have been established in the rural areas; an amount of Rs.406.36 crores has been disbursed as loans to the neighborhood groups; the further sum of Rs.719.23 crores has been mobilized as a thrift fund; and, an amount of Rs.1825 crores has been disbursed to the members.[34] Equally good work has been done by several non-governmental organizations in the field of microcredit.

Although no indices have been developed by the state government to measure the empowerment of women via microcredit, in quantitative terms, both men and women I interviewed in Kerala agreed that the microcredit group members have acquired a new sense of self-confidence and courage that was hitherto unknown to them. The question that remains is: Has this newfound self-confidence empowered women to resist violence or has it led them to generate new forms of violence? The answer is, it has done both.

---

34 Kerala State Planning Board, *Economic Review 2006*, <http://www.keralaplanningboard.org> (accessed October 9, 2007).

Bibliography

Ahmed, Syed Masud. "Intimate Partner Violence against Women: Experiences from a Woman-focused Development Programme in Matlab Bangladesh." *Journal of Health, Population, and Nutrition* 23, No. 1 (2005): 95–101.

Bhagwati, Jagdish N. *In Defense of Globalization*. 73–91. New York and Oxford: Oxford University Press, 2004.

Bograd, Michele. "Feminist Perspectives on Wife Abuse: An Introduction." In *Feminist Perspectives on Wife Abuse*. Edited by Kersti Yllö and Michele Bograd. 11–26. London: Sage Publications, 1988.

Dobash, Rebecca E., and Russell P. Dobash, R.P. "The Politics and the Policies of Responding to Violence Against Women." In *Home Truths about Domestic Violence: Feminist Influences on Policy and Practice. A Reader*. Edited by Jalna Hanmer *et al*. 187–204. London and New York: Routledge, 2000.

Freeman, Michael D.A. *Violence in the Home*. Farnborough: Saxon House, 1979.

Friedman, Milton. "Foreign Economic Aid: Means and Objectives." *The Yale Review* 47, No. 4 (1958): 500–16.

Greenfeld, L.A., Rank, M., Craven, D., Klaus, P., Perkins, C., Ringel, C., Warchol, G., Maston, C. and Fox, J. *Violence by Intimates: Analysis of Data on Crimes by Current or Former Spouses, Boyfriends, and Girlfriends*. Washington DC: US Dept of Justice, Office of Justice Programs, Bureau of Justice Statistics, 1998.

Hadi, Abdullahel. "Women's Productive Role and Marital Violence in Bangladesh" *Journal of Family Violence* 20, No. 3 (2005): 181–9.

Hanmer, Jalna. "Domestic Violence and Gender Relations: Contexts and Connections." In *Home Truths about Domestic Violence: Feminist Influences on Policy and Practice*. 9–23.

Hashemi, Syed M., Schuler, S.R., and Riley, A.P. "Rural Credit Programmes and Women's Empowerment in Bangladesh." *World Development* 24, No. 4 (1996): 635–53.

Hawkesworth, Mary E. *Globalization and Feminist Activism*. Lanham: Rowman & Littlefield Publishers, 2006.

Hondagneu-Sotelo, Pierrette. *Doméstica: Immigrant Workers Cleaning and Caring in the Shadows of Affluence*. Berkeley: University of California Press, 2001.

Jeganathan, Pradeep. "A Space for Violence: Anthropology, Politics and the Location of a Sinhala Practice of Masculinity." In *Community, Gender and Violence*. Edited by Chatterjee, Partha and Pradeep Jeganathan. 37–65. New York: Columbia University Press, 2000.

Jejeebhoy, Shireen. "Wife-beating in Rural India: A Husband's Right? Evidence from survey data." *Economic and Political Weekly* 33 (1998): 855–62.

Kabeer, Naila. "Conflicts over Credit: Re-evaluating the Empowerment Potential of Loans to Women in Rural Bangladesh." *World Development* 29, No. 1 (2001): 63–84.

Kerala State Planning Board, *Economic Review 2006*, <http://www.keralaplanningboard.org>.

Koenig, Michael A., *et al*. "Women's Status and Domestic Violence in Rural Bangladesh: Individual-and-Community-Level Effects." *Demography* 40, No. 2 (2003): 269–88.

Mallick, Ross. "Implementing and Evaluating Microcredit in Bangladesh." *Development in Practice* 12, No. 2 (2002): 153–63.

National Crime Records Bureau. *Crime in India 2005*. <http://ncrb.nic.in/crime2005/home.htm>.

Obeyesekere, Gananath. *The Cult of the Goddess Pattini*. Chicago: The University of Chicago Press, 1984.

Parrenas, Rhacel Salazar. *Servants of Globalization: Women, Migration, and Domestic Work*. Stanford: Stanford University Press, 2001.

Ptacek, James. "Why Do Men Batter Their Wives?" In *Feminist Perspectives on Wife Abuse*. 133–57.

Rapp, Rayna. "Family and Class in Contemporary America: Notes toward an Understanding of Ideology." In *Rethinking the Family: Some Feminist Questions*. Edited by Barrie Thorne and Marilyn Yalom. 168–87. New York: Longman, 1982.

Sassen, Saskia. "Global Cities and Survival Circuits." In *Global Woman: Nannies, Maids and Sex Workers in the New Economy*. Edited by Barbara Ehrenreich and Arlie Russell Hochschild. 254–74. New York: Metropolitan Books/Henry Holt, 2003.

Sato, Hiroshi. "India. NGOs: Intermediary Agents or Institutional Reformers?" In *The State and NGOs Perspective from Asia*. Edited by Shinichi Shigetomi. 57–71. Singapore: Institute of Southeast Asian Studies, 2002.

Schuler, Sidney Ruth, and Hashemi, Syed M.. "Credit Programs, Women's Empowerment, and Contraceptive Use in Rural Bangladesh." *Studies in Family Planning* 25, No. 2 (1994): 65–76.

Schuler, Sydney Ruth, Hashemi, Syed M., Badal, Shamsul Huda. "Men's Violence against Women in Rural Bangladesh: Undermined or Exacerbated by Microcredit Programmes?" *Development in Practice* 8, No. 2 (1998): 148–57.

PART II
Enclosures and Exposures

Fashioning a healthy mixture of activist and scholarly accounts, the present part contains a series of revelatory "exposures" of diverse manifestations of gender violence (physical, representational, situational, and others) in the contexts of violent conflict and its aftermath. The authors in this part pay specific attention to the possibilities of local and global redressing of these issues.

The part opens with a chapter by Rose Shomali Musleh, General Director of the Women's Affairs Technical Committee, Palestine, in which she reflects on the multiple tasks of the Palestinian women's movement in the socio-political, legal, economic, and human rights context of Palestine today. Shomali highlights the issues that immediately affect and complicate Palestinian women's rights: Israeli surveillance and control mechanisms in the West Bank; variables of legislation; and exterior and interior political dynamics. The effects of conflict on everyday lives and gender relations are also the topic of Meredeth Turshen's chapter, where she examines the hybrid experiences of Algerian adolescents in their positions as both victims and perpetrators in the Algerian civil war. Her penetrating analysis of Algerian society during the civil war and its aftermath discloses how the rebel GIA army's employment of or appeal to male adolescents shifted gender relations between Algerian men and women, politically as well as domestically. The activist, dissident, and scholar Svetlana Slapšak moves beyond the traditional considerations of conflict-related crimes to probe the discursive incarceration of women (by men and women alike) and the ways in which hegemonic concerns of conflict situations can mitigate the representation of feminism in a nation. Slapšak's chapter likens the rapid increase in misogynist discourse during the conflict in former Yugoslavia to a *post-festum* reluctance to take responsibility for war crimes. Finally, the relevance of Drucilla Cornell's assessment of the legislative determinants of post-apartheid society in South Africa to exploring violence and gender is revealed indirectly. Basing her insights on her activist and theoretical work on the *Ubuntu* Project, Cornell argues that the traditional, community-oriented *ubuntu* law, even though rooted in patriarchal systems of thought and practice, holds potential for a new, indigenous constitutional legislation of South Africa. According to Cornell, an *ubuntu*-informed legislation may influence the status and experience of both men and women in South Africa, but may also generate a wider corrective to the Western philosophy of jurisprudence and offer responses to local and global questions of dignity and reconciliation.

Chapter 4

People behind Walls, Women behind Walls: Reading Violence against Women in Palestine

Rose Shomali Musleh

This chapter presents an account of the efforts by the Palestinian women's movement to advocate for greater sensitivity to gender differences in new civil legislation, particularly laws that affect women's lives, such as the penal code and the family law.[1] It also deals with the effects of the barriers erected within the region and the fragmentation of the land by Israeli policies, and how women have coped with both. After introducing the background and the current socio-political, legal, economic, and human rights contexts of Palestinians, this analysis will address the constant violation of Palestinian women's human rights; this violation is contingent upon the Israeli occupation, but is also a by-product of the divergent legal contexts in various areas where Palestinian women live, in particular of the non-existence of a coherent family law that can be unequivocally applied to all Palestinian women regardless of their religion or sect.

Historical Overview and the Role of the Women's Movement in Building the State

The fact that the Palestinian women's movement today is by necessity deeply linked to the political context of Palestine gives it a different nature than that of many other women's movements in the world. This is not surprising: the existential struggle in which the Palestinian people have been engaged over the past century has shaped the character of the women's movement in Palestine.

As early as 1921, Palestinian women participated in the struggle for independence against the British Mandate and, afterwards, the Zionist colonization. The events leading up to 1948 and the official establishment of the State of Israel left a lasting impact on all Palestinians, especially on rural women who bore the brunt of displacement from their villages and carried the tremendous burdens and responsibilities of their suddenly uprooted families. The expulsion of more than 750,000 Palestinians from their homes into exile in 1948, an event called the

---

1 The author and the editors would like to thank Barbara Louton, Programme Advisor, The Women's Affairs Technical Committee, Palestine, for her work on the early drafts of this chapter and her help with the gathering and organization of the material for it.

"*nakba*" (disaster), changed the methods of building the national women's movement and influenced the national struggle.[2] Women began to reorganize themselves by prioritizing the development of practical programs to address the urgent needs of refugees. The women's movement has been markedly influenced by one additional event, the division of Palestine into three areas: Israel, the West Bank, and the Gaza Strip. Palestinians who remained in the West Bank and Gaza Strip have been subject to three different legal and political systems: Israeli, Jordanian, and Egyptian. The 1967 war, which resulted in the Israeli occupation of the West Bank and Gaza Strip, displaced another 430,000 Palestinians, some internally and most externally to Jordan.[3] During this period, women were active in defending their homeland: they participated in demonstrations, strikes, and some military operations. Some women were arrested by the Israeli government as early as 1968, and others were deported. While the novelty of women participating in guerilla operations won them attention, the majority of Palestinian women activists, especially those affiliated with political parties or the General Union of Palestinian Women (GUPW), were engaged in community work. Volunteerism and popular education were given high value in the new atmosphere of national pride. In 1987, Palestine again attracted the attention of the world with the Intifada (uprising) against Israeli domination. This first Intifada resurrected a spirit of collective power, which also spurred rapid development in the women's movement. To consolidate the gains which women had made and to make sure that women were not marginalized from prominent leadership roles they had played prior to the Intifada, 16 Palestinian women activists met at the Orient House in Jerusalem in November 1991. They demanded the establishment of a technical committee for women's affairs that would fill the gender gap in the peace negotiations.[4] In this way, the Women's Affairs Technical Committee (WATC) was established.

With the establishment of the Palestinian National Authority (PA) in 1994, many negotiating teams were institutionalized as ministries, but it was not the case with the WATC. In the absence of a ministry of women capable of defending women's rights, the WATC saw the importance of having a unified body which would defend the interests of women, ensuring that their rights are taken into account in the draft laws being prepared and that women become partners in nation-building and decision making as they had been in the struggle for independence.

---

2 The UN and the Badil Resource Center estimates the number of refugees between 750,000 and 900,000 during the period 1947–49 (*Survey of Palestinian Refugees and Internally Displaced Persons* [Jerusalem: Badil Resource Center, 2005], 15).

3 *Ibid.*, 21.

4 This demand followed the establishment of several technical committees to assist the Palestinian negotiating team in 1991, which included hundreds of Palestinian men and only a few women (Siham Barghouthi, a founder of WATC, interview by the author, September 27, 2007; WATC Annual Report, 1996, 1).

Legislative Battles

In December 1994, Palestinian women activists joined together in Jerusalem to draft a Women's Bill of Rights based on human rights laws, the Convention on the Elimination of All Forms of Discrimination Against Women (CEDAW), and the Palestinian Declaration of Independence, to demand equal civil, political, social, and economic rights for women. The document demanded, among other things, that the principles of women's legal status be incorporated into the Constitution and the legislation of the future Palestinian state, and that all forms of discrimination and inequality against women be abolished.[5]

Their demands were complicated by the legal framework governing Palestinians at the time. The PA inherited a complicated legal system where Jordanian laws governed the West Bank and Egyptian laws governed the Gaza Strip. The Personal Status Law applied in Gaza dates back to the Ottoman Empire; used during the British mandate, the law was amended during the Egyptian administration of Gaza, on February 26, 1954, and was termed the Law of Family Rights.[6] As Egypt used to follow mainly the Sahfi'i school, Gaza followed the same. In the West Bank, however, the Jordanian Personal Law number 61 was employed. Based on the Hanafi school, the law was amended on December 1, 1976, and was called the Jordanian Law of Family Rights.[7] Per the decree of President Yaser Arafat issued in Tunisia on May 20, 1994, these two laws were to be used simultaneously until they could be unified.

Many laws were unified in the PA, but, generally, the results were not gender sensitive. The Law of Family Rights in the West Bank and that of Gaza are still not unified, which splits the collective social agency of Palestinian women in those spaces. According to the Law of Family Rights effective in Gaza, the marital age for females should be established by the patriarchal criterion of women's "physical readiness" for marriage, which is considered 9 years of age. In the West Bank, the marital age is, instead, based on (again patriarchal) category of women's "mental readiness," set at 17 years of age. In light of that discrepancy, it is not surprising that the first organized demonstration led by the WATC in 1996 protested against the ignoring of the principle of equality, and demanded that all items that considered or implied women to be inferior be cancelled. Men demonstrated along with women by carrying banners in major Palestinian cities stating: "You will not take us back to the age of Hareem."[8] As the demonstrations coincided with the first-ever Palestinian elections, the demonstrators called for a quota of 30 percent of the seats to be reserved for women in the legislative council. Live radio debates concerning women's issues

---

5 "The Jerusalem Declaration: Principles of Women's Rights." Unpublished document. Jerusalem, 1994.

6 Hasan Ali Al Jojo, "The Personal Status Law between Fundamentalism and Modernism," *Al Ayyam Newspaper*, March 16, 1998.

7 Although the West Bank was already under the Israeli occupation, the religious Islamic court continued to follow the Jordanian government.

8 Originally referring to the women owned by a sultan, the term hareem is now used to describe the relationship and the space of this relationship in the family where all women who live in one house are protected and controlled by a single man.

followed, along with petitioning and much discussion in the media, and some of the candidates running for the Palestinian Legislative Council (PLC) made promises to stand by women's equal rights. After five months of intensive advocacy work, from November 25, 1995, until March 2, 1996, the Ministry of Interior announced in an official letter that men and women over the age of 18 years would not need the permission of their guardians to obtain passports, and that applied to both single and married women.[9] This was one of the first achievements of the WATC advocacy work in the field of legislation. Other achievements allowed women to: take driving lessons without bringing along a male chaperone; open bank accounts for their children; and obtain Palestinian passports in their maiden names.[10] Finally, in 1996, representatives of the WATC, the GUPW, Women's Center for Legal Aid and Counseling (WCLC), and other women's organizations, asked President Yaser Arafat to issue a decree that would raise the marriage age in Gaza. Accordingly, the age of marriage in Gaza was raised to 14.5 years, a compromise between the Shafi'i and the Hanafi schools.[11]

Another obstacle that hinders reaching a unified personal status law is the fact that the *Shari'a* religious law is applied to Muslims, who are the majority in Palestine, while Christians and Samaritans follow their own religious laws and courts.[12] Accordingly, each religious group has its own communal set of laws that govern and organize their familial relationships, such as marriage, divorce, custody, and inheritance. Among the Christian population, the Greek Orthodox follow the Byzantine law, the Latin Catholics adhere to the Roman law, and other communities such as the Armenian Orthodox and the Protestants have their own courts. The Samaritans have their own system based on their own Bible.[13] A study of the marital age in each religious group exemplifies how different laws are applied differently. The Greek Orthodox consider the marital age 14 years for males and 12 years for females, while marital age for the Samaritans for men and women is 17 and 15 years, respectively.[14] The differences in religious laws and courts lead to various problems in the cases of intermarriages. According to the *Shari'a*, a Christian woman is allowed to get married to a Muslim without changing her religion, but she loses her rights in inheritance and custody in cases of divorce and death of the spouse. To marry a Muslim woman, a Christian man must convert to Islam. A Samaritan woman is not allowed to marry outside of her community (even a Samaritan man), whereas a Samaritan man can marry Samaritans outside of his community provided the priest approves. While all other laws are civil, the family law is still based on various religious interpretations. This

---

9 WATC Annual Report, 1996, 2.

10 The last advancement was not effectuated due to Israeli requirements not to change the name registered in the Israeli records. WATC Annual Report 1996, 2 and 7.

11 Haleema Abu Soulb, a lawyer at WCLC, interview by the author, Ramallah, September 10, 2007.

12 Sana' Aranki, "A Review of Samaritan Religious Law from a Gender Perspective," unpublished document, WATC, 2004, 3.

13 Samaritans are remnants of an old Palestinian sect that call themselves "the real Israel" and live in Nablus in the West Bank. They were represented by one seat in the first Palestinian Legislative Council.

14 Aranki, *op. cit.*, 15.

situation hinders not only the legislation and implementation of a unified Palestinian family law, but also the passing of related laws.

In 1997, the WCLC, a member of the WATC, came up with a daring initiative known as "The Model Parliament," where modifications and amendments of laws were proposed in public meetings held in several towns in the West Bank and Gaza between August 1, 1997, and March 30, 1998. Eighty-eight men and women, equally represented, were invited to hold public debates about existing laws, especially the family law. This led to a good deal of public debate and media attention. A number of mosques were mobilized to attack those in charge of the Model Parliament.[15] One religious leader, Sheikh Hamed Al Bitawi, accused "secular" centers of being instruments of the West mobilized to sabotage "good Palestinian culture and traditions." The women leaders in particular were accused of being anti-Islamic and Westernized.[16] Islamic leaders claimed that "these women want to marry four husbands."[17] In the meantime, the WATC contacted all political parties to gain their support for the initiative. Most leftist political parties voiced their support for "women's right to freedom of expression," and one party voiced its full support. However, the biggest political Party (Fateh) did not take a clear stand, although there were some strong supporters of the Model Parliament among its young legislative council members.[18]

A few weeks after the meetings of the Model Parliament concluded, President Arafat formed a committee of male religious leaders and one woman from the Islamic Al-Khalas Party, to draft an amendment to the Palestinian family law based upon Islamic *Shari'a* with the age of marriage as 18 years for all.[19] This committee drafted a proposed family law and went through its first reading; however, the law is still in draft form and it has never been approved. Chief Judge Tayseer Al Tamimi prepared another draft with amendments such as raising the marital age or placing conditions on marrying more than one woman, to be presented to the PLC. The draft was attacked by the right wing in the Islamic movement and it has not been presented for discussion at the PLC. The women's movement considers this document a transitional step. A lot of advocacy is still needed towards this strategic goal, a unified civil family law.

A similar dynamics applies to the Penal Code. The draft Penal Code used in the West Bank is still the old Jordanian Penal Code number 16 issued in 1960; in Gaza,

---

15 Ali Khalaf, "In a Panel Discussion in Abdal Nasir Mosque in Al Bira City, Jarrar Warns about the Model Parliament Danger," *Al Hayat al Jadeeda* (April 28, 1998), 3.

16 Mustafa Ali Sabri Al Bitawi, "The Parliament Is a Conspiracy against Islam," *Al Risaleh Newspaper* 44 (March 5, 1998), 5.

17 In Islam, men can marry up to four women at the same time, with conditions.

18 There are lessons to be learned from the experience of the Model Parliament. For example, such an initiative should never be the task of one or more independent organizations but, rather, of the whole women's movement and should be undertaken only when the full support of society has been gained. In this particular case, it would have been prescient if the whole initiative had started from a reformation of religious laws and had concluded with a call for a unified, gender-sensitive Palestinian law for women, raising issues such as the marital age, domestic violence, divorce, and custody one at a time.

19 Abu Soulb, *op. cit.*

the British mandate law number 74 for the year 1936 is still being used. It is worth mentioning that the Jordanian and the Egyptian penal codes were both amended in 2002 to consider honor killing as a crime; however, in Palestine, the old versions are still in use. The Penal Code was reviewed by the Palestinian women's movement and discussed at the level of the civil society where items of discrimination were identified and alternative items that are gender-sensitive were provided with justification for each change. The document of the Penal Code was submitted to the PLC as a document of civil society in April 2003; however, it was shelved and it has become invalid. Since the current application does not entail the prevention of violence against women, the number of "honor killing" cases has increased.[20] For instance, Article 340 with its two items provides a lesser sentence to a father, brother, son, husband, or other relatives guilty of this crime. Also, Article 62 of the same law gives parents the right to beat their children as per the norm. This norm's excuse provides the legal justification for killing, because any parent can commit a crime with impunity per this law. Two cases show the unfairness which women suffer due to this law. A young girl (16 years old) from Abu Qash near Ramallah was killed by her mother after she gave birth to a baby, despite the fact that she had been raped by her two brothers (19 and 21, respectively); the brothers were sentenced for less than five years. The second case is from Ramallah where a girl was killed by her father because somebody from another religion proposed marriage to her. In the two cases, the father and the mother were released based on Article 62.[21]

Furthermore, no policies or procedures exist to deal with cases of violence against women; rather, they are considered misdemeanors (*junha*) and are not dealt with seriously. What makes the situation worse is the fact that cases of violence against women are sometimes dealt with through tribal legislation, which has grown stronger in the last three years due to decrease in security and the absence of the rule of law. The tribal legislation is not gender-sensitive and its solutions are frequently not in the best interest of the woman or the child. Such ideologies contradict the Basic Law and the Declaration of Independence that state that all citizens should enjoy equal rights in a democratic system based on social justice, equality, and non-discrimination.

The third law that affects women concerns the establishment of a quota system for women for elected positions. Affecting the women's possibilities to reach the decision-making levels, the issues surrounding this law clearly demonstrate the importance of legislation. Until the elections of 2005, no women were represented in the local councils in Gaza, and only 65 women were appointed in the West Bank. Building on the experience of the 1996 appointment, it was assumed that only a few women would nominate themselves in the 2005 elections. However, 100 women nominated themselves in the 26 local councils identified for the first phase in the West Bank. Faced with this situation, those who were against the quota felt threatened and

---

20 "Honor killing" is a crime whereby a woman is killed because she is accused or suspected of being engaged in a sexual behavior outside the institution of marriage. "Honor" in this context reflects the power relationship in the family and the gender-based discrimination where a woman has no control over her body.

21 Abu Soulb, *op. cit.*

started to form alliances to change the law; those who supported the quota sought the PLC support. Fortunately, Jamila Saidam and Hanan Ashrawi, two strong PLC members, changed their stand in favor of the quota, and this became a turning point in the process of promoting women in decision-making levels. Accordingly, on August 13, 2005, a 20 percent quota was instituted for local councils and municipalities based on Law 10 of 2005, which formed the basis of the rounds three and four of the local council elections which adopted the system of proportional representation (national lists). By the end of the round four of the local council elections, a dramatic increase in the representation of women in leadership took place, demonstrating the crucial role of legislation in promoting women's political participation and protecting their rights. As a result, 512 women became members of 262 local councils (compared to 65 women before the elections).[22] Since 2005, women have taken a great leap forward in terms of their roles in the regional public arenas as they have been elected to leadership positions in almost every village. The women's movement has worked hard to ensure that women members of local councils are well trained to prove themselves in their communities.

PLC Elections and Consequences

As for the quota of women in the PLC, the battle was different due to changes introduced to the electoral system. The women's movement advocated for a proportional representation system with a 20 percent quota for women instead of the old elections system (simple majority) which was excluded to districts and had no quota. However, a compromise was reached to combine the old and the new systems. On June 18, 2005, the PLC ratified amendments to the elections law to increase the number of PLC seats from 88 to 132 and introduced a mixed electoral system in which 50 percent of seats would be elected through the majority system directly from the districts and the other 50 percent would be elected through the proportional representation system/lists, with a quota of 20 percent of the lists' seats to women.[23] The results of the elections of January 26, 2006, showed the importance of a quota system in women's ability to reach the PLC. Not a single woman could make it at the district level in the absence of a quota. However, it must be mentioned that 17 women succeeded through the quota, which is 25.7 percent of the quota-allocated half of the seats (66 seats); this is a high percentage compared to 5.7 percent overall in the first PLC.

After the results of the elections of January 2006 were out, a delegation representing the WATC, GUPW, and representatives of human rights organizations met with the Head of the Local Council, Dr Azeez Dweik, and submitted a memorandum demanding that the achievements of the women's movement, especially the quota,

---

22 Central Elections Commission—Palestine, "Electoral System—Local Elections," <http://www.elections.ps/template.aspx?id=333> (accessed October 15, 2007).

23 Central Elections Commission—Palestine, "Electoral System—PLC Elections," <http://www.elections.ps/template.aspx?id=143>; "Legislation, Electoral Laws," Central Elections Commission, Elections Law No 9 (2005). <http://www.elections.ps/template. aspx?id=23> (accessed October 15, 2007).

should not only be maintained but also broadened to include all administrative and decision-making levels. In addition, the memorandum emphasized that all laws be based on principles of equality and nondiscrimination as specified in the Declaration of Independence and the Basic Law.[24] Following that visit, the WATC invited the new members of all parliamentary bodies represented in the PLC to two meetings, one in Ramallah and one in Gaza. In both meetings, the expectations of the women's movement from the new PLC were voiced and the demands of the PLC members from the women's movements were identified. Two issues were defined as urgent: to examine how gender fits in the Palestinian and Islamic cultures, and how to integrate gender in policies, laws, budget, and development. The head of the local council participated in the first meeting, but was unable to attend the second one since he was arrested by the Israeli army. Since then, the PLC has been almost frozen.

Unfortunately, the results of the PLC elections that were won by Hamas were not well received by the international community. The decision of the international community to boycott the results of the Palestinian elections has not only seriously undermined democracy, but also affected Palestinian women at a critical moment in the women's movement. With resources suddenly withdrawn, women at local councils have been left without the means to deliver on their promises to their communities. There are about 120,000 public servants who were not paid due to the financial siege on the new government. This means that at least 600,000 persons suffered directly, considering that the average minimum size of the family among Palestinians is five. Many families could not afford paying for the services and women had to make up for the limitation in income by completing the services themselves, which added to their load of work. Many women had to sell their personal belongings, move to live with their in-laws, or plant their garden to secure food. The situation has been made worse by the increased unemployment, which has forced men to stay home. Many women have complained about the additional violence that they face resulting from the unemployment of men.[25]

In addition to the international political and economic boycott, Israeli military and paramilitary forces abducted a large number of key members of both the Palestinian government and the PLC. Compounded, these political moves have halted the efforts of the Palestinian women to reform legislation for gender equality. In addition, the general strike in the public sector, which included the judiciary system in the West Bank and Gaza during 2006 and the first half of 2007, had a negative effect on Palestine's civil stability and, in particular, on the situation and status of women in their communities. The lack of civil security has strengthened conservative tribal ideologies, and these have now taken a lead in determining the moral framework of Palestinian culture. Some clans have armed themselves and have taken over the role of the national authority in their local areas, and this has contributed to the increasing civil unrest, making tensions within the Palestinian society difficult to control. The

---

24 The meeting with Dr Azeez Dweik, took place in Ramallah, PLC premises, March 8, 2006.

25 Cf. Afaf Zibda, *AlUnf Did AlMara'a in Muhafathet Tulkarem* [*Violence against Women in Tulkarem Governorate*] (Ramallah: The Palestinian Working Woman Society for Development, 2005), 30 *et passim*; translation by the author.

strengthening of tribal legislation has also contributed to the increase in violence against women.

Foreseeing the possibility of clashes between the two dominant political parties, Hamas and Fateh, the Palestinian women's movement advocated the creation of a national unity government capable of taking a stand against the civil unrest and growing violence against women and demanded a return to the rule of law based on human rights and democracy throughout 2006 and in the first half of 2007. With Hamas taking control of Gaza in June 2007, the geographical separation between Gaza and the West Bank has been transformed into a political separation where there are essentially two different governments ruling Palestine and none of them has full control over the borders surrounding, resources within, or mobility in their separate regions. In particular, the deterioration in the Palestinian political situation has brought more violence against women in the Gaza Strip. For example, five cases of "honor killings" took place in Gaza only in the first days of July 2007,[26] which is a huge number compared to previous months. This development urged the Coalition for the Penal Code, represented by the WATC, GUPW, WCLC, Miftah, Palestinian Women Studies and Al Haq, to meet on September 19, 2007, to prepare a memorandum to be submitted to President Mahmoud Abbas. The memorandum proposes the issue of an urgent presidential decree which would cancel the two articles that encourage honor killing (340 and 62) and treat honor killing as committing a murder.

Finally, although the Palestinian women's movement had defended the democratic choice of the Palestinian people that brought Hamas to power in the January 2006 elections, it has publicly rejected the undemocratic means used by Hamas in taking control of institutions in the Gaza Strip. The women's movement looks at democracy in its wider applications, beyond the electoral polls, as a process that is associated with a human rights perspective, good governance, the rule of law, and tolerance of others regardless of their religion, beliefs, and sex, as stated in the Palestinian Basic Law. At a press conference on July 18, 2007, the Palestinian women's movement made a statement expressing their concerns over the recent activities of Hamas, and the same day they submitted it to the Central Council of the PLO in Ramallah.[27] In their statement, the women called for the unity of the Palestinian people and stressed the importance of not allowing for the continued geographical separation between the two territories. At this point, the Palestinian women's movement is trying to balance two equally urgent activities: an engaged participation in general socio-political issues in Palestinian society and the promotion of the concerns of Palestinian women in particular.

Israeli Laws and the Splitting of Families

Although many laws affect Palestinian women's well-being, the most powerful laws that govern their daily lives are, in fact, the Israeli military laws. The geographical

---

26 The Palestinian Independent Commission for Citizen's Rights, Report of July 8, 2007, <www.piccr.org/dmdocuments/PICCR/LatestNews/nashrettamoz.pdf>.

27 See Nai'la Khalil, "GUPW and the Women Organizations Submit an Initiative to Get Out of the Current Crisis," *Al Ayyam Newspaper* (July 19, 2007).

separation between Gaza and the West Bank prevents any close interaction between these two parts of the country. The political distance between the Palestinians of the West Bank and Palestinians living on the other side of the green line also inhibits communication between them. Many West Bank Palestinians have family among the approximately 1.5 million Palestinians living behind the "green line."[28] Family members cannot visit their relatives in Israel and technically Palestinians in Israel are not allowed to enter Gaza or the urban centers of the West Bank. The situation becomes more complicated in cases of marriage between Palestinians on the different sides of the green line. In 2003, the Israeli Parliament passed the Citizenship and Entry law banning Palestinians from the Occupied Palestinian Territories (OPT) from living in Israel with Palestinian spouses who have Israeli IDs or in occupied East Jerusalem. In the OPT, "the policy is implemented without reference to any law," which has caused some Palestinians with foreign spouses to leave the OPT in order to enjoy a normal family life. In addition, Palestinian Jerusalemites would lose their residency and their right to ever live in Jerusalem again if they were to move out of the city. If they move, "[they] are considered non-residents by the Israeli authorities and are denied the right to re-enter Jerusalem."[29]

Israel's recent policies pose a particular threat to thousands of Jerusalemite women married to men from Gaza and the West Bank. If they were to visit their families in Jerusalem, they would be forced to surrender their Jerusalemite documents to the Israeli Ministry of Interior, which means losing their Jerusalem ID. The situation is made even more complicated by the fact that Israel does not consider Palestinian Jerusalemites as citizens of Jerusalem, but as residents; as such, they can lose their residence at the discretion of Israel. Ahlam, a Jerusalemite women married to a man from Gaza, is facing a number of complications. She states:

> The Israeli authorities are now creating new regulations to make sure that all Jerusalemites' legal papers and documents that relate us to Jerusalem are revoked. This is one of the worst policies of discrimination ever followed by any authority.[30]

The intervention of the Israeli policy also extends to the OPT. Those who visited the PA territories before 2000 and applied for a family union never got their documents back as a kind of "punishment" for the Intifada. As a result, the mobility of about 35,000 people is limited. "M" (whose name is withheld at her request) came to Palestine on a visitor's visa and applied for family unification, which would allow her to live in Palestine with her husband. However, her request was denied by the Israeli authorities each time she applied. She lost all her legal rights as a Palestinian: she

---

28 The "green line" refers to the 1949 Armistice Line between Israel and the West Bank drawn by the UN after the State of Israel was established in 1948.

29 All quotes, Amnesty International, "Israel/Occupied Palestinian Territories: Right to Family Life Denied, Foreign Spouses of Palestinians Barred" (March 21, 2007), <http://www.amnesty.org/Library/index/ENGMDE150182007?open&of=ENG-ISR> (accessed October 15, 2007).

30 Al Majd Press Office, "Jerusalemites Married to Gazans May Lose Jerusalem Residency," *Voice of Women* (February 22, 2007), <http://www.watcpal.org> (accessed October 15, 2007).

is deprived from traveling and leaving the country to visit her family—essentially, from living a normal family life. "M" says:

> The situation that I remember most vividly was when I was pregnant with our first child. During my pregnancy, I was unable to receive prenatal care because I was unable to get through the Israeli checkpoints to get to the hospital without an ID. I was also forced to give birth to our son in our home, and there were some complications during the birth. Although we tried to get him to the nearest hospital, by then it was too late and he died. Every day I am haunted by the memory of him, and, as a mother, I do not know if I can ever forgive myself for not protecting him.[31]

The right to citizenship or residency is problematic also for spouses from countries where advanced visas are not even required to enter Israel. Before the second Intifada (2000), Palestinians married to foreigners had to leave the country every three months to renew their visas, but now, they are not even allowed to renew them, and often they are forced to leave the country or hide. Those living with their spouses against Israeli regulations fear being deported, and hence remain confined to their homes and towns.

Israel controls the borders of the West Bank and Gaza and the movement of the Palestinian families between cities and towns through a complex system of control which involves a number of physical barriers to movement, including checkpoints where Israeli soldiers give Palestinians selective, and sometimes arbitrary, permissions to cross the border between Israel and Palestine to access their jobs, homes, schools, universities, hospitals, and family. In April 2007, the United Nations Office for the Coordination of Humanitarian Affairs (OCHA) recorded 539 permanent physical barriers and a weekly average of 175 temporary barriers to Palestinian movement erected by Israel in the West Bank—an area of 2,262 square miles. Checkpoints and Jewish settlements are often constructed in long columns through Palestinian communities to serve as another wall severing those communities. In addition, Israeli-only bypass roads, which offer quick and convenient commutes to Israel for Jewish settlers, carve right through Palestinian communities to create more impassable barriers.[32]

The largest barrier, however, is the "Separation Wall" which has been in construction on the OPT land since June 2002. When finished, the 7- to 9-meter high, 770 km long wall would confiscate more than 46 percent of the Palestinian land in the West Bank according to the published maps. The width of the Separation Wall depends on the isolated land between the Separation Wall and the 1949 Armistice Line. Until April 2007, the Separation Wall has taken 43.6 percent from the total area of the West Bank.[33] Some call it the Apartheid Wall, or Segregation Wall, but to

---

31 WATC, "Life without Legal Identity: A Journey into Pain," Voice of Women (July 9, 2007), <http://www.watcpal.org/english/display.asp?DocID=184> (accessed October 15, 2007).

32 OCHA, "West Bank Closure Count and Analysis" (September 2006), <http://www.ochaopt.org/documents/Closure_count_analysis_sept06.pdf>.

33 ARIJ, "Monitoring Israeli Colonization Activities in the Palestinian Territories" <www.arij.org> (accessed September 12, 2007).

Palestinians living on either side of the wall, it is a separation line not between the Israelis and the Palestinians, but between the Palestinians and their land, work, basic services, and members of their family.

The case of Nazlet Issa, a village close to Tulkarem in North of the West Bank, exemplifies this situation. Though small, Nazlet Issa used to have 202 commercial shops which employed 400 people from other villages, and the town's municipality was considered affluent. That dynamic changed when the Separation Wall was built. The wall divided Nazlet Issa into two and destroyed its commercial market, confiscating the agricultural land and destroying houses. The whole economy of the village collapsed suddenly. Whereas 350 people used to work in Israel, now only 80 people aged 30 and more are given three-month permits to work in Israel. However, they are not allowed to use the gate to cross to Israel: they have to use the Al-Tybeh checkpoint to enter Israel, which is about 30 km from Nazlet Issa, and then to go back again almost to the place from which they started on the other side of the wall. The rest of the people who are younger than 30 years or those who have been refused permits smuggle themselves into Israel to work, and by doing so, are at risk of being arrested. Those without a permit smuggle themselves through the wall by traveling 50 km from Nazlet Issa to Jerusalem and back to the other side of the wall (which is another 50 km) in order to come to a point that does not exceed 20 meters from where the journey began.[34]

The wall creates additional difficulties for Nazlet Issa. The gates allow only 62 people to cross to the west side and 22 students to go to schools on the east side, and that only during certain hours. The 62 people have to prove that they own land on the other side of the wall to be able to use the gate, and, even so, they are only allowed to enter the other side during harvesting or olive picking. Not more than two persons from the same family are usually allowed to cross the gate, and the time they are allowed to remain on the other side is never enough to finish the work. On the other hand, workers who do not get permits stay for prolonged periods in Israel to lessen their chances of being caught at a checkpoint. Because men are away most of the time from their families, the town of Nazlet Issa has been called the "women's town." In effect, as the wall cuts the town into two halves, the town looks as if the houses were built in the wall. Those who work on the other side of the wall must climb the roofs of their homes to speak with their families. One woman describes the situation: "I see my husband every day, but he is far to reach." A child said: "I see my father, but I can't hold him."[35]

The wall, interspersed Jewish settlements, and Israeli-only roads serve the purpose of changing, not only the face of the land, but its demographics. John Dugard, Special Rapporteur of the Commission on Human Rights in Palestine described the wall as designed to strengthen the position of the settlers by incorporating half of the settler population in the West Bank and East Jerusalem. He also warned that the complete construction of the wall would see 54 illegal Israeli settlements built on

---

34 Afaf Zibda, WATC coordinator in the north of the West Bank, interview by the author, August 25, 2007.

35 *Ibid.*

the Palestinian West Bank land, and 142,000 settlers incorporated into Israel.[36] This situation not only complicates the daily life of Palestinians, but makes it difficult to maintain a collective identity and ideals of a unified state. Former United States President Jimmy Carter observed:

> The wall is designed to complete the enclosure of a severely truncated Palestine [...]. It is obvious that the Palestinians will be left with no territory in which to establish a viable state, but completely enclosed within the barrier and the occupied Jordan River valley.[37]

Finally, in terms of gender relationships, the study conducted by the Women's Affairs Center in Gaza in 2006 showed a correlation between Israeli occupation and the increase in domestic violence against women in Gaza. This study confirmed the results reached by Afaf Zibda in the years 2004–05, in the Tulkarem area in the north of the West Bank. Zibda observes that the ideology of the occupation can be read, firstly, in terms of its psychological effect on Palestinian women; secondly, with regard to its effects on the parents and, specifically, husband within a family; and, thirdly, through its consequences on the community.[38] In terms of psychological violence, the occupation has affected women either through the absence of their husbands (due to their imprisonment, death, and so on) or by their husbands' loss of jobs due to closures or checkpoints. This situation has affected women in one unique sense: they have become more closely watched by society. "Rowa," a 22-year-old woman who married at the age of 16 and now is the wife of a Palestinian prisoner serving a life sentence, states:

> I am from a rural society where women are not supposed to leave their houses in the absence of their husbands. Not being able to leave my house, I can't go back to school. I am not allowed to visit my husband to discuss the issue with him and I do not want to make my in-laws angry. I am afraid that this situation will go on for a long time. I have become very nervous in my treatment to my children. I have lost weight. I want to get out and learn but I can't.[39]

Another form of violence against women resulting from the political developments in the region lies in the increase in women's responsibilities as a consequence of the absence of their spouses. Amal, another woman whose husband is wanted by the Israelis, states: "The burden is too much now. I do everything, and this tires me psychologically and physically." Tamam, whose husband has lost his job, describes her husband's changed mental condition: "Now everything is a reason to make him angry. He can't control his temper and starts yelling at our children for no reason. We started to fight about everything."[40]

---

36 ARIJ, *op. cit.*

37 Jimmy Carter, *Palestine: Peace Not Apartheid* (New York: Simon & Schuster, 2006), 196.

38 Afaf Zibda, *Violence*, 27.

39 *Ibid.*, 60.

40 *Ibid.*, 28.

Concluding Remarks

The fragmentation of land, the division of people by Israeli policies, and the separation of families have left their mark on every aspect of Palestinian life, pushing families to emigrate both out of Israel and out of the Palestinian territories. The June 2007 events in Gaza have not only exacerbated the divisions among Palestinians themselves, but they have further moved them away from realizing the dream of an independent democratic Palestinian state where all citizens are equal regardless of their religion or sex. In this context, the Palestinian women's movement today is confronted not only with the continued emergency condition of the women in the West Bank and Gaza, but also with the possibility of a civil war and the absence of the rule of the law.

In this crisis, as in all other crises, women carry the burdens and sustain their families, not only economically and socially, but also morally. As always, it is women who play a unifying role in addressing conflicts among parties and in moving Palestinians closer to their national dream: in the middle of the current crisis, the Palestinian women's movement has been consolidating efforts to advocate for a national unity government. It seeks to establish a dialogue as the only means to resolve conflict and for the rule of law to ensure civil peace. Such efforts reinforce the interconnections between the cause of women and the nation's cause.

Bibliography

Abu Soulb, Haleema. Interview by Rose Shomali Musleh. September 10, 2007.

Al Bitawi, Mustafa Ali Sabri. "The Parliament Is a Conspiracy against Islam." *Al Risaleh Newspaper*. March 5, 1998.

Al Jojo, Hasan Ali. "The Personal Status Law between Fundamentalism and Modernism." *Al Ayyam Newspaper*. March 16, 1998.

Al Majd Press Office. "Jerusalemites Married to Gazans May Lose Jerusalem Residency." *Voice of Women* 259 (February 22, 2007). <http://www.watcpal. org>.

Al Mezan Center for Human Rights. Press Release No. 2007/83. July 10, 2007. <www.mezan.org>.

Amnesty International. "Israel/Occupied Palestinian Territories: Right to Family Life Denied, Foreign Spouses of Palestinians Barred." March 21, 2007. <web. amnesty.org/library/Index/ENGMDE150182007?open&of=ENG-ISR>.

Aranki, Sana'. "A Review of Christian Religious Laws from a Gender Perspective." Unpublished document: WATC, 2004.

—— "A Review of Samaritan Laws from a Gender Perspective." Unpublished document: WATC, 2004.

ARIJ. "Monitoring Israeli Colonization Activities in the Palestinian Territories." September 12, 2007. <www.arij.org>.

—— *An Atlas of Palestine: The West Bank and Gaza*. Bethlehem: Applied Research Institute—Jerusalem, 2000.

Badil Resource Center. *Survey of Palestinian Refugees and Internally Displaced Persons.* Jerusalem: Badil Resource Center, 2005.

Bakr, Isam. Hadetha. "Incident." *Voice of Women*, No. 274. September 20, 2007.

Barghouthi, Siham. Interview by the author. September 27, 2007.

Carter, Jimmy. *Palestine Peace Not Apartheid.* New York: Simon & Schuster, 2006.

Central Elections Commission, "Electoral System, Electoral Laws." <www.elections. ps>.

Central Elections Commission—Palestine, "Electoral System—Local Elections," <http://www.elections.ps/template.aspx?id=333> (accessed October 15, 2007).

—— "Electoral System—PLC Elections," <http://www.elections.ps/template. aspx?id=143>

—— "Legislation, Electoral Laws," *Elections Law No 9* (2005). <http://www. elections.ps/template.aspx?id=23> (accessed October 15, 2007).

Dweik, Azeez. Interview by WATC. Ramallah, PLC premises. March 8, 2006.

"The Jerusalem Declaration: Principles of Women's Rights." Unpublished document. Jerusalem, 1994.

Khalaf, Ali. "In a Panel Discussion in Abdal Nasir Mosque in Al Bira City, Jarrar Warns about the Model Parliament Danger." *Al Hayat al Jadeeda.* April 28, 1998.

Khalil, Nai'la. "GUPW and the Women Organizations Submit an Initiative to Get Out of the Current Crisis." *Al Ayyam Newspaper.* July 19, 2007.

The Palestinian Independent Commission for Citizen's Rights. "July Report, 2007." <http://www.piccr.org/dmdocuments/PICCR/LatestNews/nashrettamoz2007. pdf>.

United Nations Office for the Coordination of Humanitarian Affairs (OCHA 2007). "Occupied Palestinian Territory." <http://inpalestine.blogspot.com/2007/02/un-report-compares-israels-actions-to.html>.

—— "West Bank Closure Count and Analysis." <http://www.ochaopt.org/documents/ Closure_count_analysis_sept06.pdf>.

Women's Affairs Technical Committee. Annual Report 1996. Unpublished document. Ramallah: WATC, 1997.

—— "Life without Legal Identity: A Journey into Pain." Voice *of Women.* July 9, 2007. <http://www.watcpal.org/english/display.asp?DocID=184>.

Zibda, Afaf. *AlUnf Did AlMara'a in Muhafathet Tulkarem* [*Violence against Women in Tulkarem Governorate*]. Ramallah: The Palestinian Working Woman Society for Development, 2005.

—— Interview by the author. September 27, 2007.

Chapter 5

Algerian Adolescents Caught in the Crossfire

Meredeth Turshen

The focus of this chapter is the experience of Algerian adolescents as both victims and perpetrators in the violent years of the last decade of the twentieth century. Gender shaped and sharpened the experience in that era. That adolescents are fighters, that they participate in warfare in other ways (as spies, lookouts, couriers, and plants, for example), that they transport weapons and matériel even when they are not trained to use them, are all well-established facts. In Algeria, older teenaged boys and young men did all of these things and more. Teenaged girls appear uniformly as victims: there are no documented cases of teenaged girls participating in any armed groups.[1] The sole exception is the girls living in the forest camps of the armed bands with guerrillas who kidnapped and enslaved them, required them to cook and clean, and forced them to provide sexual services.[2] Girls never carried arms and never went on raids, as girls in similar circumstances did in conflicts in Mozambique, Sierra Leone, Uganda, and elsewhere. Some women, called "*fisistes*," did support the FIS (*Front islamique du salut*, Islamic Salvation Front, the main Islamist political party) and marched in support of the FIS agenda, and some wives of combatants did live in the forest camps; but no reporter (male or female) ever identified a girl or woman in any attack. The absence of women in the conflict of the 1990s contrasts strikingly to the enlistment of young women, some still in their teens, in the bloody eight-year struggle for independence.[3]

Active fighting began in 1992, after the military interrupted the elections and took control of the government. An estimated 80,000 to 100,000 people lost their lives in the 1990s. Precise figures of total deaths do not exist. Partial data are available for children. From 1994 to 1998, 1,241 children lost their lives, including 189 infants; out of that number, 422 children were killed in explosions that targeted populated areas; the number of wounded and disabled children in this period was 128; and 3,000

---

1 Most interpreters believe that Islamic law forbids Muslim women to take active roles as combatants in warfare. However, many exceptions are well known: Palestinian women have participated in suicide bombings, Kashmiri women have been found in the front lines of the conflict between India and Pakistan, and Algerian women and teenaged girls participated in the war for independence against the French.

2 As a signatory to the United Nations Convention on the Rights of the Child, Algeria defines women as above age 18 years and girls as below that age.

3 Meredeth Turshen, "Algerian Women in the Liberation Struggle and the Civil War: From Active Participants to Passive Victims?" *Social Research* 69, No. 3 (2002): 889–911.

children were psychologically affected.[4] A ten-year retrospective study published in the *Journal Algérien de Médicine* found a doubling of child victims of domestic violence consulting health services between 1987 and 1988, and 1997 and 1998.[5] Sporadic guerrilla attacks continued into the next decade: about 500 people died between January and September 2004.

In the 1990s a myriad of competing armed groups operated in the name of Islam.[6] The main group, the GIA (*Groupe Islamique Armé*, Armed Islamic Group), distinguished itself from 1993 by its extreme cruelty and savagery. It attacked civilians indiscriminately, abducted and killed foreigners, planted bombs in public places, set upon and killed travelers at false roadblocks, and committed numerous massacres in villages and towns. On a single night in August 1997, the GIA massacred 100 to 300 women, children, and men in Haï-Raïs, and in September it slaughtered 64 in Beni-Messous and 100 to 200 in Bentalha.[7]

A Brief Account of Modern Algerian History through a Gendered Lens

France conquered Algeria in 1832, bringing new concepts of masculinity in a conquest carried out mainly by groups of men; the French also exploited Algerians sexually, a common feature of conquest. The French settled their new colony, and by the end of their occupation some 900,000 to 1,000,000 *pieds noirs* returned to France. Algerian men experienced the French occupation as emasculating, and women saw their social status fall.[8] Conquest and settlement disrupted all the structures of Algerian society, and gender orders were no exception.[9] One example of such disruption is the land seizures, especially in Kabylia (the home of ethnic Berbers) after the 1871 uprising, which resulted in gendered labor migration (the grand exodus of men).[10] Women lost heavily in land transactions, as men (both French and Algerian) manipulated to despoil them of their property. Another example is the missionary attacks on local gender arrangements as Catholic missionaries established outposts in many parts of Algeria, gathering up orphans and converting them. French colonialism established

---

4 *Arabic News*, May 22, 1998.

5 "La santé publique et la prise en charge des victimes de violence," *Journal Algérien de Médicine*, December 1998.

6 It is important to distinguish "Islam" from "Islamism"; in contrast to Islam, a politically and socially diverse monotheistic world religion, Islamism is a political project. Some Islamist movements are transnational; others, like that in Algeria, are primarily national opposition movements. Islamism invokes the religious values of Islam to justify and legitimize political action and political arrangements.

7 Anissa Barrak, "Les faits, à travers la presse algérienne," *Confluences Méditerranée* 25 (1998): 11–20.

8 Marnia Lazreg, *The Eloquence of Silence*: *Algerian Women in Question* (New York and London: Routledge, 1994).

9 Robert W. Connell, *The Men and the Boys* (Cambridge: Polity, 2000).

10 From 1871 to 1882, 347,268 hectares transferred to French colonies, and from 1887 the French-imposed juridical system enlarged land appropriation (Omar Carlier, *Entre nation et jihad*: *Histoire sociale des radicalismes algériens* [Paris: Presses de la foundation nationale des sciences politiques, 1995]).

new gender orders in Algeria and brought new gendered institutions: armies, state structures, bureaucracies, corporations, capital markets, schools, law courts, and transport systems, to name a few.[11] The French disbanded traditional Qur'anic schools (*madrassas*) and established new schools for boys; few girls enrolled before the 1930s. These new gendered institutions directly reconstituted masculinities and femininities in the country, transforming men into women and women into prostitutes, according to Marnia Lazreg.[12]

Algeria won its independence from France in 1962 after a cruel eight-year war in which more than one million people died. The war challenged both colonial and Algerian gender arrangements: women enlisted to help the guerrilla struggle, which deliberately cultivated masculine hardness and violence.[13] After the war Algerian society honored, even revered, male fighters, and the press and political leaders constantly evoked the heroism of the martyrs; their image certainly had an impact on the next generation's ideas of masculinity.[14] Society did not similarly honor women fighters until Djamila Amrane, herself a veteran, published the first study of them in the early 1990s and a spate of autobiographies began to appear in print.[15]

The process of decolonization ushered in a further round of disruption of the gender hierarchies of the colonial order. New national and international contexts took community-based gender orders another step towards the reorientation of femininity and masculinity, what R.W. Connell refers to as the masculinities of postcolonialism and neoliberalism.[16] Neoliberalism has an implicit gender politics. For example, the model entrepreneur is male, and austerity programs, which attack the welfare state, weaken the position of women. Furthermore, the unregulated activities of transnational corporations place strategic power in the hands of particular groups of men; Connell identifies these men in terms of the masculinity of businessmen in transnational corporations. He says that increasing egocentrism, conditional loyalties, a declining sense of responsibility for others, increasing libertarian sexuality, and a growing tendency to commodify relations with women mark the businessmen.[17]

---

11 Connell, *op. cit.* Fadhma Aith Mansour Amrouche, in *L'Histoire de ma vie*, describes how the French overturned local gender arrangements: she relates how her mother used the colonial legal system to resist the attempts of her dead husband's family to take away her children, as was their right under Islamic law (I am indebted to Richard Serrano for this example).

12 Lazreg, *op. cit.*

13 Carlier, *op. cit.*

14 The GIA and other Islamist armed bands deliberately tried to imitate the style of the independence fighters (see, Carlier, *op. cit.*, 379–409, for a sophisticated analysis of violence in Algeria).

15 D.D. Amrane Minne, *Femmes au combat: la guerre d'Algérie* (Algiers: Éditions Rahma, 1993). A number of survivors are beginning to tell their stories and publish their memoirs (see, for example, *El Moudjahid* August 23, 2001; Louisette Ighilahriz, *Algérienne* [Paris: Fayard/Calmann-Levy, 2001]; *L'Authentique* March 19, 2001; and *L'Espace d'Algérie* November 8, 2000).

16 Connell, *op. cit.*

17 *Ibid.*

With independence Algerian women secured citizenship, equal rights to coeducation and health services (both free), and entry to the professions. For this chapter, the most important point is the impressive gains in girls' education: by 1994 to 1995, girls comprised 46 percent of primary and 50 percent of secondary school students; women comprised one-half of university graduates; 50 percent of doctors (and only 48 percent of nurses), one third of judges, and 30 percent of lawyers.[18] By 2004, over 90 percent of girls were in primary school and more girls than boys enrolled in secondary school (gross ratio 77 percent boys, 83 percent girls).[19]

What Happened to Girls in the 1990s?

From the beginning of the decade, it was clear that girls and women were both targets and pawns in the power struggles between the Islamists and the government. On April 20, 1990, the FIS organized a march of several hundred thousand to present their platform to the government of President Chadli Benjedid. Among the points was a call for the application of *Shari'a* law,[20] a code that would further curtail women's rights in rapidly urbanizing and industrializing Algeria, and the acceleration of educational "reform" to protect schools from non-Islamist influences like coeducation and mixed groups in school lunchrooms. Other aspects of the FIS platform included actively discouraging women from working outside the home, and creating separate administrative services, public transport, and beaches for women and men.

Fatwa (religious commandments based on scholarly legal decisions in Islamic societies) singling out women followed in rapid succession. A 1994 FIS *fatwa* legalized the killing of girls and women not wearing the *hijab* (which in Algeria consists of a scarf that hides the hair and neck, and a full-length robe—"veil" is not an accurate translation); another *fatwa* legalized kidnapping of women and temporary marriage. According to the FIS, Muslim women have rights to (religious) education, respect, inheritance, freedom of opinion, the vote, and the right to refuse an imposed husband. They do not have the right to work outside the home, become political leaders, or participate in sports. They should not wear makeup, perfume, fitted clothes, and also should not mingle with men in public. Rather, as Leila Hessini notes, they should wear the *hijab* "which not only establishes the distinction between masculine and feminine but underscores the separation between public and private."[21] According to the monthly newsletter *El Mounquid* (*The Holy Warrior*), which is the official

---

18 Fatima-Zohra Oufriha, "Femmes algériennes: La révolution silencieuse?" *Maghreb-Machrek*, (November/December 1999).

19 The United Nations Children's Fund, *The State of the World's Children 2006* (New York: United Nations, 2006).

20 *Shari'a* is the law system inspired by the Qur'an, the Sunna, and other parallel traditions. For the purposes of this chapter, the importance of *Shari'a* lies in domestic judicial fields like family, marriage, and inheritance.

21 Leila Hessini, *Living on a Fault Line: Political Violence Against Women in Algeria* (Cairo and New York: Population Council and the United Nations Development Fund for Women, 1996), 8.

journal of FIS, the *hijab* distinguishes Muslims from non-Muslims; it is obligatory for Muslim women and not an individual decision.

The pressure on girls became intense, and the Islamists made an example of non-conforming girls to warn others of the consequences. The Islamists had warned Katia Bengana, a 17-year-old high school senior in Blida, to cover herself, but she told her mother, "Even if one day I will be assassinated, I will never wear *hijab* against my will. If I must wear something, it will be the traditional dress of Kabylia, rather than the imported *hijab* they want to force on us."[22] On February 28, 1994, a group of men ambushed, shot, and killed Katia as she left school. This story illustrates the agency of young women: Katia defied the Islamists. It also introduces the factor of ethnicity: Katia identifies herself as Berber from Kabylia.[23]

Although Islam proclaims the primary importance of the family as the basis of the community of Muslims, Islamism disrupts family life. Far from reasserting "traditional family values," Islamism turns children against parents by encouraging them to spy on their parents and report on such non-Islamist activities as drinking alcohol, smoking cigarettes, and watching television. This religious justification gave boys and young men new powers over girls, both their sisters at home and schoolmates on the street. The arms which the men carried backed those powers. Finally, with the *fatwa* authorizing kidnapping and temporary marriage, Islamism now disguised rape. ("Temporary marriage" is a Shi'a practice that is not part of Algerian religious traditions.[24]) Yamina, a 16-year-old from Bathia, a village at the foot of the Ouarsenis mountains, was forced to wear the *hijab* (to defend herself against the threats of Islamists) and to quit school when the "*intégristes*" who were installed in her village burnt it down.[25] In December 1994, Nebaâ, the *emir* of the

---

22 Véronique Taveau, *L'Algérie dévoilée* (Paris: Plon, 1999), 141.

23 Space precludes a discussion of the ethnic dimensions of the Algerian conflict, a project discussed elsewhere (Meredeth Turshen, "Algerian Women in the Islamist and Berberist Struggles," paper presented at the meeting of contributors to *Gender and Democratization in Warring Societies* (ed.), by Maureen Hays Mitchell and Jill A. Irvine, Colgate University, October 6, 2006). We need to integrate into our analyses of ethnic conflict the findings of research on gender relations in ethnic groups and the social location of ethnic groups in society, especially minority groups. Our understanding of gender shifts in war-torn societies depends on analyses that recognize the social construction of gendered ethnic identities, and the ways in which conflict distorts both gender and ethnic identities and may even encourage a further cycle of aggression and revenge. When conflict destabilizes identities, aggression may seem a strategy to resolve gender relations and ethnic order.

24 Observers, including Muslim scholars, have condemned rape, the abduction of young women, often for weeks at a time, and their subjection to repeated abuse and violence of various kinds in what their kidnappers called "temporary marriages." The Algerian delegate told the United Nations Commission on the Rights of the Child that the so-called "temporary marriage" was permitted by Shi'a Islam but was completely unknown in and prohibited by Sunni Islam. It has been noted that "temporary marriage" was also contrary to Algerian national legislation (United Nations Committee on the Rights of the Child, *Summary Record of the 388th Meeting: Algeria*, June 4, 1997).

25 "*Intégristes*" is a term commonly used in Algeria to describe Islamists. The term "fundamentalist" is less often used. For a discussion of the terminology used in Algeria, see, Meredeth Turshen, "Pan-Islamism, Militarism and Women," *Journal of Asian and African*

band, forced her into a temporary marriage with his lieutenant Haroun, despite her father's protest.[26] The night of the ceremony Haroun raped her in her family home while holding a knife at her throat. Over the next two months, he repeatedly beat her with a belt and raped her. Then government forces killed him in a shoot out, and seven months later Yamina gave birth to a son whom both the village and the state regard as illegitimate.[27]

As this story shows, the sanction of armed Islamism enabled young men to take wives—or sexual partners. The account also illustrates the impotence of older men who are forced to cede power and authority to younger men, an inversion of the traditional age hierarchy. Because the young men carried arms and because they had ejected moderate *imams* who would have condemned such behavior, villagers believed they could not stop the bands or survive a confrontation. Algerian feminists have led an unsuccessful campaign to force the government to acknowledge raped women and the children born of rape as victims of the war.[28] Such an acknowledgment would both entitle the women to reparations and enable villagers to accept them and their children.[29]

Armed bands also abducted and raped young schoolgirls in the course of the conflict: Algerian women's groups documented about a dozen cases of abduction, rape, and throat-cutting of 14-year-old girls, but there were also cases of atrocities committed against much younger children. Amal Boumediene, a journalist who writes for the Algerian French-language daily *El-Watan*, told Faye Bowers, a reporter for the *Christian Science Monitor*:

> I will never forget the look on Hadjira's (an Algiers victim of terrorism) face—all of the fear and suffering in the world. She had been kidnapped and held for two months by fundamentalists, along with 10 other little girls—one only 10 years old—and raped several times a day in the name of Islam.[30]

Studies (special issue *Africa and Globalization: Critical Perspectives*), 25, no 3/4 (2004): 458–9.

26 The title *emir* means commander. The use of "lieutenant" is an example of guerrillas' copying of the military ranking of Algerian fighters in the war for independence.

27 Nacera Belloula, *Algérie, le massacre des innocents* (Paris: Fayard, 2000), 36–8.

28 Nadia Mellal, "Femmes violées par les terrorists: silence et humiliation," *Liberté*, June 16, 2005.

29 *El Watan*, March 3, 2002. Abortion is illegal in Algeria. In 1998 the government formally asked the highest religious body, the High Islamic Council, to allow abortions for women whom terrorists have raped. The government told the United Nations Secretary-General's panel that in such cases abortions were permissible only if a doctor certified that the woman's health was at risk. Many women told the panelists that they thought this was demeaning to them (United Nations, *Report of the panel appointed by the Secretary-General of the United Nations to gather information on the situation in Algeria in order to provide the international community with greater clarity on the situation in the region*, Department of Public Information DPI/2007, sales no. F.99.I.4, September 1998).

30 Faye Bowers, "Islamists Strike at Women in Algeria War," *Christian Science Monitor*, June 28, 1995.

Although the choice to rape schoolgirls in particular was opportunistic, it was also a statement about the rejection of secular (as opposed to religious) education of girls and a condemnation of coeducation.

Families often rejected girls who survived rape, forcing them to leave home and seek shelter at one of the centers created by feminists in the cities. But not every girl suffered that fate. Fatima-Zohra Karadja, a psychologist who runs a center for traumatized children in Algiers, described a massacre in which armed bands kidnapped ten girls and women aged 16 to 24 years. Five days later, searchers recovered the bodies of eight: the killers had mutilated the girls and thrown their bodies into a nearby well. One girl survived and spent several months recovering in a psychiatric hospital. There she told her doctors that her friends had been gang raped, tortured, enslaved, and suffered all sorts of humiliations, but she repeatedly insisted that she had escaped rape. She returned to her village, which connived to maintain her version of the events, thus assuring her rehabilitation and reintegration.[31] This fascinating story portrays village solidarity across the usual gender and generational divisions during an extremely stressful time of conflict.[32]

In addition to exerting pressure on girls to conform to the new Islamist regulations issued in *fatwa*, forcing girls into temporary marriage, and raping girls during raids, guerrillas also abducted girls and took them to their camps in the mountains. One girl named Mériem described life in captivity in this way:

> Captured women did not have the right to wash or to comb their hair. We were not allowed to pray, or to cover our hair, or wear a veil. Girls like me who had worn *hijab* no longer had the right to do so. All of the daily [religious] duties became privileges granted only to the so-called free women, the wives, mothers, or sisters of the terrorists.[33]

The Islamist guerrillas treated the girls as non-Muslims, perhaps as a way to justify their inhumane treatment of them. The fighters declared that only the women related to them were true Muslim women, and they treated their kin with respect.[34]

The fate of girls in the camps was sometimes far worse than what Mériem described. Fella Zouaoui of Sidi Moussa was 14 years old when Khaled Ferhah, a GIA operative who coveted her, organized a raid on her home in order to kidnap her and take her to his camp as "war booty." In the course of the raid, his band

---

31 Fatima-Zohra Karadja and Nadia Korso-Bioud, "Violence, les possibles reparations," *Insaniyat* 10 (January-April, 2000): 51.

32 Karadja recounted this story at the WHO Workshop on Violence against Women in Situations of Armed Conflict, Naples, Italy, October 12, 2000, and the UNICEF representative asked her whether the returning of the girl to her village was not analogous to sending a victim of domestic violence back to her abusive partner. Karadja replied that reintegration in village life was preferable to the miserable alternative—life in a home for abandoned girls. (I was acting as interpreter for Karadja.)

33 Mériem Chréa (March 1998), as testified to Nacera Belloula, *op. cit.*, 116.

34 V.G. Julie Rajan (personal communication) has suggested that this might be an instance of "othering," that Islamists were establishing a new norm of femininity according to their dictates. My reading of the situation is different. These girls were Algerian Muslims, and the guerrillas were indulging in the raw use of brutal power; the men (whose piety was questionable, according to the press reports) degraded and dehumanized their compatriots.

murdered all the members of her family at home (three happened to be in town that day). According to GIA rules, Khaled first had to offer Fella to Zouabri, the group's *emir*, who raped her every night for a week and then assigned her to Khaled. Khaled thought he would then keep her for himself and spare her the gang rape reserved for most captives. His comrades' disapproval put both of their lives in danger. Khaled tried to flee with Fella, but the band intercepted and beheaded him on the spot. They tied Fella with wire and dragged her back to Tala-Acha, the camp where Zouabri condemned her to death. Blaming her for Khaled's attempted escape, the guerrillas tied her, spread-eagled, to an iron gate on the ground where they gang raped her daily. Dozens of terrorists stomped on her and shouted, "To hell with the sorceress!" Her torturers tore out one of her eyes and stabbed her repeatedly. After 12 days, Zouabri took a sword and cut Fella's body in two. Although no one has ever found her corpse, we know Fella's fate because Djamila, another captive of the same group, escaped to tell it.[35] The Islamists blamed Fella, the girl they kidnapped, for tempting their comrade, and they held her responsible for his murder, which they committed. This philosophy is of a piece with the insistence that women dress modestly lest men lose their self-control.[36]

Reports of these incidents circulated widely in Algeria, spreading fear and influencing girls' behavior, especially in towns and cities. The newspapers (of which there are many in Arabic, French, and Tamazight [Berber]) carried these stories. In an effort to mobilize public opinion, some of the feminist groups opposed to FIS compiled press clippings of atrocities in annual volumes that they distributed widely. Many girls took the stories as a warning rather than a rallying cry; they internalized these messages and most of them acted to protect themselves by conforming to the new Islamist strictures. Young men also internalized the fact that the government never captured or tried those responsible for the rapes; in other words, they learned that they could behave with impunity in ways that parents, religious elders, and the state would not have tolerated earlier.

Islamism empowered some young men, who joined guerrilla bands, which offered a kind of work and access to money, rewards in the form of women, and a lifestyle much richer than what they had known. For some girls the allure of a life alliance with young men they perceived as powerful was irresistible. Marriage to the leader of an armed band promised wealth and status. Nadia (a pseudonym), who came from a poor peasant family in Haï Bounab, was 16 years old when she met Ahmed Chaabani, who became a GIA *emir* under Antar Zouabri. Recounting her marriage, Nadia told Baya Gacemi that her husband had more money working with Zouabri than he would have earned from a regular job.[37]

---

35 Belloula, *op. cit.*

36 Lazreg describes Algerian men's paradoxical behavior: men wished to pry women away from the strict code of sexual conduct in order to have easier access to their bodies, but, when they were no longer convinced of their primacy over women, they wanted to see the code maintained (Lazreg, *op. cit.*, 192).

37 Baya Gacemi, *Moi, Nadia, femme d'un émir du GIA* (Paris: Éditions du Seuil, 1998), 133–4.

The GIA ran rackets, in which they extorted a "tax for the revolution" from all the inhabitants; with this money they could afford to dress in name-brand clothes and wear Reeboks, Nikes, or Filas. They also ate well; Nadia described the elaborate meals she prepared for Ahmed's band. The men stole some of the goods from the houses of the people they killed. Nadia related how Ahmed and his followers once furnished a house for her with a truckload of furniture, a stove, blankets, sheets, dishes, and large baskets of food stolen from two *patriotes* (men enrolled in communal self-defense groups armed by the government) whom they had murdered the night before. Nadia adds, "Nothing but expensive products, foreign brands. Everything was new. There was even a washing machine, which I never used because I didn't know how to."[38]

What Happened to Teenaged Boys in the 1990s?

It is best to ask questions about the experiences of teenaged boys and young men in the economic, political, and social contexts of contemporary Algeria. In the context of limited economic alternatives resulting from the imposition of structural adjustment in the 1980s, the country experienced increased poverty and unemployment for the first time since its independence. In the context of limited political expression, in 1988 people rioted against structural adjustment and voted against the corrupt government in two sets of elections (municipal in 1990 and national in 1991). The military staged a *coup* to keep the state from falling into the hands of the Islamists, and the Chadli government fell. In the context of the social unrest, young men confronted a combination of unfavorable circumstances: they could not marry because of a housing crisis, because they had no jobs, and because girls remained longer at school and did not marry before graduation (the average age at first marriage for women is now 27 years).[39]

In these contexts, the *intégristes* easily and relentlessly infiltrated education, sports, and social mores. In their attacks on the so-called "un-Islamic behavior," the *intégristes* banned smoking: the effect on poor young boys who commonly earned money selling cigarettes on the street was to deprive them of their only income. Boys also lost their cultural diversions. The Islamists not only closed the conservatory of music in Algiers, the capital of Algeria, but the FIS even denounced the popular music of *raï* sung by women and men.[40] *Raï*, they said, was immoral and distracting from worship. The AIS (*Armée Islamique du Salut*, Islamic Salvation Army) shot

---

38 *Ibid.*

39 Meredeth Turshen, "Armed Violence and Poverty in Algeria," The Armed Violence and Poverty Initiative commissioned by the UK Department for International Development Centre for International Cooperation and Security, Department of Peace Studies at Bradford University, November 2004, <http://www.brad.ac.uk/acad/cics/projects/avpi/>.

40 The musical form of *rai* came together in the 1920s and 1930s; women on the margins of urban and small-town culture in West Algeria, with the center in Oran, developed *rai* in an extremely complex musical landscape rendered yet more complicated when the French introduced jazz and cabaret and as Arabic women singers like Umm Kulthum and Asmahan rose to superstar status (Richard Serrano, personal communication).

and killed some of its practitioners (for example, the GIA assassinated Cheb Hasni from Oran in 1994), and the FIS cancelled the Oran *raï* festival in 1993.

A counter to Islamist attempts at censorship, television programs arrived unedited from France, Spain, and Italy via satellite. Islamists objected to foreign films featuring nudity that channels mixed in with news and other programming. An Islamist edict condemned television viewing and banned satellite dishes. A measure of the effect of this *fatwa* is the stagnant number of 68 televisions per 1,000 people in Algeria, as compared to the increase in 1998 from 81 sets per 1,000 in 1990 to 198 sets per 1,000 in Tunisia, and the increase in Morocco from 102 to 160.[41] Placing this marker in the context of the changes which television has brought to the lives of Algerians, it is worth underscoring that even in the poorest urban homes, television is an essential fixture of everyday life, and it is women's most important form of entertainment and source of information.[42]

The armed bands recruited young men and teenaged boys who joined these groups for a variety of reasons. Yet, this conflict was not a youthful rebellion; the leaders were all adult men.[43] Some youths joined the bands to escape army service or to revenge a family member whom the military had jailed or killed. In other cases, Islamists tricked youths into joining (for example, a combatant would use a teenager as a lookout and then persuade him that the military had observed him and were now looking to pick him up, stating "it is better to come with us and be safe"). Another ruse was the promised trip to Mecca, which ended up in an Al Qaeda training camp in Afghanistan.[44] Some teenagers were brainwashed, as we have learnt from court proceedings in which the prosecution produced induction tape recordings as evidence; the techniques used will be familiar to those who have studied cult induction procedures.

As in every conflict of some duration, the fighters distorted the political economy and provided some employment opportunities, albeit often in illegal activities. Some of the older teenagers were already involved in moving contraband. Young smugglers, called *trabendistes*, who were Islamist sympathizers aided the armed bands. From moving consumer goods, they turned to more dangerous trafficking in arms and drugs. Just as arms smuggling supplied the fighters, drug smuggling expanded the use of drugs (hashish, cocaine, and *kif*); commentators link drug use to the conflict, noting that the traffic has become entrenched and professionalized.[45]

The armed Islamist bands ran rackets; they collected "taxes" as mentioned previously, and they stole goods from shops. Moreover, for a time they controlled the main arteries of the country. The roadblocks they maintained allowed them to check

---

41 United Nations Development Programme, *Human development report* (New York: United Nations, 2000).

42 Lazreg, *op. cit.*

43 The two leaders of the FIS are Abbassi Madani, born in 1931, and Ali Belhadj, born in 1956. In 1991 Belhadj would have been 35 years of age.

44 Many of the fighters in the GIA were veterans of the Afghan wars. About 2,000 who had trained with the CIA in the 1980s returned to Algeria, bringing the ideas of the Taliban as well as their tactics.

45 *El Watan*, July 21, 2002, and May 16, 2004.

the movement of goods from the ports to the interior, diverting what they needed.[46] The connections with local "mafias," who were involved in smuggling and other illicit economic activities, intensified even as the armed movements' political and social bases contracted. In September 1998, at the peak of the massacres that were the turning point in the war, arms smuggling was critical to guerrilla operations. *El Watan* reported on September 5, 1998 that Hassan Hattab, a GIA *emir*, was believed to have activated contacts with his men abroad to smuggle weapons from a European port into Algeria.

When the Algerian military eventually picked up the armed groups that recruited teenaged boys, a number of detainees aged between 16 and 18 came before the criminal courts, but any penalty imposed on them took account of their age. The courts did not impose the death penalty. (Algeria suspended capital punishment in October 1993.) Judges usually placed minors involved in terrorist activities in special institutions for the re-education and rehabilitation of juvenile delinquents. The problem of terrorist groups training younger children was very marginal; no children under the age of 14 were involved.[47]

Younger boys, like girls, were mainly victims of the conflict. Fatima-Zohra Karadja, the psychologist who runs a center for traumatized children in Algiers and also heads the National Association for the Support of Children in Difficulty, recalls the case of one boy in Bouinam, a village south of Algiers in an area called the "triangle of death." This boy was the sole survivor among 11 school children when gunmen attacked their school bus. She notes of the boy: "He never talks about what happened, or draws anything about the massacre. But he is living with something incredible and tough [...]. He is always tense and wakes up every night and is terrified."[48] Karadja's center takes care of boys like him and attends to the girls who have survived abduction and rape.

La Mixité

The Algerian term for coeducation is *la mixité*. It has been a principle of public education since colonial times, and the new government vigorously reaffirmed it after independence. During the 1990s, the Islamists attempted to undermine this principle.

Where they controlled villages, Islamists shut public schools. Bombs destroyed schools in many other places where Islamists did not control public education, where coeducation persisted and girls mixed with boys in lunchrooms, where the curriculum included French language classes, and where girls participated in sports. In September 1994, the GIA called for a boycott of schools and issued a *fatwa*

---

46 Luis Martinez, *La guerre civile en Algérie* (Paris: Karthala, 1998).

47 Testimony of the Algerian Delegate, United Nations Committee on the Rights of the Child, *op. cit.*, note 24 above.

48 Scott Peterson, "Amid Algeria's Massacres: Conquering Fear to Help Children," *Christian Science Monitor*, January 9, 1998.

forbidding all children from going to school.[49] Women defied the ban and sent their children to school, despite real and threatened reprisals such as school burnings and murders of teachers. Women brought their sons and daughters to classes and stood in front of schools in solidarity with teachers and in defense of coeducation.[50]

In 1998, a year when general violence had already begun to subside, Islamists bombed 17 schools, bringing the total close to 700 and the murder of teachers to 200. The numbers would have been higher, but, by then, students knew to report suspicious packages. Consequently, in El-Biar on January 21, 1998, pupils discovered a bomb that security services were able to defuse 20 minutes before it was set to go off.[51]

In 1993 young people founded an association, RAJ (*Rassemblement-Action-Jeunesse*) to defend *la mixité* and freedom of speech.[52] The activities of the

Figure 5.1   Children in front of a primary school in Haï Raïs, Algeria, bombed in 1997 (photograph taken by Meredeth Turshen on April 27, 2001; reproduced by kind permission of Meredeth Turshen).

---

49 In Algeria, school is free and compulsory for children. There are about 7.5 million children currently in schools.

50 Josette Alia, "Récit: ce jour-là ..." *Le nouvel observateur*, No. 1576. January 19–25, 1995: 7–10, 9.

51 Observatoire National des Droits de l'Homme, *Rapport annuel: 1999* (Algiers: Observatoire National des Droits de l'Homme, 1999).

52 Francois Germain-Robin, *Femmes rebelles d'Algérie* (Paris: Les Éditions de l'Atelier, 1996), 91–7.

group range from trips to the beach (boys and girls together), through organizing concerts—even in Bad El Oued, the Algiers neighborhood dominated by the FIS— to distributing condoms and talking about AIDS. They publish and sell a newspaper, *Vie-RAJ*. Their express desire is to create a space in which they can break down the separate worlds of men and women, the state of affairs which they regard as a kind of apartheid lived by the older generation.

Interpretations

The conjunction of militarism and Islamism in an already patriarchal society changed gender relations, not only between adult men and women, but also between adolescent boys and girls. Militarism and Islamism have in common the usurpation of the roles and prerogatives of civil society. The infusion of military values in civil society has particular implications for women's and girls' democratic rights, as does the imposition of Islamist tenets. Military regimes limit democratic freedoms in the name of national security and employ secrecy to protect their decisions from civilian review; thus, holding the military accountable for their actions in times of war is difficult even in democratic societies, as we well know. Islamism imposes a strict interpretation of religious law to the exclusion of civil law.

It would be, however, false to suggest that militarized Islamism contrasts with a secular civilian Algerian government. Political power has always been in the hands of the military in Algeria. The Algerian military, like militaries everywhere, has used the threat of internal disorder to justify its rule. William B. Quandt observes: "The military's relatively cohesive organizational structure has given it a comparative political advantage; and petrodollars have helped to keep soldiers in place by giving an unpopular regime a means of buying acquiescence from many citizens."[53] The response of the government to the Islamist attacks was fierce repression: arrests, the internment of suspects in camps, and the "disappearance" of prisoners.[54]

Both Islamism and the military are masculine, male-dominated institutions; both are patriarchal in the sense that they are gendered, hierarchical systems of social and sexual control; both install sex-segregated societies with sharp sexual divisions of labor. Patriarchal traditionalism, Islamism, and militarism all control girls and women to accomplish their goals. Cynthia Enloe explains, "Militaries need women to provide commercial sex to soldiers, to be loyal military wives, to fill jobs working in the defense industry, and for the military."[55] Islamism places women at the center of family life, which is the foundation of Muslim society. The patriarchal organizational structures of Islamism, the military, and many nationalistic cultures, are consonant and mutually reinforcing. In combination, militarized Islamism

---

53 William B. Quandt, "Algeria's Uneasy Peace," *Journal of Democracy* 13, No. 4 (2002): 20.

54 Amnesty International, "Algeria: Truth and Justice Obscured by the Shadow of Impunity" (New York: Amnesty International, 2000).

55 Cynthia Enloe, *Maneuvers: The International Politics of Militarizing Women's Lives* (Berkeley: University of California Press, 2000), xii.

in patriarchal cultures minimizes and marginalizes the multiple roles of girls and women in society.

What happens to adolescent gender relations in times of conflict and war, especially in Muslim societies affected by Islamism? The literature describes the impact of war on "children and youth." When authors make a distinction between boys and girls, they examine the genders separately, not in relation to one another, recounting only the different impact on girls and boys. I found no information on what happens to gender relations, on how conflict and war affect the interaction of girls and boys and the power relations between them. One obvious change is that the social spaces in which boys and girls can meet—which is so important in sex segregated societies where dating is not the custom—become even more limited. If, as in Algeria during *la décennie noire*, gunmen patrol the streets, school is suspended, or classes and lunchrooms are segregated, if sports are curtailed and beaches for women are separated from those for men, all of these venues of interaction between girls and boys are closed. Closed, too, then, are the spaces for nonviolent gender interaction.

Bibliography

Ait Mohand, Achour. *Projet d'élaboration d'un manuel d'intervention auprès de l'enfance traumatisée.* Algiers: Institut National de Santé Publique, 1999.

Alia, Josette. "Récit: ce jour-là ...." *Le nouvel observateur*, No. 1576, January 19–25, 1995: 7–10.

Amnesty International. "Algeria: Truth and Justice Obscured by the Shadow of Impunity." New York: Amnesty International, 2000.

Arabic News. "1,241 children victim of terrorism since 1994." May 22, 1998. <http://www.arabicnews.com/ansub/Daily/Day/980522/1998052217.html>. Accessed August 25, 2007.

Barrak, Anissa. "Les faits, à travers la presse algérienne." *Confluences Méditerranée* 25 (1998): 11–20.

Belloula, Nacera. *Algérie, le massacre des innocents.* Paris: Fayard, 2000.

Bowers, Faye. "Islamists Strike at Women in Algeria War." *Christian Science Monitor* 87, No. 149. June 28, 1995: 1, 2c.

Carlier, Omar. *Entre nation et jihad: histoire sociale des radicalismes algériens.* Paris: Presses de la foundation nationale des sciences politiques, 1995.

Connell, Robert W. *The Men and the Boys.* Cambridge: Polity, 2000.

El Moudjahid. August 23, 2001.

El Watan. "Familles victimes du terrorisme : en quête d'une reconnaissance légale." March 3, 2002.

Enloe, Cynthia. *Maneuvers: The International Politics of Militarizing Women's Lives.* Berkeley: University of California Press, 2000.

Gacemi, Baya. *Moi, Nadia, femme d'un émir du GIA.* Paris: Éditions du Seuil, 1998.

Germain-Robin, Francois. *Femmes rebelles d'Algérie.* Paris: Les Éditions de l'Atelier, 1996.

Hessini, Leila. *Living on a Fault Line: Political Violence against Women in Algeria.* New York and Cairo: Population Council and the United Nations Development Fund for Women, 1996.

Ighilahriz, Louisette. *Algérienne.* Paris: Fayard/Calmann-Levy, 2001.

Karadja, Fatima-Zohra and Nadia Korso-Bioud. "Violence, les possibles réparations." *Insaniyat.* January–April 2000: 45–53.

L'Authentique. March 19, 2001.

Lazreg, Marnia. *The Eloquence of Silence: Algerian Women in Question.* New York: Routledge, 1994.

L'Espace d'Algérie. November 8, 2000.

Martinez, Luis. *La guerre civile en Algérie.* Paris: Karthala, 1998.

Mellal, Nadia. "Femmes violées par les terrorists: silence et humiliation," *Liberté,* June 16, 2005.

Minne, D.D. Amrane. *Femmes au combat: la guerre d'Algérie* (Algiers: Éditions Rahma, 1993).

Observatoire National des Droits de l'Homme. *Rapport Annuel: 1999.* Algiers: Observatoire National des Droits de l'Homme, 1999.

Oufriha, Fatima-Zohra. "Femmes algériennes: la révolution silencieuse?" *Maghreb-Machrek.* November–December 1999.

Peterson, Scott. "Amid Algeria's Massacres: Conquering Fear to Help Children." *Christian Science Monitor.* January 9, 1998.

Quandt, William B. "Algeria's Uneasy Peace." *Journal of Democracy,* 13, No. 4 (2002): 15–23.

Taveau, Véronique. *L'Algerie dévoilée.* Paris: Plon, 1999.

Turshen, Meredeth. "Algerian Women in the Liberation Struggle and the Civil War: From Active Participants to Passive Victims?" *Social Research* 69, No. 3 (2002): 889–911.

—— "Pan-Islamism, Militarism and Women." *Journal of Asian and African Studies (Special Issue on* Africa and Globalization: Critical Perspectives) 25, No. 3/4 (2004): 458–9.

—— "Armed Violence and Poverty in Algeria." The Armed Violence and Poverty Initiative Commissioned by the UK Department for International Development, Centre for International Cooperation and Security, Department of Peace Studies at Bradford University, November 2004. <http://www.brad.ac.uk/acad/cics/projects/avpi>.

—— "Algerian women in the Islamist and Berberist struggles." Paper presented at the meeting of contributors to *Gender and Democratization in Warring Societies.* Edited by Maureen Hays Mitchell and Jill A. Irvine. Colgate University, October 6, 2006.

United Nations. *Report of the panel appointed by the Secretary-General of the United Nations to gather information on the situation in Algeria in order to provide the international community with greater clarity on the situation in the region.* Department of Public Information DPI/2007, sales no. F.99.I.4, September 1998.

—— Committee on the Rights of the Child. *The initial report of Algeria* (CRC/C/28/Add.4). 1997.

—— *Summary record of the 388th meeting: Algeria.* June 4, 1997. CRC/C/SR.388. 1997.

United Nations Children's Fund, *The State of the World's Children 2006.* New York: United Nations, 2006.

United Nations Development Programme. *Human development report.* New York: United Nations, 2000.

Chapter 6

The After-War War of Genders: Misogyny, Feminist Ghettoization, and the Discourse of Responsibility in Post-Yugoslav Societies

Svetlana Slapšak

Gender, War, and Responsibility

A marked gap in modern European historiography is still women's history, or gendered historiography. On the other hand, historiography is the least popular and slowest expanding discipline in the otherwise booming European gender studies. Unacceptable today, traditional historiography was based on the concept of self-sufficient, unquestioned universality; the latter masked the lack of "othering" subjects of history. This "lack" is, in fact, the result of various types of manipulation and occlusion of othering subjects, including the commodity of turning a blind eye. Even today, there are a number of serious and comprehensive historical studies that simply do not take account of the largest othering subject—women. Yet, in the time-spaces of *entangled histories (histoire croisée)*,[1] the outcome and the very argumentation of historiographic research do not work epistemologically if gendered history is not engaged. In a rather elliptical way—which is also a way to shorten an extensive introduction—my aim in this chapter is *inscribing back*. This action is multi-leveled: inscribing back in the blank spots of historical maps, left there as the traces of a clumsy passage of self-centered cultural colonialism, mainly Anglo-American; inscribing back on the wrinkled, almost petrified pages of national historiographies; and, inscribing back into the actual scenarios of re-arranging histories according to power-directed demands.

The last seems to be the most dangerous, because it involves a massive re-composition of memory. Just one example should suffice. A recent trend in almost all post-socialist/"new" European countries is to turn tables in the assessment of

---

1 For an illuminating discussion of the *histoire croisée* approach, its methodological implications and its empirical developments, see Michael Werner and Bénédicte Zimmermann, "Beyond Comparison. *Histoire Croisée* and the Challenge of Reflexivity," *History and Theory* 45 (2006): 30–50. Drawing on the recent debates about comparative history, transfer studies, and connected or shared history, the notion of *histoire croisée* deals with empirical inter-crossings consubstantial with the object of study, and the operations by which researchers themselves cross scales, categories, and viewpoints.

World War II, to represent quislings, Nazi-collaborators, traitors, dead or survivors, as representatives of alternative decision making in hard times. It is a skillfully made scenario that includes the notion of democracy (everyone's right to personal decision), the relativization of the historical context (and henceforth how "free" is the decision to collaborate in extermination of your own people or other peoples), a fogging of issues (collaboration was, as a rule, part of the wartime behavior of the rich, powerful, conservative and exploiting—Church, industrials, police, politicians); and, the forging of new, manipulative narratives (resistance fighters allegedly demanded or ordered fratricide, rupture of family ties, communism instead of patriotism, and so on).

Apart from an easily detectable twist of history in the countries that massively participated in World War II on the fascist side and where the Soviet Russians are officially presented as occupiers since 1944–95, there is a specific scenario for countries in which the Soviet Russians, even if present for a short while in the final war operations, did not figure ever since: the countries of former Yugoslavia. The initiative to re-compose historical memory started in the 1980s in Slovenia and Serbia, and took the form of a demand to make the dead equal, to make peace between the living, to pay due respect to victims of the post-war atrocities over those who previously had chosen a wrong side in the war.[2] In Croatia, the similar but much more virulent process, involving deeper historical wounds (the only concentration camp during World War II was in that region), has been eventually contained by the present day democratic state institutions; but the discourse of *ustashi*, the infamous Croat Nazi movement, is still floating on the fringes of the public sphere. Everywhere, the sites of the execution of Nazi-collaborators have been sacralized, marked with monuments, annual meetings and rituals, the relatives or survivors have become visible, since they have been given the opportunity to speak up. In Slovenia, a special archaeology of hidden burials has been developed, more as a scene of enacting a power-play of new historians who capitalize on the media effect of skulls and old people in tears in front of cameras. The methodology of discovering these burials is totally arbitrary and is based on randomly chosen memories of locals. The recognition and identification data are not clear and the evidence is smothered in excessive emotions. Even an amateur can ask themselves whether a presumed victim of communist violence might have been, in fact, a victim of Nazi or fascist violence, for the chronological distance would be just months, or even weeks. Which forensic procedure can exactly determine the ideological orientation of bone remains, if there are no signs of uniform or other material indicators, before the DNA tests have been done to confirm at least the family ties? There is a rather short passage

---

2 The inter-ethnic atrocities of World War II in Yugoslavia, including the extermination of Jews (by local quisling forces in Croatia and Serbia, by Hungarian and German occupation forces in Vojvodina and Macedonia) and of Serbs and Roma in Croatia (especially in the Jasenovac concentration camp in Croatia), were an important issue of the post-war communist cultural production (education, literature, film, theatre). In an attempt to avoid the allocation of ethnic guilt to any nation in the new multi-ethnic state, the focus was placed on the individual, class, and ideological aspects of responsibility. This multi-sided concept of responsibility was gradually abandoned over the next few decades. The first sign of revisionism was a long and futile debate about the number of victims at Jasenovac in the mid-1980s.

from the initiative to uncover the censored parts of the war and post-war history, to a vulgar re-writing of history to serve actual political goals, which unfortunately but necessarily comprise a quick building-up of ignorance. Is it possible to build-up ignorance at the same speed as knowledge? Whatever the answer, the propaganda manipulation is threatening both historic re-examination of World War II history and the part of the European intellectual heritage of thought about war responsibility, genocide, violence, bare life—Theodor Adorno, Jean-Paul Sartre, Hannah Arendt, Giorgio Agamben, and many others—and, separately from these thinkers, Simone de Beauvoir; for the horrors of war made de Beauvoir think and write about one horror which was not listed: patriarchy.

The revisionist scenarios embedded in the actual political power-struggles also have a co-lateral narrative function: the creation of a cultural space inhabited with metaphoric notions. Along with the revisionist World War II history, there comes the denial of changes that occurred after 1945 in former Yugoslavia. The most important among these now contested social transformations—because visualized as the major symbol of changes—is the new position of women. The recourse to the institutionalized religion, Church, family values, and the patriarchal containment of women characterize the narrative of the newly proposed "good guys" of World War II. This narrative serves as a paradigm for today's gender politics in the countries of former Yugoslavia. In Croatia, Serbia, and much less in Slovenia, the new World War II narratives have been directly used to accommodate, familiarize, and stereotype the gender relations in the more recent war that accompanied and followed the decomposition of Yugoslavia. The obvious necessity to scare away women from a basic demand of not diminishing the already acquired human rights generated imposing imagery and aggressive public discourse, which can be defined as misogyny in the majority of cases. Denying responsibility for the war, so characteristic of the public climate in Serbia today, is therefore entangled in gender politics. As a consequence, gender sensibility is connected and associated with people and discourse engaged in taking responsibility for war crimes. The reaction to the responsibility-demands is always the same—brutality and the discourse of hatred. The activity of "inscribing back" in this case means not only re-revising history, but also engaging in open local-political struggle. The aims of the latter are, paradoxically, not much higher than the barely satisfying, onerous recall of things already thought, achieved, resolved. But there is an additional intellectual benefit of such an endeavor: to introduce one's innovative gender studies methodology, to question feminist epistemology, and to re-read running theories from a different ground-level point. Last but not least, this contribution activates the "postcolonial joy" of presenting a case familiar to few.

Historicizing Misogyny

Violence in the conceptually and actually hyphenated spheres of the intimate and the extimate invokes for me misogyny in the first place. It may be a personal confrontation with the past non-admissible pleasures, for instance enjoying reading openly misogynist authors, like Bernard Shaw and Friedrich Nietzsche. But, beside the ambivalent satisfaction of critically scrutinizing one's own roadmap on the eve of the old age, there is a need to revisit and revise the aspects of misogyny and to compare and draw similarities between different contextual articulations of the phenomenon. I would oppose the position of Marina Blagojević, the editor of the collection *Mapping Misogyny in Serbia: Discourses and Practices*, that misogyny does not need argumentation about the causes because it is simply there, and that misogyny in post-communist cultures is non-systematic, non-institutional, and rather a spontaneous than a normative feature.[3] While Blagojević's collection is an excellent, richly documented piece of feminist academic work, a seminal reading for anyone interested in gender studies in the region, I would propose a different view of misogyny: as a predictable weapon of culturally different patriarchies in similar contexts. Misogyny can be systematized because it comes from a previous systematization and experiences of at least two centuries of modern history, and it is always institutionalized. These features of misogyny were strikingly prominent in the infamous case of Croatian "witches" in 1992–93, an event in which political insiders and the leading structure of PEN Croatia plotted a real conspiracy in order publicly to humiliate five renowned women in literature, feminist and pacifist activism, theory, and journalism.[4]

The closest comparable case of massive misogyny is certainly the culpabilization of women in former socialist countries of the Soviet bloc for their share in supporting communism.[5] The irrationality of such an argument is fascinating: women slept with communists and bore children to them; hence, they should be deprived of all rights given to them by communists. Here "the communists" appear as a mythical group of seducers and manipulators, and obviously men today do/did not have anything in common with them. They (the citizens of today's countries) want to establish a new, "democratic" order, in which women will sleep with men in power and bear children to them without any reward or right. This re-evaluation is accompanied by a discourse highlighting that the new condition will be much better for women. This is, of course, a very simplified picture. Yet, if, in 2006, the Slovenian Minister for Work and Family proposes a program on fertility/birth rate which re-introduces, after a half of a century, limitations to and payment for abortion, accompanying this proposition with a detailed description of fertility-risks caused by modern clothing of women, excluding, parenthetically, any other idea how to boost fertility rate (for instance, by liberalizing

---

3 Marina Blagojević (ed.), *Mapping Misogyny in Serbia: Discourses and Practices* (Belgrade: AZIN, 2004).

4 The case concerns the media-ostracization of several women authors (Slavenka Drakulić, Rada Iveković, Jelena Lovrić, Vesna Kesić, and Dubravka Ugrešić) on the grounds of their being "insufficiently patriotic" in 1992–93. The media-action involved the publishing of private data and the discourse of hatred, expressed in the titles such as "Croatian Witches Rape Croatia," and it engaged many Croatian intellectuals in a game of public denunciation. See Meredith Tax, "The Five Croatian 'Witches': A Casebook on 'Trial by Public Opinion' as a Form of Censorship and Intimidation" (1993) <http://www.wworld.org/archive/archive.asp?ID=157> (accessed October 20, 2007).

5 See Nanette Funk, "Feminism East and West," 1–14, and "Women and Post-Communism," 318–30, in *Gender Politics and Post-Communism* (ed.), by Nanette Funk and Magda Mueller (New York and London: Routledge, 1993).

immigration), then the fear of the constant return of systematized, institutionalized, and orchestrated misogynist discourse, fantasies, and measures is confirmed.[6]

Patriarchal crisis management, at least in the century of world wars, seems regularly to include misogynist invention as a major cultural product: after World War I popular and high-brow culture were full of images of menacing and castrating female figures, vampires-vamps, heartless suffragettes, or simply women who survived the war. Wounded, sometimes castrated, and certainly psychologically shattered men were meeting upon their return civilian women whose experiences were markedly different from theirs, even if they worked in the war industry, as nurses, or if they replaced men in all kinds of public services.[7] To topple this, radical change in fashion and body politics made women more mobile, independent, careless, and free. So when only 20 years later World War II broke out, the boys were ready: even with more participation in war efforts and in war actions than ever before, Western women were pushed back into homes, fashion made them less mobile, popular culture reinvented sin and guilt, and the backlash was completed with the discursive invention of a (dangerous, unnatural, immoral, and thirsty for commodity) communist woman of the East. Misogyny seems to be an inevitable component of the dominant public discourse during social crisis and war, at least in the twentieth century, and it is richly registered in the media and the popular culture.

Besides being a sign/symptom, can misogyny also be more seriously entangled in reasons, motives, and causalities of crisis and wars? We can think about it in terms of *brutalization*, which is an answer to a situation, but at the same time it releases a whole chain of responses. As a part of brutalization strategies, misogynist narratives, along with other discursive inventions of internal enemies, give the illusion that there is an enemy that can be defeated, and release an aggressive energy that can be shared at less cost and effort, and with more fun and security, than the action at the war front. This substitute for the actual engagement with the war is, then, ideal to control the situation back home, to re-introduce patriotism "at home" and thereby stealthily to recapture/recover the patriarchal self-esteem. Misogynist narratives are not a by-product of war and crisis, but the central public discourse pattern available for initiating such situations, their prolongation, and their reproduction, whenever there is a need for it in the centers of production of public discourse. Cultures with strong patriarchal indexes, which might have been corrected by recent and strong repression of patriarchy (like in former communist regimes), keep these indexes "frozen," but ready for the immediate re-introduction of misogyny into culture; they can count on a large number of zealous cultural translators of all genders. Mechanisms of repetition and pleasure enable the dissemination of misogyny up to a stage in which a participant in this *cultural intimacy* ritual does not notice it above or outside the set of stereotypes they are using.[8] The dangerous rationality

---

6 Due to an extremely negative response to this proposal, Janez Drobnič, the Slovenian Minister for Work, Family and Social Matters, had to step down on December 1, 2006.

7 Margaret Higonnet (ed.), *Behind the Lines: Gender and the Two World Wars* (New Haven: Yale University Press, 1987).

8 Michael Herzfeld, *Cultural Intimacy: Social Poetics in the Nation-State* (New York and London: Routledge, 2005).

of stereotypes lies exactly in this: the content of a narrative is not subdued by the process of understanding, but it affects and orients emotions and motions.

Situating Misogyny

One of the greatest "blanks" in today's gender studies is certainly the gendered or women's history of the Balkans. This situation is exacerbated by the ongoing discussions/conundrums about how we actually define the Balkans and the never-ending struggle with the stereotypes that abound not only in the media, but also in academic discourse. Only recently some attention has been paid to the theorizing on gender and the Balkans by the youngest generation of scholars.[9] Now it may be necessary to make an interdisciplinary link between Balkan studies (Balkanology) and gender studies, and to explore anthropological continuities (at least inside patriarchy), following the epistemological pattern offered by the modern development of ancient women's studies from ancient studies. The historic perspective of women in the Balkans would easily work with hypotheses about continuities, really long continuities, based on recognizable patriarchal patterns which have been repeated and modified in different cultural contexts and at different times, since the earliest historic periods. Is it admissible for a feminist today even to pay attention to the concept of patriarchal patterns? I am afraid it is, when it comes to historiography: the deconstruction of patriarchy, but also a research into the niches available to women in some forms of patriarchy, are necessary to write women's history.

A possible historical approach is to contextualize and analyze the key terms of a certain time-space. Misogyny itself could be such a term. Since misogyny is infrequently used in referential domains (at least it is not understood as a generally acceptable term in the dominant public discourse), it cannot be readily observed. Because of this discursive non-presence, the researcher's possibilities to establish a semantic history of the term are minimal. Hence, the term has been applied to a situation in a public discourse as a kind of *isoseme*—the concept carrying the same meaning in different contexts. Using an *isoseme* is a strategy of cultural translation: a well known term is used to enlarge the space of analogy, to internationalize and transfer meanings. In the case of misogyny, the cultural translation and transfer of meaning are done by feminists. By itself, the term "misogyny" evokes a critical approach, but it seriously lacks theoretical background and, frankly, it does not inspire theorizing. Women-hating and women-haters may have gained an ambivalent kind of charm in literature, but there is certainly no place for misogyny in politically correct public discourse. Consequently, it can be detected only in public discourses or cultures without any established political correctness.

I propose that the actual presence of misogyny in public discourse is also an important symptom of cultural readiness for war, or presence of war-culture in a seemingly pacified culture. This is the case of several post-Yugoslav cultures, most obviously that of Serbia. To clarify this bold presumption, I would like to

---

9 Jelisaveta Blagojević, Katerina Kolozova, and Svetlana Slapšak (eds), *Gender and Identity: Theories from and/or on Southeastern Europe*, (Belgrade: Women's Studies and Gender Research Center, 2006).

present a personal experience instead of an argument, being not able to find a fully scientifically established explanation of the relation between human words and actions. In the 1980s, the prevailing Western schools of interpretation of text (but also older Russian theory, especially formalism) insisted on the arbitrary relation between the author and the text, following the post-de Saussurean formula about the relation sign–signified. To my situatedness then, in the dissident circles of former Yugoslavia, the argument about the arbitrariness was not only convincing, but also useful. In fact, this was the authority on which myself and others have based our defense of authors (and non-authors) exposed to state repression because of the things they said or published. We could quote established international authors, theorists, and philosophers—many of them already translated in former Yugoslavia—and show that "our" authors could not have been responsible for their own text, because any reading is legitimate. In our own work in humanities and social sciences, that also helped us reject rigid interpretations of biographical causality in somebody's work, which we then sensed (with sane reasons) as a remnant of the Stalinist way of thinking. The communist propaganda in Yugoslavia was dead at that time, and this could explain our candid assumption that the *multiplicity of different readings* based on knowledge and education may protect us from propaganda effects. Only a couple of years later, I had to change my position quite radically. Many of my dissident peers became rabid nationalists and were producing discourse which deeply affected people, pushing them to persecute, rob, or even kill the other, convincing them of the supreme collective rationality of such acts, which should not be punished, but rewarded. The nightmare of words passing to action was there, and no theory was available to explain it. I had to face the new reality with a new toolbox, and it is still rather empty: contemporary philosophy is still over-populated with acrobats of the arbitrary while the ethical reflection on responsibility is rare. On the far side of relevant thinking about words and actions, The Hague International War Crime Tribunal has established some criteria for war crimes related to the use of words: in the Rwanda trials, radio shows in which the houses of people to be persecuted and killed were indicated on air were taken as the evidence of criminal activities. In the recent legal process against Vojislav Šešelj, a suspected war criminal whom I had protected against the state repression in 1984–86,[10] the need to produce evidence, for instance a video with the inflammatory speech connected directly to action by place, time, and clear indication of the intended and then perpetrated crime, is still procrastinating the passing of sentence (at the time of writing).

This is what I have to keep in mind when I am thinking of the discursive presence of the term misogyny in the public discourse and the cultural readiness for war: do the term and the behavior meet on the ground of discursively subjugated/inarticulated? Does that mean that readiness for war is always existent? Is there a discursive spark that causes a socio-cultural switch-on? Some of my research into this topic went

---

10 First in my rubric in the journal "Književna reč" in 1984, then in my capacity as the President of the Committee for Protection of Freedom of Expression at the Writers' Association of Serbia in a series of petitions in 1986–89.

into the direction of rhetoric and stylistics;[11] some of it, presented here, went into the direction of contextualizing discursive strategies. I do not have definitive answers, but there are arguments for the link between discursive invention in the public sphere and collective actions in both directions of my research.

Yugoslav socialism persisted (more visibly during the first 20 years of its existence, 1945–65) in its political, cultural, and symbolic use of women: their new rights, positions, visibility, political participation, and signs of power were everywhere. The female body, very much like the Soviet female body, was the visual sign of the new social order in mass culture. Communist ideology is, undoubtedly women-friendly, at least in its many programmatic texts. The strategies of committing to this ideology and the strategies of avoiding the ideological demands alternated at quite a dynamic pace. Paradoxically, when the ideological constraints were loosening up, and the more liberal mentality prevailed, patriarchal discourse was gaining ground. A good example of this dynamics is the case of Yugoslav communist guerrillas (partisans) who had engaged masses of women into an open feminist movement during World War II, and then let them down after several years: women gained enormous visibility in political and Party bodies, as MPs, mothers, and widows in black in the first rows at conferences, congresses, war crimes tribunals, cultural events—all of which was cut short after Tito's break with Stalin in 1948.[12] The Yugoslav communists feared that women's masses could turn in favor of the Soviet type of communism and challenge the Yugoslav resistance to Stalin. As a consequence of internal purges in Yugoslavia, many women were sent to concentration camps organized for the Soviet sympathizers. There they were kept under harsh conditions for several years, some up to 15 years. Many did not survive torture, hunger, and humiliation.[13] The Anti-fascist Front of Women (AFŽ), founded in 1943, which had 100 times more members than the Communist Party by the end of the war, was silently dismissed

---

11 Jelena Petrović and Svetlana Slapšak, "Sex/gender Distinction, Uses and Abuses in South Slavic Languages in the Multilingual Balkan Region. Serbian/Croatian/Bosnian in Their Comparative Setting," in *The Making of European Women's Studies: A Work in Progress Report on Curriculum Development and Related Issues in Gender Education and Research*, Vol. 5 (ed.), by Rosi Braidotti, Edyta Just, Marlise Mensink (Utrecht: Utrecht University, 2004), 80–85.

12 Before World War II, the Yugoslav Communist movement had its major support base in educated urban women. With the beginning of the war, forced to organize guerrilla actions outside the cities, the partisan guerrilla started a huge action of propaganda among another population of women—uneducated rural women—and the success was enormous. Along with women's support in logistics, health care, and food providing, the process of "enlightening" women about their rights and the bright communist future went on in the most unprivileged of conditions. In the post-war period, women conducted voluntary work of reconstruction, education, and health and humanitarian care.

13 Most concentration camps organized for the presumed pro-Soviet sympathizers, such as Goli otok or Pančevo camp, had special departments for women. Among the many books of fiction, history, and memoirs concerning these camps, only one woman published her memoirs: Ženi Lebl, *Ljubičica bela* [*White Violet*] (Gornji Milanovac: Dečje Novine, 1990).

in 1952.[14] Women were given only representative, symbolic roles in the communist power system ever since.

Yugoslavia's subsequent history demonstrates the harm that can be done to women over a long time-span, by introducing patriarchal mentalities through media and culture and by combining them with Western consumerist dispositions. The ambivalence and hypocrisy of their position were felt by women early enough to provoke dissatisfaction; it engendered a search for more inspiring feminist goals and texts, such as the French feminist theory, but also a massive retreat of women into the patriarchal world and values, a backlash (consumerism + patriarchy) which occurred with economic reforms in the 1970s. In the cultural space of Yugoslav dissidence feminism was never raised to be an important issue, so it had to seek its own political program, and, by the end of the 1980s, this new activist agenda was formulated as the fusion of pacifism and multiculturalism, if possible in an integrated Yugoslav space.[15] In the 1990s, while dissidence dissolved in the nationalist narratives, with only a few individuals proposing peaceful solutions, the Yugoslav feminists never split, even during the most terrible war actions and inside the most dangerous war zones.[16] In all the warring regions of former Yugoslavia, the blame was placed on these activists: feminists were seen as "national traitors." The abovementioned affair with women writers, activists and journalists proclaimed "witches" in Croatia in 1992–93 ended in a court process that was eventually won by these women. In Serbia, however, misogynist discourse has remained prominent in media, culture, even science. It was reinforced during the NATO intervention in 1999, and it gradually shaped the ruling public discourse. The latter is based on two intertwined principles: the emphasis on women's responsibility (as "traitors" in the recent war) and the denial of men's responsibility.

The women working in institutions dealing with human rights and war crimes have been especially targeted. They have been continuously denounced as whores, crones, perverted-lesbians, foreign mercenaries, and so on in Serbian media, movies, books, and articles since 1991.[17] A striking example of this gender politics is a commentary by a popular Belgrade columnist in a leading state-controlled daily, *Politika*, just after the NATO bombing stopped: "The NATO generals are like Mother Theresa, compared to Serbian feminists!"[18] The author goes on to argue that the greatest threat

---

14 Lydia Sklevicky, *Konji, žene, ratovi* [*Horses, Women, Wars*] (Zagreb: Ženska infoteka, 1996).

15 See Biljana Dojčinović-Nešić, *Odabrana bibliografija radova iz feministicke teorije/ zenskih studija 1974–1996* [*Selected Bibliography of Works in Feminist Theory/Women's Studies 1974–1996*] (Belgrade: Centar za ženske studije, 1996).

16 For testimonies, publications, and documents in English on the wartime cooperation of women from different parts of former Yugoslavia, see: <http://www.womenngo.org. yu>; <http://www.awin.org.yu>; and <http://www.zenstud.hr>. See also Svetlana Slapšak, "Yugoslav War: A Case of/for Gendered History," in *War Discourse, Women's Discourse* (ed.), by Svetlana Slapšak, (Ljubljana: Topos, 2000), 17–68.

17 Svetlana Slapšak, "Representations of Gender as Constructed, Questioned and Subverted in Balkan films," *Cinéaste* 32, No. 3 (2007): 37–40.

18 As stated by the journalist Bogdan Tirnanić. Cf. Svetlana Slapšak, "Im Innern der populistischen Maschinerie: Eliten, Intellektuelle, Diskurslieferanten in Serbien 1986–2001,"

for Serbian men was—Serbian women. In this case, women function as a collective screen of culpabilization, with a twofold use: to project a collective patriarchal anger and frustration, reinforced by a displacement of male "culpability" for cowardice during the war years onto women, and to use this imaginary screen to hide and silence the dark side of collective memory. This negative representation of women coincides with the Serbian refusal to take responsibility for the war. This massive socio-cultural phenomenon can be compared to the representational petrification of women in socialist Yugoslavia—with a minus-index.[19]

Feminist Ghettoization and Backlash Activism

A voluntary retreat from the public discourse during the recent war was perhaps the only way to keep the existing feminist institutions functional in an openly unfriendly atmosphere, both in Serbia and in Croatia. In a situation in which state funding was both impossible and unwanted, and the only flow of resources was coming from the outside, this institutional ghettoization was the most important part of the survival-package. Within this strategy, the predictable divide between the academic and the activist groups took place by the end of the war (1995–97). Scarcely and reluctantly accepted as a source of information even in the oppositional (anti-Milošević) press, Serbian feminists survived without visible impact on the public discourse for almost ten years: activist feminists kept alive the politics of gender tolerance in their inner circles, and academic feminists could express their views in rare domestic and some international publications. Even invisible, they could not avoid a massive attack on feminists and women generally during the last Balkan crisis in 1999 and 2000. The feminist practices over this period could be described only as pacifist, aimed at re-establishing the links with other feminist organizations across the new borders, helping victims of war and production of numerous texts, studies, and reports in *samizdat* format. The only activity lacking from this picture is the actual participation in the local public discourse, for instance polemics with the war advocates or critique of the intellectual elites for their part in collaborating with the regime. Given feminists' limited or non-existent access to the media, it is hard to criticize the strategy of ghettoization even on these grounds. However, keeping a low profile in the space of public discourse and establishing a withdrawal into an academic or low-level activist niche is not very productive in a culture that still conceives of itself as a homogenous whole. For, although some *actants* in this

---

in *Rechtspopulismus. Österreichische Krankheit oder europäische Normalität?* (ed.), by Wolfgang Eismann, (Vienna: Czernin, 2002), 199–220.

19 Cf., Marina Blagojević (ed.), *Ka vidljivoj ženskoj istoriji: Zenski pokret u Beogradu 90-ih [Toward a Visible Women's History: Women's Movement in Belgrade in the 1990s]* Belgrade: Centar za ženske studije, 1998; Svetlana Slapšak, "Feminizm i pisarstwo kobiet na polu minowym: paradygmat jugosłowiański i postjugosłowiański w perspektywie synchronicznej i diachronicznej" ["Feminism and Women's Writing in a Minefield: Yugoslav and Post-Yugoslav Paradigm from the Synchronic and Diachronic Perspective"], in *Literatury słowiańskie po roku 1989: nowe zjawiska, tendencje, perspektywy, Vol. 2: Feminizm* (ed.), by Ewa Kraskowska (Warsaw: Kolor Plus, 2005), 137–68.

culture may be ghettoized, they would be taken into account at the moment when "enemies" are needed, in the time of crisis.

The question remains: does it get better with the changes? The massive anti-war coalition in Serbia dissolved after the fall of Milošević in 2000. The discrepancy of political goals and expectations was such that the Europe-oriented Serbian PM Zoran Djindjić was assassinated in 2003. The cultural fragmentation divided former allies against Milošević into the two opposed groups along the issue of responsibility. The majority of former pacifists and critics of the regime made compromising arrangements with the nationalists by arguing that there was enough pain and suffering for the Serbian people and that the demand for responsibility, and especially the demand of the International Tribunal for war crimes in The Hague, was "destabilizing" to the fragile democracy in Serbia. The minority of "radical critics" demanding the responsibility account was labeled "traitors" once again, this time by their own former peers; they were excluded from the new public discourse, the access to which was never precluded to national extremists.[20] I am not arguing that a more visible feminist presence in the public sphere could have changed the course of history. I am just highlighting an extremely discomforting reality, and the question which still remains open: that of the feminist active participation and share-demanding in any socio-cultural context.

Thus I will close this discussion by addressing the attendant phenomenon of backlash activism. I will use statements by two female intellectuals from the region as case-studies to show the pervasiveness of misogynist discourse and its self-productive power even within women's discourse itself. The first statement is by Slovene Renata Salecl, from her book *Spoils of Freedom*:

> The sad fact is that no serious feminist movement exists in post-socialist countries. There are few feminist groups with any public impact. There are several reasons for this lack of feminism. First, no feminist tradition existed under socialism. Second, as is well known, socialism was a very patriarchal society, in spite of the official claim that it solved the woman question. Furthermore, feminism did not emerge after the fall of socialism because women perceive it as being un-feminine.[21]

The second statement is by Biljana Srbljanović, a renowned playwright from Belgrade, in a radio show on Radio B92:

> And I am mad at Šešelj and Milošević because they are the reason for the presence of Carla del Ponte and that Hartman woman in my life. I am mad because these two bitches are constantly present in my life and they are incessantly preaching to me. My theory is that the association "Freedom" and Koštunica are paying Carla del Ponte [...] to smear the Hague Tribunal. When Hartman comes and says, "What kind of a country you are, you don't even have a government," that is like [they] told her, "Here is the money, please tell it like this." Isn't my theory logical? I cannot understand that people are promoting their job in such an idiotic way. So what if we do not have a government? First, we have it,

---

20 On this divide, see Sonja Biserko, *Tačka razlaza* [*The Point of Divide*] (Belgrade: Helsinški odbor Srbije, 2002).

21 Renata Salecl, *The Spoils of Freedom. Psychoanalysis and Feminism after the Fall of Socialism* (London: Routledge, 1994), 4.

secondly, so what if we do not have it, it is none of your business, go look after your own. Go judge the criminals, don't lecture me [...]. I bet that Karadžić and Mladić give a few pennies to those two to go around and smear the Hague Tribunal.[22]

Ten years separate these two extreme statements. While the self-promoting motivation apparent in both cases is of no interest to the debate on misogyny, the discursive strategies and the calculation about the presupposed knowledge and receptiveness of the targeted audience are more interesting in the context of my discussion. According to Renata Salecl, feminism never happened and is non-existent in the region. Facts do not support this statement: there were many grassroots women's organizations that found their way out of the war-defined aims and modes of acting, many centers for women's and gender studies outside the official academe have been founded, there has been a strong movement of conquering the academic institutions in Croatia and Serbia, and there is a solid 20 years of continuity of presence of gender and women's studies in the academic setting of Slovenia. Are we observing two separate worlds? In the case of both Salecl and Srbljanović, we are indeed dealing with discursive inventions of "colonized worlds," which include strategies and manipulative techniques to ensure the inventor's future benefits and exclusive rights of exploitation. True, these two statements should also be put in the context of the transition in the region, of the improvised survival-kits for the new capitalist rules on the market, rising right-wing ideologies, insecurity, and so on. But they do, in their own ways, speak of women's history, and of almost impossible tasks that the regional feminist thinking and movements are still facing.

Salecl starts with a "sad fact" that no serious feminist movement exists in post-socialist countries. The fact is "sad" because Salecl is an interested feminist, the one that does not fall under the rubric of this sad state of affairs: in other words, Salecl is immediately representing herself as a genuine and probably the only feminist coming from the post-socialist countries. She argues that there are few feminist groups with any public impact. This (1994) is the time of war in former Yugoslavia (I leave out the rest of the post-socialist world, since Salecl's main interest is in that region), and feminist groups are very visible: the Croatian "witches," Women's Center in Zagreb, Women in Black, Women's Center in Belgrade, Belgrade Circle and its affiliated feminist activists, and many, many others—local women's NGOs are proliferating in Bosnia and Croatia. In fact, being the favorite target in the media, nationalist and non-nationalist, they are constantly present in the public sphere and they represent an important portion of the political opposition to Milošević's regime in Serbia. Their auto-ghettoization, as I discussed previously, invites an elaborate academic interpretation, not censorship. It is women who took over the streets in the 1993–94 protest in Belgrade because men were hiding in fear of draft. Salecl's statements are an obvious disinformation, or worse. Further allegation that no feminist tradition existed under socialism is, likewise, erroneous, as my previous discussion has showed. Since Salecl did not make the effort of doing a routine research work on this

---

22 Biljana Srbljanović, Interview, Radio B92, February 20, 2004. Carla del Ponte is The Hague Tribunal war crime head investigator; Florence Hartman is del Ponte's spokeswoman; Vojislav Koštunica is President of Serbia.

subject, the doubt remains that she did not want to do it in order to present herself as a unique existing feminist from former Yugoslavia.

Finally, Salecl is right in underscoring that socialism was deeply patriarchal. Yet, there were great differences between the Yugoslav social situation and the gender conditions in the countries of the former Soviet bloc, for Yugoslav patriarchy was deeply contaminated with consumerist freedom—a state that cannot be compared with that in any country of the bloc. Finally, Salecl argues that the lack of feminism is based on the fact that women perceive feminism as un-feminine. No doubt that this rather trivial stereotype is largely in use, especially in the so-called yellow press, women's magazines, and conservative public discourse. But are these the reasons not to expect feminism in, say, the United Kingdom or the United States? Or is Salecl just manipulating a misogynist and colonial stereotype about women from this region, who are supposed to be less clever, politically and culturally retarded, and therefore more likely to succumb to the threats and seduction from conservative political circles and consumerist culture alike?

Ten years later, the situation defies all possible predictions. The map of feminist movements, pacifist, political, social, health and therapy oriented, cultural, and academic, is richer than anybody in the region could have hoped for. This is true even for the most extreme case, that of Serbia, where the rich feminist area unfortunately does not meet official politics in any point of public life. Culturally, they often represent two different worlds of discourse, meaning, emotions, understanding, and symbols. Biljana Srbljanović belonged to the anti-Milošević majority before October 2000; she was even tried and sentenced for slander after she publicly stated that the film director Emir Kusturica had received funds for making his film *Underground* from Milošević's government. But in her statement cited here, Srbljanović expresses views that are quite close to the present inflammatory misogynist discourse in the Serbian media. Carla del Ponte of The Hague Tribunal and her assistant are quoted as "bitches," a term that has a long and uneasy folkloric and anthropological history in the region. Del Ponte and Hartman become "implicated" in an eccentric imaginary plot in which war criminals and Serbian right-wing politicians pay these women to denigrate the legal institutions for which they are working. The two professional women are represented as pawns, deprived of power, hungry for (very little) money, and despicable in every way. Moreover, they haunt Srbljanović's private life, they are nothing but a nuisance. Srbljanović is proud of her government, in whatever condition it might be—even non-existing—which gives an unpleasant nationalist undertone to her exaggerated statement.

Where does this immeasurable hatred against the two women come from? Since October 2000 in Serbia, the former allies in the fight against Milošević's regime and the war have split, as I showed earlier in this chapter. Consequently, the perception of The Hague Tribunal, formerly understood as the only hope for the punishment of war criminals, shifted toward a rather negative image in which it figures as a kind of a maverick institution that intervenes on the local level and destabilizes a laboriously established balance of forces. Del Ponte and her assistant's gender are politicized according to the local narratives of women "traitors," "foreign mercenaries," and generally persons dangerous for (in this case, Serbian) men.

We recognize this behavior as one of the usual misogynist strategies, but why should it be gendered in such an extreme way? The answer to this question could be sought in the recognition of the similarity of strategies used by Salecl and Srbljanović to muffle the real dimensions of war in the region. While Salecl presents the war in recognizable, stereotyped terms of Western media, Srbljanović avoids the war issue, and insists on private and personal commodity as the main, and maybe the unique, victim of war: Del Ponte unnerves *her*, Srbljanović, by pursuing war criminals. Life is simpler and more pleasant with war criminals on the loose. This kind of self-censorship of memory was one of the basic survival techniques in socialist times. The appropriation of this strategy is the clue to the success of the Srbljanović's *Diary* during the NATO bombing of Serbia in 1999, which was published in several European journals (for example, Italian *La Republica*). This is a diary of a well-to-do city girl who is disturbed by bombing in her daily routine, hygiene, shopping, going to trendy places, and even making love. It is written from a self-centered perspective and with an amount of carelessness about the other. It must be said that such an error in perception and reading of culture is colossal: the trauma of war, as described by male nationalist authors from the region, is deeply inscribed in gender relations. The omission of noticing this state of affairs by women themselves is highly indicative of the inadvertent appropriation of misogynist discourse by women themselves.

Salecl's argument about feminism being "un-feminine," and Srbljanović's use of the term "bitch" converge in an unexpected way. Srbljanović's use of strong street language is very un-feminine, indeed representative of misogyny, slandering the very impersonations of the policy that irrevocably separates genders in the local context. Using daring paradoxes, both Srbljanović and Salecl, although separated by ten years and very different positions, manipulate the potential of the negative imaging of feminism to project themselves against this deliberately darkened screen.

Conclusion

This analysis of discourses on war and gender, male and female, has shown that the main specificity of the area, when it comes to feminism and gender, lies in conceptualizing, contextualizing, and presenting the war. It is a fascinating case, quite challenging for the epistemology of gender studies, of a concept/context mutual work and formation. This state of affairs confirms that specific knowledge, blending of local (native) input and theoretical dialogue into the same referential framework, is absolutely necessary in the future planning of gender and feminist studies. For superficial homonymy can produce deep misunderstanding and it can be a fertile ground for manipulative misogynist strategies, as seen in the Salecl–Srbljanović case.

Bibliography

Biserko, Sonja. *Tačka razlaza* [*The Point of Divide*]. Belgrade: Helsinški odbor Srbije, 2002.

Blagojević, Jelisaveta, Katerina Kolozova, and Svetlana Slapšak (eds), *Gender and Identity: Theories from and/or on Southeastern Europe*. Belgrade: Women's Studies and Gender Research Center, 2006.

Blagojević, Marina (ed.), *Ka vidljivoj ženskoj istoriji: Ženski pokret u Beogradu 90-ih [Toward a Visible Women's History: Women's Movement in Belgrade in the 1990s]*. Belgrade: Centar za ženske studije, 1998.

—— (ed.), *Mapping Misogyny in Serbia: Discourses and Practices*. Belgrade: AZIN, 2004.

Dojčinović-Nešić, Biljana. *Odabrana bibliografija radova iz feministicke teorije/ zenskih studija 1974–1996 [Selected Bibliography of Works in Feminist Theory/ Women's Studies 1974–1996]*. Belgrade: Centar za ženske studije, 1996.

Funk, Nanette. "Feminism East and West," 1–14, and "Women and Post-Communism," 318–30. In *Gender Politics and Post-Communism*. Edited by Nanette Funk and Magda Mueller. New York and London: Routledge, 1993.

Herzfeld, Michael. *Cultural Intimacy: Social Poetics in the Nation-State*. New York and London: Routledge, 2005.

Higonnet, Margaret (ed.), *Behind the Lines: Gender and the Two World Wars*. New Haven: Yale University Press, 1987.

Lebl, Ženi. *Ljubičica bela [White Violet]*. Gornji Milanovac: Dečje Novine, 1990.

Petrović, Jelena, and Svetlana Slapšak. "Sex/gender Distinction, Uses and Abuses in South Slavic Languages in the Multilingual Balkan Region. Serbian/Croatian/ Bosnian in Their Comparative Setting." In *The Making of European Women's Studies: A Work in Progress Report on Curriculum Development and Related Issues in Gender Education and Research*. Vol. 5. Edited by Rosi Braidotti, Edyta Just, Marlise Mensink. 80–85. Utrecht: Utrecht University, 2004.

Salecl, Renata. *The Spoils of Freedom. Psychoanalysis and Feminism after the Fall of Socialism*. London: Routledge, 1994.

Sklevicky, Lydia. *Konji, žene, ratovi [Horses, Women, Wars]*. Zagreb: Ženska infoteka, 1996.

Slapšak, Svetlana. "Yugoslav War: A Case of/for Gendered History." In *War Discourse, Women's Discourse*. Edited by Svetlana Slapšak. 17–68. Ljubljana: Topos, 2000.

—— "Im Innern der populistischen Maschinerie: Eliten, Intellektuelle, Diskurslieferanten in Serbien 1986–2001." In *Rechtspopulismus. Österreichische Krankheit oder europäische Normalität?* Edited by Wolfgang Eismann. 199–220. Vienna: Czernin, 2002.

—— "Feminizm i pisarstwo kobiet na polu minowym: paradygmat jugosłowiański i postjugosłowiański w perspektywie synchronicznej i diachronicznej." ["Feminism and Women's Writing in a Minefield: Yugoslav and Post-Yugoslav Paradigm from the Synchronic and Diachronic Perspective."] In *Literatury słowiańskie po roku 1989: nowe zjawiska, tendencje, perspektywy, Vol. 2: Feminizm*. Edited by Ewa Kraskowska. 137–68. Warsaw: Kolor Plus, 2005.

—— "Representations of Gender as Constructed, Questioned and Subverted in Balkan Films." *Cinéaste* 32, No. 3 (2007): 37–40.

Srbljanović, Biljana. Interview. Radio B92. February 20, 2004.

Tax, Meredith. "The Five Croatian 'Witches': A Casebook on 'Trial by Public Opinion' As a Form of Censorship and Intimidation." (1993) <http://www. wworld.org/archive/archive.asp?ID=157>.

Werner, Michael, and Bénédicte Zimmermann. "Beyond Comparison. *Historie Croisée* and the Challenge of Reflexivity." *History and Theory* 45 (2006): 30–50.

Chapter 7

A Call for a Nuanced Constitutional Jurisprudence: South Africa, *Ubuntu*, Dignity, and Reconciliation[1]

Drucilla Cornell, in collaboration with Karin Van Marle

Introduction

What I hope to do in this chapter is first to try to reconfigure the relationship between dignity and *ubuntu*, and then show how we might rethink this relationship in some crucial court cases and activist projects in South Africa. The notion of dignity comes from Immanuel Kant's distinction between who and how we are as sensible beings in the world, subjected to determination by the causal laws of nature in our lives as sensual creatures.[2] Yet in our lives as creatures capable of making ourselves subject to the law of the categorical imperative, we can also make ourselves legislators of the moral law and moral right. We are free and as free we are of infinite worth. The categorical imperative in Kant is a demand put on us that could be succinctly summarized as follows: who I am only has a claim to dignity because I comply my life with who I should be, and the categorical imperative is a practical imperative that commands the "should be." Since it is only in the realm of morality that we find our freedom, there is no contradiction in Kant between subjecting ourselves to that command and our freedom.

Dignity as an Ideal

Many thinkers, particularly feminists, have questioned Kant in terms of his dualism: the dualism between the noumenal and the phenomenal self. Yet on a much broader understanding of Kantian insight, it turns on the notion that dignity itself, since it is part of practical reason and not theoretical reason, is inevitably related to the ideal

---

1 This chapter has come into being through the integration of two texts: Drucilla Cornell, "A Call for a Nuanced Constitutional Jurisprudence: *Ubuntu*, Dignity, and Reconciliation" (*Suid-Afrikaanse Publiekereg/South African Public Law* 19 (2004): 666–75), and Drucilla Cornell and Karin Van Marle, "Exploring *Ubuntu*—Tentative Reflections" (*African Human Rights Law Journal* [2005]: 195–220). The author and the editors would like to thank Karin Van Marle for allowing them to reproduce the portions of the latter text.

2 See, generally, Immanuel Kant, *Groundwork of the Metaphysics of Morals* [*Grundlegung zur Metaphysik der Sitten*], (1785).

of humanity, an ideal which is inseparable from freedom. But our freedom need not be defined so rigidly as in Kant, as only the subject of moral reason placed under the categorical imperative. Our dignity and the demand for its respect can stem from actual resistance, but also from the broken dreams that mark our commitment to moral ideals. Painted with a very broad brush, dignity inheres in the evaluations we all have to make of our lives, the ethical decisions we consciously confront, and even the ones we ignore. Dignity lies in our struggle to remain true to our moral vision, and even in our wavering from it. In the case of South Africa, those who broke under torture did not lose their dignity, precisely because they cannot lose their dignity, since it is a postulate of practical reason that can never be fatally undermined by our actual existential collapse before horrifying brutality. As Zora Neale Hurston's character, Nanny, in *Their Eyes Were Watching God* describes dignity:

> Ah was born back due in slavery, so it wasn't for me to fulfill my dreams of whut a woman oughta be and to do. Dat's one of de hold-backs of slavery. But nothing can't stop you from wishin'. You can't beat nobody down so low till you can rob'em of they will. Ah didn't want to be used or a work-ox and a brood sow and Ah didn't want mah daughter used dat way neither.[3]

Again, if we give Kantian dignity its broadest meaning, it is not associated with our actual freedom but with the postulation of ourselves as beings who not only can, but must, confront moral and ethical decisions, and in making those decisions, we give value to our world. In the context of South Africa, the remembrance of the postulation of dignity as an ideal that we can never lose is particularly important, for dignity simply is at the level of the ideal. Dignity and its respect is also a demand placed on us as we shape our practical, ethical, and political reality. It is human beings in their practical activity who give value to the world. In Kant, freedom is inscrutable; if it could be reduced to a set of positive characteristics, it would no longer be freedom, but would come to be known as a cognizable object falling under the laws of nature. Beyond the inscrutability of our freedom, dignity and the respect it demands does not require the elaboration of common identities and shared characteristics, with the corresponding boundaries of who is in and who is out. Indeed such an elaboration goes against the grain of dignity since all value scales that attempt to codify the meaning of richer identities have long been associated with the hierarchical brutality of colonization and patriarchal ideologies. It is important to note here that dignity is an ideal, not a value, because unlike a value it cannot be weighed; there is no such thing as thick and thin dignity.

It is precisely because dignity remains at the level of an ideality associated with the ideal of humanity that it is difficult to use it as a sole justification for what is known as second- or third-generation rights, especially in the case of South Africa.[4]

---

3 Zora Neale Hurston, *Their Eyes Were Watching God* (New York: Harper & Row Publishers, 1990), 15.

4 As initially proposed by Karel Vašák and subsequently elaborated at the International Institute of Human Rights in Strasbourg, human rights may be divided into three generations: the first-generation human rights are related to liberty and the right to participate in political life; the second-generation human rights deal with equality/equity (for example, right to

But I want to make a stronger point here, which is that dignity should not be used as the ideal or translated into a legal principle to justify such rights at all. The reason for this is that we undermine both the ideal and critical aspect of dignity when we attempt to say and elaborate the conditions under which it can be lost. This, for example, is the problem with Martha Nussbaum's attempt when she seeks to elaborate what a fully human life is, with its attendant understanding that if we ("women") are denied certain conditions, we are subject to violence of specific kind: we lose our dignity, because we are no longer "dignified."[5] Feminist conflations between dignity and what is dignified are particularly problematic, for then there is the danger of denying dignity to other women because of the oppressive conditions under which they live. We seek to say that those conditions should be changed in the name of their dignity and not because they have lost their dignity due to those conditions. This distinction may seem subtle, but I believe it is crucial for both transnational feminism, and for the jurisprudence of South Africa. However, dignity is enough for a wide range of cases—as we shall see hereafter, it certainly can be used to reject state imposed execution as constitutionally legitimate. We can move from Kant to the rejection of the death penalty because, as in suicide, the subject of rights is annihilated, and without at least an idealized subject of rights, there can be no rights in the first place.

Elsewhere I have defended a revision of the Kantian notion of dignity, so as to reconcile Kant with the right to die.[6] But for now, I want to emphasize that for Kant, the notion of law and the founding principle of legality can only be a hypothetical experiment in the imagination, in which self-legislating human beings contracted to their own restraint on the basis of mutual accordance of each other's dignity as free persons, are limited only by the internal restrictions of dignity as an ideal. As a result, Kant could not himself easily justify anything close to second- or third-generation rights. Throughout a philosophical lifetime, John Rawls sought to demonstrate that perhaps we could take the Kantian hypothetical social contract so as to reach much more sweeping egalitarian conclusions.[7] Whether or not he was successful is open to debate. But my point here is somewhat different: it is simply that even in Kant, let alone in his predecessors and contemporaries, modern Anglo-European political philosophy presumes, at least on the level of the individual, a social contract as the only legitimate constitutive power of a constituted government. The definition of a legitimate legal authority turns on this idealized social contract with its highly specific understanding of how a bill of rights and other constitutional mandates can be legitimated only from within this imagined basis of a contract with an imagined, already individuated, individual. This understanding of law through social contract

---

be employed, right to housing and health care, right to unemployment benefits, and so on); and the third-generation human rights include rights such as collective rights, right to self-determination, right to economic and social development, right to participation in cultural heritage, and others (editors' note).

5 See, generally, Martha Nussbaum, *Women and Human Development: The Capabilities Approach* (Cambridge: Cambridge University Press, 2000).

6 Drucilla Cornell, "Who Bears the Right to Die," in *Sovereignty and Death* (ed.), by Adam Thurschwell, forthcoming.

7 See, for one, John Rawls, *A Theory of Justice* (Cambridge, Mass.: Harvard University Press, 1971).

is, in my opinion, simply inadequate to the second- and third-generation rights guaranteed in the South African Constitution.

Kant can get us to the notion of democracy as friendship, but only in the following sense: I am your friend because I am a friend to myself, as a being who can make himself or herself a person who struggles to make what I am, who I should be.

Ubuntu

The Judge Yvonne Mokgoro has summarized the many notions of what *ubuntu* may be as follows:

> Generally, *ubuntu* translates as *humaneness*. In its most fundamental sense, it translates as *personhood* and *morality*. Metaphorically, it expresses itself in *umuntu ngumuntu ngabantu*, describing the significance of group solidarity on survival issues so central to the survival of communities. While it envelops the key values of group solidarity, compassion, respect, human dignity, conformity to basic norms and collective unity, in its fundamental sense it denotes humanity and morality. Its spirit emphasises respect for human dignity, marking a shift from confrontation to conciliation.[8]

Irrespective of its evident relevance, *ubuntu* is a controversial value or ideal in South Africa. Philosophers such as Augustine Shutte have forcefully argued that *ubuntu* should be adopted as a new ethic for South Africa.[9] On the other hand, critics of *ubuntu* have made a number of arguments against those who would make *ubuntu* an essential ethical ideal or moral value in the new South Africa. Broadly construed, those criticisms range from the claim that *ubuntu* was once a meaningful value but now gives nothing to young South Africans to the claim that *ubuntu* is inherently patriarchal and conservative. Still others argue that *ubuntu* is such a bloated concept that it means everything to everyone, and as a bloated concept it should not be translated into a constitutional principle. Although *ubuntu* was included in the epilogue of the interim constitution there have not been many attempts to incorporate *ubuntu* into post-apartheid jurisprudence. Where courts have referred to *ubuntu* they treated it as a "uni-dimensional" concept and not as a philosophical doctrine.[10]

The debate whether or not *ubuntu* can be translated into a justiciable principle turns not only on the definition one gives to *ubuntu* but also on how and why *ubuntu* can be considered an "African" or "South African" value, or an embodiment of "African" philosophy.[11] One crucial aspect of "African" philosophy which is articulated by

---

8 See Yvonne Mokgoro, opinion in *State v. Makwanyane & Mchunu* (1995), <http://www.constitutionalcourt.org.za/uhtbin/cgisirsi/20071014193136/SIRSI/0/520/J-CCT3-94> (paragraph 308), 101. The Khosa proverb *"umuntu ngumuntu ngabantu"* translates: "a person is a person through persons."

9 See Augustine Shutte, *Philosophy for Africa* (Milwaukee, WI: Marquette University Press, 1995), especially chapters 10 and 11.

10 Marius Pieterse, "'Traditional' African Jurisprudence," in *Jurisprudence* 442 (ed.), by Christopher J. Roederer and D. Moellendorf (Lansdowne: Juta and Co, Ltd, 2004).

11 In March 2004, The *Ubuntu* Project, a project developed out of the Stellenbosch Institute for Advanced Studies, held a one-day conference in March 2004 to discuss the role of

anthropologists, theologians, and philosophers, who disagree on every other aspect of "African" philosophy, is its focus on metadynamics and the relationship, or active play of forces, as the nature of being. Whatever else it may be, *ubuntu* implies an interactive ethic in a profound sense, or an ontic orientation in which who and how we can be as human beings is always being shaped in our interaction with each other. This ethic is not then a simple form of communalism or communitarianism, if one means by those terms the privileging of the community over the individual. For what is at stake here is the process of becoming a person or, more strongly put, how one is given the chance to become a person at all. The community is not something "outside," some static entity that stands against individuals. The community *is* only as it is continuously brought into being by those who "make it up." The community, then, is always being formed through an ethic of being with others, and this ethic is in turn evaluated by how it empowers people. In a dynamic process the individual and community are always in the process of coming into being. Individuals become individuated through their engagement with others, and their ability to live in line with their capability is at the heart of how ethical interactions are judged. However, because we are gathered together in the first place by our engagements with others, a strong notion of responsibility inheres in *ubuntu*. Since our togetherness is actually part of our creative force that comes into being as we form ourselves with each other, our freedom is almost indistinguishable from our responsibility to the way in which we create a life in common with each other. If we ever try to bring *ubuntu* into speech, we might attempt to define it as this integral connection between freedom and empowerment, which is always enhanced and indeed only made possible through engagement with other people.

This interactive, ontic orientation reveals how freedom can be understood as indivisible, as Nelson Mandela wrote.[12] Without all of us transforming ourselves so as to be together in freedom, our individuality will be thwarted since we will all be bound, if differently so, in a field of unfreedom. Mandela writes:

> A man who takes away another man's freedom is a prisoner of hatred. He is locked behind the bars of prejudice and narrow-mindedness. I am not truly free if I am taking away someone else's freedom, just as surely as I am not free when my freedom is taken from me. The oppressed and the oppressor alike are robbed of their humanity.[13]

In Mandela's interpretation, then, the dynamic, interactive ethic that *ubuntu* expresses has as much to do with reshaping of our humanness through the modality of being together as it does with defining what are, for example, the essential attributes of our humanity that make us moral beings. This understanding that our humanness

---

ubuntu in the new South Africa, and, particularly, the feasibility of translating *ubuntu* into law. One of the panels at the conference focused exclusively on the question of whether *ubuntu* is a South African value, and even more broadly an African value or ideal, and what this would mean for the future of the South African Constitution.

12 Cf., "Freedom is indivisible. The chains on any one of my people are the chains on all of them. The chains on all of my people are the chains on me" (Nelson Mandela, *Long Walk to Freedom* [Backbay Books, 1995], 624).

13 *Ibid.*

is shaped in our interactions with one another and within a force field created and sustained by those interactions explains one of the most interesting aspects of *ubuntu* that will be discussed later—the notion that one's humanness can be diminished by the violent actions of others, including the violent actions of the state.

These ideals are understood well by those who pursue the *Ubuntu* Project in its ethnographic and anthropological aspects. The efforts of this project include multiple interviews conducted by and with young black South Africans regarding the meaning and significance of *ubuntu* to them. Not surprisingly, in addition to the ethnographic and jurisprudential aspects of the project, there emerged an activist dimension. A group of young women, who were initially conducting interviews on the meaning of *ubuntu* in local townships, organized themselves into a committee to found an *ubuntu* women's center. The result is the founding of *Ubuntu* Women's Center in Khayamandi in 2004.

The attempt to articulate and interpret the meaning of *ubuntu* and the struggle over its political, ethical, and practical importance in the new South Africa, however, demands an interdisciplinary inquiry that not only fuses grassroots activism, anthropology and philosophy, but is also reflected in legislation. In her most theoretically innovative moments, Judge Yvonne Mokgoro has suggested that *ubuntu* provides us with a notion of the founding of the principle of law very different from the practices in the Western societal contract tradition described above. The Law of law or the founding principles of legality are not reducible to the internal limiting principles of the social contract, based on maximizing the negative freedom of all. Instead, the Law of law is rearticulated to recognize that democracy as friendship can only be found in solidarity by reinforcing the community that sustains it:

Ubuntu(-ism), which is central to age-old African custom and tradition however, abounds with values and ideas which have the potential of shaping not only current indigenous law institutions, but South African jurisprudence as a whole. Examples that come to mind are: The original conception of law perceived not as a tool for personal defense, but as an opportunity given to all to survive under the protection of the order of the communal entity; communalism which emphasises group solidarity and interests generally, and all rules which sustain it, as opposed to individual interests, with its likely utility in building a sense of national unity among South Africans; the conciliatory character of the adjudication process which aims to restore peace and harmony between members rather than the adversarial approach which emphasises retribution and seems repressive The lawsuit is viewed as a quarrel between community members and not as a conflict; the importance of public ritual and ceremony in the communication of information within the group; the idea that law, experienced by an individual within the group, is bound to individual duty as opposed to individual rights or entitlement. Closely related is the notion of sacrifice for group interests and group solidarity so central to ubuntu(ism); the importance of sacrifice for every advantage or benefit, which has significant implications for reciprocity and caring within the communal entity.[14]

---

14 Judge Yvonne Mokgoro, "*Ubuntu* and the Law in South Africa," in *Seminar Report of the First Colloquium: Constitution and Law, Potchefstroom Electronic Law Journal*, vol. 1 (Johannesburg: Konrad-Adenauer-Stiftung, 1998).

Ubuntu, understood as an ideal irreducible to that based in an imagined social contract, could potentially promote a different set of ideals for interpreting the Bill of Rights in South Africa. Such an interpretation would not have to swim upstream, against the grain of negative liberty implied in the Western social contract tradition.

Now we could rephrase the Kantian language of friendship through *ubuntu* as follows. In Kant, I am a friend to myself because of the dignity of my humanity. Under *ubuntu*, I am a friend to myself because others in my community have already been friends to me, making me someone who could survive, and therefore be in the community. It is only because I have always been together with others and they have been with me that I am gathered together as a person and sustained in that self-gathering. We have a responsibility to that community that is irreducible to one on one correspondence between rights and duty, because I am not at all a person without this community. Obligation and duty in this sense go beyond that allowable under social contract theory. This more sweeping sense of obligation can help us understand how the beneficiaries of racism can be held responsible for correcting it, even by asserting and defending what at first glance might seem as an unequal, and because unequal, unfair position *vis-à-vis* other members of the community—for example, they may be expected to pay higher electricity bills than black South Africans.

But it is not only its ability to defend a notion of obligation that goes beyond social contract that makes *ubuntu* a highly relevant conceptual framework. It is the emphasis on the just quality of the community and the enhancement of that just quality that distinguishes *ubuntu* from other notions of community that reduce it to an imagined social contract between already individuated persons. In her opinion in the *Khosa* case Mokgoro did not justify her decision through the use of *ubuntu*, yet her conclusions in the case reflect an *ubuntu* inspired jurisprudence. In this decision the court had to confront a challenge to a certain provision of the Social Assistant Act 59 of 1992. The applicants in both matters were Mozambique citizens who were permanent residents in South Africa. In the case of the first applicant, the mother applied for two child support grants for her children under the age of seven and another grant, a care dependency grant, for a 12-year-old child who suffered from diabetes. The second applicant applied for an old age grant. The applicants in both matters were denied the grants because they were not citizens of South Africa. The applicants argued that sections 26, 27, and 28 of the South African Constitution use the word "everyone" in the first two cases and the words "every child" in the third case, and that delimiting access to social service grants violated not only their dignity but also the Constitution in which it is written that "everyone" is eligible. In a decision to uphold the validity of an order of the High Court, Mokgoro ruled that the court had the responsibility to read the words "permanent resident" into the challenged sections of the Social Security Act.

Mokgoro could have limited the reach of her decision to the group before her, the Mozambiquans. There is a tragic past that the South Africa of apartheid rule shared with Mozambique. Many of the freedom fighters of the African National Congress, including members of a guerrilla army formed by Mandela, fled to Mozambique and based their operations there. The result was an ongoing set of military interventions into Mozambique that violated the integrity of the country and that continues to make life in Mozambique difficult.[15] Due to this tragic past, Mokgoro could have made a special exception for Mozambiquan refugees but she chose not to rest her decision on that past or the special responsibility that might grow out of it. Instead, she took the message of the Constitution to heart because the relevant sections gave the rights to "everyone," and that "everyone" was the word that demanded interpretation. She ruled:

> This Court has adopted a purposive approach to the interpretation of rights. Given that the Constitution expressly provides that the Bill of Rights enshrines the rights of "all people in our country," and in the absence of any indication that the section 27(1) right is to be restricted to citizens as in other provisions in the Bill of Rights, the word "everyone" in this section cannot be construed as referring only to "citizens."[16]

Here Mokgoro explicitly rejects the "American" solution to this problem, which is to treat "citizens" differently from "non-citizens." Indeed, the respondents argued that many "developed" countries, and not just the United States, made distinctions between "citizens" and "non-citizens" in the granting of social welfare grants. Mokgoro distinguished her own decision from the US Supreme Court by arguing that the reasonableness by which differentiations and exclusion in legislations are judged in South Africa is of a much higher standard of judicial review than those used by the US Supreme Court, which is based on rationality. But what makes Mokgoro's decision particularly important is that she not only emphasizes the wrong done to the individuals, but she also insists that the purposive nature of the South African Constitution is rooted in the promotion of a just community, a just community which again is irreducible to a social contractual and "rational" understanding of the relationship between rights and duties. Thus, she ruled that the Court should not just make sure that the change takes place now so that the destitute individuals should get their grants (although, of course, Mokgoro is very much concerned that they do get their grants), but also that the change should be enforced by the Court to bring into being a just and equitable community. Mokgoro writes:

> At the time the immigrant applies for admission to take up permanent residence the state has a choice. If it chooses to allow immigrants to make their homes here it is because it sees some advantage to the state in doing so. Through careful immigration policies it can ensure that those admitted for the purpose of becoming permanent residents are persons who will profit, and not be a burden to, the state. If a mistake is made in this regard, and the permanent resident becomes a burden, that may be a cost we have to pay for the constitutional commitment to developing a caring society, and granting access to socio-economic rights to all who make their homes here. [...] The category of permanent residents who are before us are children and the aged, all of whom are destitute and in need of social assistance. They are unlikely to earn a living for themselves. While the self-sufficiency argument may hold in the case of immigrants who are viable in the job market

---

15 One classic example is that a relatively large amount of Mozambiquan land is still heavily mined. The mines were installed by the South African government under apartheid and now those lands are of little industrial or agricultural use.

16 Yvonne Mokgoro, opinion in *Khosa v. The Minister of Social Development* (2004), <http://www.lhr.org.za/projects/refugee/ConCourt%20judgements/khosa%20full%20 judgement.pdf> (para 47), 31.

and who are still in the process of applying for permanent resident status, the argument is seemingly not valid in the case of children and the aged who are already settled permanent residents and part of South African society.[17]

The best way to understand Mokgoro's argument is that permanent residents, through their actual engagements with South Africa, have become a part of the ethical interactions that make up the country and that they, as a result, should be considered part of the promise for justice offered by the Constitution. Mokgoro did not use the word *ubuntu* here, but when she writes that additional burden must be assumed by citizens and that others who do not have those burdens still have equal right to access to social benefits, she is not only promoting a fair community but, as she writes, she is advancing a caring community. And this close connection between a just and caring community is part and parcel of her understanding of what the *nomos* of the new South Africa demands of its citizens. This *nomos* seems to be based on honoring what Simone Weil characterized as "sacred in every human being": an indomitable expectation, "in the teeth of all experience of crimes committed, suffered, and witnessed, that good and not evil will be done to [him/her]."[18] What may have influenced Mokgoro's decision is thus a striving for a caring society. That the inspiration for this politics and ethics could be the notion of *ubuntu* is hinted at in the following excerpt from Mokgoro's judgment: "Sharing responsibility for the problems and consequences of poverty equally as a community represents the extent to which wealthier members of the community view the minimal well-being of the poor as connected with their personal well-being and the well-being of the community as a whole."[19]

The closest we come to this ideal of *ubuntu* in the European tradition is in Hegel, where the objective community, or *sittlichkeit*, always precedes and constitutes the subject of rights. Hegel, of course, did not deny subjective rights, as we understand them—as first-generation rights defended through dignity—and neither does Yvonne Mokgoro. But I would like to suggest here that to understand Mokgoro at her most provocative is to grasp her argument that African ideals of solidarity and mutual sustenance could potentially provide a new and important way to think about the Law of law, or the grounding principles of legality itself. G.J. van Niekerk makes a similar argument in her defense of the idea that the basic principles of indigenous law remain implicated in a different notion of the ground of law, one that is "foreign" to social contract theory.[20] She describes those principles as the harmony of the collectivity, the principle of the superhuman or spiritual forces superior to the human, and what she calls the identity postulate. The identity postulate is an odd way for her to name her principle, since her point is that transformation and indeed

---

17 *Ibid.* (para. 65), 40.

18 Simone Weil, "Human Personality," *Simone Weil: An Anthology* (ed.), by Sian Miles (New York: Grove Press, 1986), 51.

19 Mokgoro, *Khosa* (para. 74), 47.

20 G.J. van Niekerk, "A Common Law for Southern Africa: Roman Law or Indigenous African Law?" in *Roman Law at the Crossroads* (ed.), by J.E. Spruit, W.J. Kamba, and M.O. Hinz (Kenwyn: Juta & Co. Ltd., 2000), 83.

contradictory ways of thinking can be taken into these principles in a "both-and" ethical attitude that can seek harmony without rationalization.

In some of the most sophisticated postcolonial theory today, this "both-and" attitude is defended as being against the historicism that, following Hegel, seeks to tell us that we must reject as an anachronism pieces/aspects of our lives, including, for example, the belief in spiritual and agential beings in the world of humans, because they can be thoroughly replaced with the rationality of the mature enlightenment which becomes secular at the level of ontology. Dipesh Chakrabarty, for example, argues that this "both-and" attitude is what allows us to keep alive contemporaneous "future nows" in Heidegger's sense, which can be present at hand and yet, seemingly contradictory.[21]

Ubuntu and social contract theory are in tension with one another, but if postcolonial theory has anything to teach us, it is that that tension can be productive, even as we attempt reconfigurations of possibly divergent notions of the Law of law and the axiomatic principles it generates. It is, therefore, important to note here that when Mokgoro translates *ubuntu* into an ideal of the South African Constitution, she does so by way of what I have called a conversion principle.[22] By a conversion principle, I mean an act of recollective imagination which not only recalls the past as it remembers the future, but also projects forward as an ideal the very principles that read into the past, that is, in this case, *ubuntu*. A conversion principle generally both converts the way we understand the past, and converts or translates any current practice of interpretation as we attempt to realize it in the reconstruction of law and legal principle. Given Mokgoro's profound concern with discrimination against women, she is, on my reading of her, converting the world-view and ideal of *ubuntu* into a "caring community" law, by both recollecting it and then also re-imagining it in accordance with a Constitution that is explicitly teleological and thus performative, in that it attempts to actualize the democratic values of human dignity, equality, and freedom. In turn, this re-imagining reconfigures the interpretation of the Constitution itself. A proposal for such reconfiguration can be found in Mokgoro's opinion in the case *State v. Makwanyane & Mchunu*, the first case of the new South African Constitutional Court, and one which defined what bearing the interim Constitution of South Africa had on capital punishment. In her concurring opinion, Mokgoro asserts that the death penalty is a form of vengeance incompatible with *ubuntu*. She goes on to explain:

> With the entrenchment of a bill of fundamental rights and freedoms in a supreme constitution however the interpretive task frequently involves making constitutional choices by balancing competing rights and freedoms. This can often only be done by reference to a system of values extraneous to the constitutional text itself where these principles constitute the historical context in which the text was adopted and which helped to explain the meaning of the text. The constitution makes it particularly imperative for

---

21 See, Dipesh Chakrabarty, *Provincializing Europe* (Princeton: Princeton University Press, 2000).

22 See, Drucilla Cornell, *Transformations: Recollective Imagination and Sexual Difference* (New York: Routledge, 1993), 37–40.

courts to develop the entrenched fundamental rights in terms of a cohesive set of values, ideal to an open and democratic society.[23]

Certainly, there are questionable aspects of *ubuntu* as a customary law, particularly for feminists, such as, for example, the endorsement of the notion of subsidiarity. Subsidiarity, as the philosopher Augustine Shutte has defined it, carries with itself a benevolent paternalism that has often treated women in customary law as if they were minors under the care of their husbands.[24] It is evident that her feminist aspirations would lead Mokgoro to question subsidiarity, at least as it applies to women. But she does so by reminding us that social custom, including the day-to-day on the ground status of women, is dynamic, even if at times certain aspects of customary law have become rigidified. Thus there are sources within the practice of social custom itself that can be imagined and re-imagined so as to reconfigure the norms of customary law. As I understand her, Mokgoro is proceeding from two directions. The first is to convert *ubuntu* into a constitutional principle and thereby to synchronize it with dignity. The second is to re-imagine *ubuntu* from within the *practices* of customary law, as they are engaged in by women themselves.

Of course, there is a more limited way to read Mokgoro, but one that I think is unfair to her more sweeping arguments that African values, such as *ubuntu*, are important in any jurisprudence that will seek to justify second- and third-generation rights. The more limited—or more localized—way to read Mokgoro is to argue that she is simply defending the notion that, as a matter of equality, we should respect the role and importance of African values in a society which has completely repudiated the very notion that black Africans had anything of ethical worth to add to the legal or moral culture to which they were subjected. Judge Albie Sachs has clearly joined Mokgoro in this more limited understanding of *ubuntu* in his opinion in the *State v. Makwanyane & Mchunu* case. He states that the implementation of *ubuntu* as a constitutionally acknowledged principle, means, above all, "giving long overdue recognition to African law and legal thinking as a source of legal ideas, values, and practice." He concludes, "We cannot, unfortunately extend the equality principle backwards in time to remove the humilities and indignities suffered by past generations, but we can restore dignity to ideas and values that have long been suppressed or marginalized."[25]

While Sachs has been criticized for establishing no normative basis for his system of human rights,[26] I want to suggest provocatively that, similarly to Mokgoro, the

---

23 Mokgoro, opinion in *State v. Makwanyane & Mchunu*, para. 302 <http://www.constitutionalcourt.org.za/uhtbin/cgisirsi/20071014193136/SIRSI/0/520/J-CCT3-94>, 99.

24 Augustine Shutte, *Ubuntu: An Ethic for a New South Africa* (Pietermaritzburg: Cluster Publications, 2001), 107, 148, 182.

25 Albie Sachs, opinion in *State v. Makwanyane & Mchunu*, para 365, 114.

26 See, Albie Sachs, *Protecting Human Rights in a New South Africa* (Oxford: Oxford University Press, 1991) and Sachs, *Advancing Human Rights in South Africa* (Oxford: Oxford University Press, 1992). For criticism of Sachs's work, see Dennis Davis, "Deconstructing and Reconstructing the Argument for a Bill of Rights within the Context of South African Nationalism," in *The Post-Apartheid Constitutions* (ed.), by Penelope Andrews and Stephen Ellmann (Johannesburg and Athens: Witwatersrand University Press and Ohio University

spirit of *ubuntu* does actually reside in Sachs's jurisprudence. It pervades, specifically, Sachs's attempt to "harmonize"—the word he often uses—the particularly difficult right of cultural belonging and religious belief; this is evidenced in his argument in the *Prince* case in which the young Rastafari practitioner thought to be a lawyer entered into the official Bar of South Africa. In his language, Sachs makes it clear "that the state should walk the extra mile in protecting religious practices even if some of those practices involve illegality, in this case the smoking of dagga."[27] Sachs's point—similar to Chakrabarty's—is that this extra mile should be taken precisely because religious belief and practice and rational assessment and justification simply do not proceed at the same register, and human beings cannot and should not be called to rationalize those beliefs or clean them up through reason, unless they fall afoul of the need to affirm the basic principles of the Bill of Rights. Particularly in this case, I am suggesting that Sachs's opinion reflects the spirit of *ubuntu* in two ways that go beyond the simple recognition that dignity should have a subjective component that demands that we respect people's representations of themselves. The first way in which Sachs's opinion reflects *ubuntu* takes us back to what van Niekerk has described as the identity postulate associated with *ubuntu* thinking. What I am suggesting here is that Sachs, in this opinion, recognizes the "both-and" as an ontic orientation in the world that is sometimes difficult for Westerners to comprehend. This orientation says: I believe in the Constitution and in ancestor worship and I do not believe that these two registers can be gathered together in a coherent whole. Secondly, I am suggesting that Sachs is seeking the harmonization of legal ideals so as to respect reconciliation, social harmony, and democracy as friendship, which all put on us a strong demand.

My question to Sachs would then be why he did *not* rely on *ubuntu* in his decision to refuse the allocation of kidney machines under conditions of scarce resources, particularly since in his opinion he has insisted that the very nature of the right involved has to turn on the recognition of our actual interdependence as human beings, and on the notion of human interdependence as "defining the circumstances in which the rights may most fairly and effectively be enjoyed."[28] Instead, Sachs has relied in his opinion on Ronald Dworkin.[29] Although Dworkin's insight into the dominion of life is certainly relevant to making these kinds of decisions, Dworkin's "Western" insistence on integrity and coherence makes him reluctant ever to acknowledge tragedy as inevitable in a world in which we live under conditions of massive inequality. By contrast, *ubuntu* can not only note that interdependence, but it can also help us understand tragedy and how we were all diminished in our humanity when the young man who could not afford the costly dialysis treatments died.

Press, 2001), 194–223; and, Mahmood Mamdani, *Citizen and Subject* [Princeton: Princeton University Press, 1996], 131–2 *et passim*).

27 See Sachs, opinion in *Prince v. President of the Law Society of the Cape of Good Hope* (2001), <http://www.constitutionalcourt.org.za/Archimages/755.PDF> (para. 149), 105.

28 See Sachs, concurring opinion in *Soobramoney v. Minister of Health (Kwazulu-Natal)* (1997), <http://hei.unige.ch/~clapham/hrdoc/docs/soobramoney.pdf> (paras 50–59), 28–34. For the details of the case, see the same document.

29 See Ronald Dworkin, *Life's Dominion* (New York: Vintage Books, 1994).

In African philosophy, *ubuntu* is associated with *seriti*, which names the life force by which a community of persons are connected to each other. In a constant mutual interchange of personhood and community, *seriti* becomes indistinguishable from *ubuntu* in that the unity of the life-force depends on the individual's unity with the community. As the philosopher of *ubuntu* Gabriel Setiloane explains, "it is as if each person were a magnet creating together a complex field. Within that field any change in the degree of magnetization, any movement of one, affects the magnetization of all."[30]

In my interviews in South Africa, this concept of *seriti*, as a force-field that shapes who we can be and diminishes us if we cannot live up to the demand for care and responsibility that it imposes upon us, was emphasized again and again; it importantly informs the *ubuntu* gender activism. The *seriti* principle holds that we have actually physically lost something, we are, in a sense, drained of our humanity, if we allow one of us to be denied access to a kidney machine simply because he or she can no longer afford it. In her opinion in *Makwanyane*, Judge Mokgoro seems to rely on something like this notion of *seriti*, when she claims that the toll of vengeance is not only felt by the one murdered, but extends to those who murder him or her, and beyond that to all those who live in a society shaped by that kind of vengeance— this is a notion exceedingly important in the process of (any) reconciliation.[31] It is difficult, if not impossible, for many legal thinkers trained in the Anglo-American tradition to live with the proposition that a legal decision can be fair and yet tragic. But I believe that this is "consistent" with *ubuntu* thinking in the "both-and" sense that I described earlier, and that the South African Constitution in particular needs to keep alive this "both-and" sense, not only because of its recent history but also because many of the socio-economic rights guaranteed by the Constitution are simply beyond their actualization in the current social and economic reality of South Africa. Keeping the ideal alive often involves marking that tragedy.

Conclusion

Ultimately a jurisprudence rich enough for the South African Constitution will have to reach beyond the ethical individualism of Ronald Dworkin, and even the radical egalitarian Kantianism of John Rawls. Social contract theory, even in its best form, can only take us so far. But it is not simply a matter of dignity that we respect indigenous traditions in South Africa, its "both-and" attitude, and the ensuing ways of social and, specifically, gender interrelating. My more provocative suggestion is that *ubuntu* thinking—and I am sure there will be many other such ideals to be recollected and re-imagined in African legal and ethical philosophy—is crucial to the fundamental purpose of the South African Constitution, which is to develop an interpretation of the Bill of Rights that goes way beyond the limited interpretation of such a bill as only a defense against state intrusion based on negative freedoms. The promotion of a democratic community of friendship that always remains to

---

30 Gabriel Setiloane, *The Image of God among the Sotho-Tswana* (Rotterdam: A.A. Balkema, 1976), 52, cited in Michael Battle, *Reconciliation: The Ubuntu Theology of Desmond Tutu* (Cleveland: The Pilgrim Press, 1997), 50.

31 See Mokgoro, opinion in *State v. Makwanyane, op. cit.*

come, even as we seek to bring it into being today, brings a nuanced jurisprudence that entails a complex reconciliation that makes it stronger—a reconciliation of the inevitable tensions between customary law and the Western ideals of liberalism, all of which should inform the Constitution.

Bibliography

Battle, Michael. *Reconciliation: The Ubuntu Theology of Desmond Tutu*. Cleveland: The Pilgrim Press, 1997.

Chakrabarty, Dipesh. *Provincializing Europe*. Princeton: Princeton University Press, 2000.

Cornell, Drucilla. *Transformations: Recollective Imagination and Sexual Difference*. New York: Routledge, 1993.

—— "Who Bears the Right to Die." In *Sovereignty and Death*. Edited by Adam Thurschwell. Forthcoming.

Davis, Dennis. "Deconstructing and Reconstructing the Argument for a Bill of Rights within the Context of South African Nationalism." In *The Post-Apartheid Constitutions*. Edited by Penelope Andrews and Stephen Ellmann. 194–223. Johannesburg and Athens: Witwatersrand University Press and Ohio University Press, 2001.

Dworkin, Ronald. *Life's Dominion*. New York: Vintage Books, 1994.

Hurston, Zora Neale. *Their Eyes Were Watching God*. New York: Harper & Row Publishers, 1990.

Kant, Immanuel. *Groundwork of the Metaphysics of Morals* [*Grundlegung zur Metaphysik der Sitten*] (1785).

Mamdani, Mahmood. *Citizen and Subject*. Princeton: Princeton University Press, 1996.

Mandela, Nelson. *Long Walk to Freedom*. Backbay Books, 1995.

Mokgoro, Yvonne. "*Ubuntu* and the Law in South Africa." In *Seminar Report of the First Colloquium: Constitution and Law, Potchefstroom Electronic Law Journal*, vol. 1 (Johannesburg: Konrad-Adenauer-Stiftung, 1998).

—— Opinion in *State v. Makwanyane & Mchunu*. (1995). Paragraphs 300–317. <http://www.constitutionalcourt.org.za/uhtbin/cgisirsi/20071014193136/SIRSI/0/520/J-CCT3-94>. 98–104.

—— Opinion in *Khosa v. The Minister of Social Development* (2004). Paragraphs 1–98.<http://www.lhr.org.za/projects/refugee/ConCourt%20judgements/khosa%20full%20judgement.pdf>. 2–63.

van Niekerk, G.J. "A Common Law for Southern Africa: Roman Law or Indigenous African Law?" In *Roman Law at the Crossroads*. Edited by J.E. Spruit, W.J. Kamba, and M.O. Hinz. Kenwyn: Juta & Co. Ltd, 2000.

Nussbaum, Martha. *Women and Human Development: The Capabilities Approach*. Cambridge: Cambridge University Press, 2000.

Pieterse, Marius. "'Traditional' African Jurisprudence." In *Jurisprudence* 442. Edited by Christopher J. Roederer and D. Moellendorf. Lansdowne: Juta and Co, Ltd, 2004.

Rawls, John. *A Theory of Justice.* Cambridge, Mass.: Harvard University Press, 1971.

Sachs, Albie. *Protecting Human Rights in a New South Africa.* Oxford: Oxford University Press, 1991.

—— *Advancing Human Rights in South Africa.* Oxford: Oxford University Press, 1992.

—— Opinion in *State v. Makwanyane & Mchunu.* Paragraphs 345–92 (1995). 110–19.

—— Opinion in *Soobramoney v. Minister of Health (Kwazulu-Natal).* Paragraphs 50–59 (1997). <http://hei.unige.ch/~clapham/hrdoc/docs/soobramoney.pdf>. 28–34.

—— Opinion in *Prince v. President of the Law Society of the Cape of Good Hope* Paragraphs 145–73 (2001). <http://www.constitutionalcourt.org.za/Archimages/755.PDF>. 100–38.

Shutte, Augustine. *Philosophy for Africa.* Milwaukee: Marquette University Press, 1995.

—— *Ubuntu: An Ethic for a New South Africa.* Pietermaritzburg: Cluster Publications, 2001.

Weil, Simone. *Simone Weil: An Anthology.* Edited by Sian Miles. New York: Grove Press, 1986.

PART III

Bordered Subjectivities, Global Connections

This part explores violence against women through the phenomenon of "the border." The editors are interested particularly in how borders complicate the discernment and recognition of certain patterns and processes constituting violence against women within and across complex spatial and subjective constructions of race, sexual orientation, and language, among others.

This part includes chapters naming and articulating the phenomenon of borders in various international contexts. Jennifer M. Green revisits the ambiguous borders among women, the nation-state, and globalization by deciphering how international legislation, and, in particular, the development of US legislation concerning sexual violence, affects women's rights globally. Sealing Cheng's and Loretta Ihme's chapters critically assess the set of processes concerning the global anti-trafficking action in which national governments and international bodies have been emphatically engaged since the late 1990s. Sealing Cheng's exploration of trafficking in South Korea highlights the often eclipsed borders between certain feminist NGOs and women who have been trafficked. Her research reveals that NGO advocacy may revictimize women involved in trafficking and migration by reporting on and representing their stories primarily through a lens circumscribed by their own needs for narratives of victimization, in effect marginalizing the voices of the women themselves. Furthering the discussion on trafficking and migration, Loretta Ihme's analysis of women trafficked in Central and Eastern Europe problematizes traditional interpretations of the multiple borders separating the trafficker from the trafficked by revealing how the nation-state itself may compound violence associated with trafficking by producing and circulating its own racist and misogynist propaganda. Finally, Angéla Kóczé's chapter considers how gendered borders within the already marginalized Roma community complicate the visibility and representation of Roma women in Europe and globally, and proposes innovative methods to counter this state of affairs.

Chapter 8

Litigating International Human Rights Claims of Sexual Violence in the US Courts: A Brief Overview of Cases Brought under the Alien Tort Statute and Torture Victim Protection Act

Jennifer M. Green

This chapter focuses on one small part of the global movement to end sexual violence and to punish those who perpetrate, command, and are otherwise complicit in rape and other types of sexual violence, or violence of a sexual nature other than rape.[1] It focuses on cases brought under two statutes in the United States: the Alien Tort Statute and the Torture Victim Protection Act. The Alien Tort Statute (ATS), 28 USC 1350, was enacted as part of the First Judiciary Act in 1789. It is a simple statute, providing that an "alien can bring a claim in tort for a violation of the law of nations."[2] In early 1992 the US Congress passed the Torture Victim Protection Act (TVPA), which reinforces the right of torture victims and relatives of people murdered by government security forces around the world to bring lawsuits in US courts.[3] The legislative history made clear that the TVPA was intended to supplement claims brought under the ATS. The TVPA allowed US citizens, as well as non-citizens, to bring claims for torture and for the extrajudicial killing of relatives. For the past 15 years, in ATS and TVPA claims, survivors and family members of those killed have brought claims in the United States courts for sexual violence as violations of customary international law arguing that these acts violate the universal prohibitions against torture and other cruel, inhuman, or degrading treatment; war crimes; and crimes against humanity. They have also brought claims for sexual slavery and forced prostitution, and have

---

1 This chapter is dedicated to the brave women and men who were plaintiffs in these cases, as well as to the many activists, legal scholars, and lawyers who have been instrumental in bringing to light and codifying the international prohibition of sexual violence, and who continue to work on these issues. A particular personal debt is owed to Rhonda Copelon, Judith Chomsky, and Beth Stephens who were my first mentors on ATS litigation and gender justice, whom I was privileged to work with on the cases discussed in this chapter, and who continue to provide insight, guidance, and support.

2 The Alien Tort Statute, 28 USC Section 1350.

3 The Torture Victim Protection Act of 1991, Public Law No. 102-256, 106 Stat. 73 (1992).

made some preliminary attempts to argue that "violence against women" and "sexual violence" are also norms recognized by customary international law.

ATS and TVPA lawsuits have resulted in numerous successes as well as defeats, at least in the legal decisions in court. Successes have included civil judgments including compensatory and punitive damage awards against foreign perpetrators living in or traveling to the United States. Defendants found liable for these abuses have included Radovan Karadžić, the former self-proclaimed leader of the Bosnian Serbs, for acts of genocide in the former Yugoslavia, and Emmanuel Constant, paramilitary leader of the Front Pour L'Avancement et le Progres Haitien (Front for Advancement and Progress of Haiti or FRAPH) in the 1990s in Haiti. Recently, courts have also recognized that corporations doing business in the United States can be held liable when they aid and abet or otherwise further sexual violence. Favorable rulings allowing claims of rape have also come from courts in cases brought on behalf of survivors of rape from Burma and Sudan, and from those seeking political asylum in the United States and subjected to sexual assault while being detained in a facility run by a company contracting with the US government.

Attempts to hold foreign governments themselves or US officials responsible have failed largely due to legal doctrines immunizing these powerful entities. The survivors of Japanese military sexual slavery during World War II brought claims in a US court but were dismissed because the court found that it could not rule on the legal claims without interfering with the US Executive branch and Congress—that this was a "political question." Efforts to hold U.S officials accountable for sexual violence have run up against provisions in US law—which limit the ability to sue US officials and the US government itself—and overbroad interpretations of these provisions by the US courts.

One largely unexplored area is whether there are also independent claims for sexual violence or violence against women. Sexual violence has been disproportionately targeted against women and other disempowered gender groups, but it should not be confused with "violence against women" or gender violence. "Violence against women" is violence targeted against women because they are women. It is part of "gender violence", or violence inflicted due to conformity or nonconformity with socially constructed gender roles—violence inflicted against women, lesbians, gays, bisexuals or transgender people, because of gender identity. A few cases in US courts have included claims of "sexual violence" and "violence against women," but no court has provided any careful analysis of these claims, and those courts which have considered the claims have rejected them in a cursory fashion. The recognition by US courts that claims of rape are violations of customary international law and can be considered to be forms of torture, war crimes, and crimes against humanity have resulted from the international advocacy and scholarship that brought violence against women to light and have led to prosecutions at the special tribunals for Rwanda and the former Yugoslavia. Similarly, developments in the US courts have contributed to this movement—building the norms of violence against women and strengthening work in other countries. This synergy has helped build a system of both codification of the norms prohibiting sexual violence and enforcement worldwide to prevent, as well as to punish, sexual violence. Hopefully, the type of advocacy that produced these changes will also be successful in building the codification and enforceability of the norms against all violence against women and gender violence.

Filartiga v. Pena-Irala: The First Human Rights Case Brought under the ATS

The ATS was virtually ignored for almost 200 years until Rhonda Copelon and Peter Weiss at the Center for Constitutional Rights used it to bring a claim on behalf of the sister and father of Joelito Filartiga, who was tortured to death when he was 17 years old. The perpetrator was Americo Pena-Irala, the Inspector General of Police in Asuncion, Paraguay. Joelito Filartiga was the target because his father, Joel Filartiga, was a prominent leader in the opposition movement to the former Paraguayan dictator, Alfredo Stroessner.[4] The claim that the Filartiga family brought was initially dismissed by the trial court because the judge felt constrained by prior decisions, but it was reversed on appeal by the United States Second Circuit.[5] In a landmark decision, the Second Circuit established that claims can be brought for an internationally recognized norm such as torture. That court laid out the standard for how a court should measure when a violation has reached the level of the "law of nations."

The significance of the *Filartiga* case is that this decision outlined the standard for international law claims that has been accepted to this day, including by the United States Supreme Court.[6] The Second Circuit held that a court examining whether a plaintiff stated a valid claim under international law should look to the current state of the law because customary international law was an evolving body of norms.[7] The court also found that torture was prohibited by the law of nations, it analyzed the international prohibition against torture, and held that:

> [...] deliberate torture perpetrated under color of official authority violates universally accepted norms of the international law of human rights, regardless of the nationality of the parties. Thus, whenever an alleged torturer is found and served with process by an alien within our borders, Section 1350 provides federal jurisdiction.[8]

The *Filartiga* court also provided a detailed analysis about how a court could analyze whether a given violation alleged by a plaintiff was in fact a violation of customary international law. The court found that international law could be ascertained by

---

4 For a discussion of the development of the *Filartiga* case, which includes interviews with the Filartiga family, the lawyers who brought the case, as well as commentary on the legal significance of the Second Circuit's decision in *Filartiga v. Pena-Irala*, see William J. Aceves, *The Anatomy of Torture: A Documentary History of Filartiga v. Pena-Irala* (Washington, DC: Bridge Street Books, 2007).

5 *Filartiga v. Pena-Irala*, 630 F.2d, 876; 880 (1980).

6 *Sosa v. Alvarez-Machain*, 542 US 692 (2004).

7 *Filartiga*, 630 F.2d at 881 ("Courts must interpret international law not as it was in 1789 but as it has evolved and exits among the nations of the world today.") This was also endorsed by the United States Supreme Court, *Sosa v. Alvarez-Machain*, 542 US 732–4.

8 *Filartiga*, 630 F.2d at 884; 878.

consulting the works of international law scholars, by the general usage and practice of nations, or by the judicial decisions recognizing and enforcing that law.[9]

The Development of Customary International Law Norms against Sexual Violence

The ruling in *Filartiga* was important for later claims for sexual violence as Alien Tort claims on a number of levels. Firstly, the court's careful explanation of what constituted international law and the recognition that international law evolves provided room for the changing norms prohibiting rape and other sexual violence and the increasing codification that sexual violence, especially rape, was a violation of international law. Significant developments in the 1990s included an increasing number of fora condemning violence against women; the establishment of the international tribunals to prosecute those who committed war crimes and crimes against humanity; the work of world conferences;[10] and increasing codification by state systems around the world. Secondly, directly related to the *Filartiga* holding about torture was the increasing acceptance in the 1990s that rape was a form of torture.

Scholars have argued that the prohibition against rape goes back to 1474.[11] The early prohibitions did not consistently characterize rape as violence against women,[12] and the condemnations themselves often emphasized women's secondary status.[13] The US codification of the customary laws of war into the US Army regulations on the laws of land warfare, known as the Lieber Code, listed rape by a belligerent as one of the most serious war crimes.[14] However, in the Hague Convention of 1907 rape was implicitly condemned as an offense against "family honour and rights."[15] The 1949 Geneva Conventions implicitly included rape as "outrages against personal

---

9 *Ibid.*, 630 F.2d at 880, citing *United States v. Smith*, 18 US (5 Wheat.) 153, 160–61 (1820).

10 World Conference on Human Rights (Vienna 1993); Beijing Conference on Women (1995); and creation of a Special Rapporteur on Violence against Women, Its Causes and Consequences. See Rhonda Copelon, "Introduction: Bringing Beijing Home," *Brooklyn Journal of International Law* 21/3 (1996): 599–604.

11 See Kelly Dawn Askin, *War Crimes Against Women: Prosecutions in International War Crimes Tribunals* (Leiden: Martinus Nijhoff Publishers, 1997), 5, n.11.

12 Rhonda Copelon, "Gender Crimes as War Crimes: Integrating Crimes against Women into International Criminal Law," *McGill Law Journal*, Vol. 46, No. 3 (2000): 217–40.

13 Patricia Viseur Sellers, "Sexual Violence and Peremptory Norms: The Legal Value of Rape," *Case Western Reserve Journal of International Law* Vol. 34, No. 3 (Fall, 2002), 287.

14 "Instructions for the Government of the United States in the Field by Order of the Secretary of War," Washington, DC (April 24, 1863); "Rules of Land Warfare," War Department Document No. 467, Office of the Chief of Staff (GPO 1917) (approved April 25, 1914).

15 "Convention (IV) Respecting the Laws and Customs of War on Land and Its Annex: Regulation Concerning the Laws and Customs of War on Land" (October 18, 1907). Annex, Article 46.

dignity" or "humiliating and degrading treatment" and an attack on honor.[16] Rape was not explicitly included as a grave breach, although on the list were "torture or inhumane treatment," and "willingfully causing great suffering or serious injury to body or health."[17] The 1977 Protocol II the Geneva Conventions mentioned "rape, forced prostitution and any other form of indecent assault" only as "humiliating or degrading treatment."[18] The developments in the 1990s recognizing that rape and other sexual violence were forms of the most condemned violations of international human rights and humanitarian law were critical in recognizing that women's rights are human rights and that gender violence constitutes one of the most pernicious forms of violence.

In addition, no real system of enforcement existed until the 1990s. In the first trials established for war crimes and crimes against humanity, rape and forced prostitution were not recognized as offenses by the Nuremberg Tribunal itself, and although rape was recognized as a crime against humanity in Local Council Law No. 10, which governed the subsequent trials of lower-level Nazis held by the Allied military powers, none were ever charged with rape.[19] The Indictment for the International Military Tribunal for the Far East (the Tokyo Tribunal) made some progress and included rape and other cruelties as "violations of recognized customs and conventions of war." Evidence of rape was used by the Tokyo Tribunal to support convictions on charges of war crimes and "crimes against humanity."[20] However, survivors of military sexual slavery by Japan have worked for decades to hold the Japanese accountable for the sexual slavery of "comfort" women during World War II.

Feminists for decades have worked for the categorization of rape as an act of violence in their domestic laws, which made major strides through the 1980s; internationally, they began to be successful in efforts to have rape recognized as a form of torture.[21] In the 1990s, feminist activists were key in bringing to the world's attention sexual violence as part of the genocide in Bosnia and Croatia, as well as in Rwanda, and the political attacks amounting to crimes against humanity in Haiti. International condemnation of the use of rape as an act of genocide in the former Yugoslavia and Rwanda was one factor leading to the creation of the international

---

16 "Convention for the Amelioration of the Condition of the Wounded and Sick in Armed Forces in the Field" (August 12, 1949), 75 UNTS 31, Article 3.

17 "Convention Relative to the Protection of Civilian Persons in Time of War" (August 12, 1949), 75 UNTS 187, Article 147.

18 UN Office of the High Commissioner for Human Rights (1977). <http://www.unhchr. ch/html/menu3/b/93.htm> (accessed November 26, 2007).

19 Adalbert Ruckerl, *The Investigation of Nazi Crimes 1945–1978* (Heidelberg: C.F. Muller, 1979).

20 R. John Pritchard (ed.), *The Tokyo Major War Crimes Trial: The Judgment, Separate Opinions, Proceedings in Chambers* (New York: Mellen Press, 2005), 49.

21 See, among others, Beth Stephens, "Humanitarian Law and Gender Violence: An End to Centuries of Neglect?" *Hofstra Law & Policy Symposium* No. 3 (1999): 87–109; Deborah Blatt, "Recognizing Rape as Method of Torture," *Review of Law and Social Change* No. 19 (1992): 821–65, see, in particular, 821, 833; and, Charlotte Bunch, "Women's Rights as Human Rights: Toward a Re-Vision of Human Rights," *Human Rights Quarterly* No. 12 (1990): 486–98.

criminal tribunals established to prosecute individuals accused of acts of genocide, war crimes, and crimes against humanity.[22] Another important piece of developing law was the line of cases in the International Criminal Tribunals for Rwanda and the former Yugoslavia. These developments were incorporated into the statute of the International Criminal Court after extended advocacy by groups such as the Women's Caucus for Gender Justice.[23]

Another important development has been the increasing recognition by US courts that rape can be a form of torture in decisions in the 1980s and 1990s, the most common context being within US prisons. For example, in 1980, the US Supreme Court stated that rape in prisons was "the equivalent of torture, and is offensive to any modern standard of human dignity."[24] In a 1988 case against the former Argentinean General Suarez-Mason, the court examined the acts committed under General Suarez-Mason's command during Argentina's "dirty war" and found that Suarez-Mason was responsible for "shock sessions that were interspersed with rapes and other forms of torture."[25] In 1994, Justice Blackmun, in a concurring opinion in the Supreme Court case *Farmer v. Brennan* stated that rape within US prisons is "nothing less than torture."[26] This condemnation has continued: for example, in a 2002 case, the court stated that "[r]ape can constitute torture. Rape is a form of aggression constituting an egregious violation of humanity."[27]

ATS Cases on Sexual Violence

Beginning in the 1990s, ATS and TVPA lawsuits began to incorporate sexual violence as part of the human rights claims brought to court. The courts ruled on claims of rape and other sexual abuse and found these claims to constitute torture, war crimes, and crimes against humanity.

Cases against Foreign Officials

1. Ortiz v. Gramajo: *Rape as a Violation of the International Prohibition Against Torture*

In 1989, Sister Dianna Ortiz, a US nun, was kidnapped and subjected to brutal torture—including rape and other sexual abuse—by security forces in Guatemala under the command of General Hector Gramajo. In 1990, Gramajo left Guatemala to study at Harvard's Kennedy School of Government. On his graduation day from Harvard in June 1991, Gramajo was served with a suit brought under the ATS and

---

22 See Kelly Dawn Askin, "Developments in International Criminal Law: Sexual Violence in Decisions and Indictments of the Yugoslav and Rwandan Tribunals: Current Status," *American Journal of International Law* Vol. 93, No. 1 (1999): 97–123.

23 For a discussion of these developments, see Copelon, *op. cit.*

24 *United States v. Bailey*, 444 US 394, 423 (1980).

25 *In Re Extradition of Suarez Mason*, 694 F. Supp. 676, 682 (N.D. Cal. 1988).

26 *Farmer v. Brennan*, 511 US 825, 854 (1994).

27 *Zubeda v. Ashcroft*, 333 F.3d 463, 472 (3rd Cir. 2002).

the TVPA by Sister Ortiz and a group of indigenous Guatemalans who were also tortured, detained, and subjected to cruel, inhuman or degrading treatment and who lost family members in Gramajo's campaign against their communities.

As part of a briefing to the court on why the case should be allowed to proceed, the plaintiffs presented an expert declaration by 27 law scholars who analyzed whether the violations charged by the plaintiffs constituted customary international law violations that were "specific, obligatory, and universal."[28] The violations charged included torture and cruel, and inhuman or degrading treatment. In the section arguing that rape was an act of torture, the declaration cited a number of statements by the US Department of State and testimony by US State Department officials before the United States Congress, and pronouncements by United Nations officials as authority that torture included rape,[29] sexual abuse,[30] and other forms of gender-based violence.[31] In its ruling, the US District Court for Massachusetts held that Gramajo was liable for the torture of Sister Diana Ortiz.[32]

2. Doe v. Karadžić; Kadić v. Karadžić: *Rape as Torture, Genocide, and War Crimes*

In the early 1990s, there were reports of the campaign of genocide in the former Yugoslavia, including widespread and systematic rape, brought up by women's organizations working in the region, journalists, and women's rights projects at international human rights organizations.[33] In early 1993, when Bosnian Serb leader Radovan Karadžić was traveling to the United States, a coalition of activists and

---

28 Affidavit of International Law Scholars, *Ortiz v. Gramajo*, reproduced in Appendix I to Beth Stephens and Michael Ratner, *International Human Rights Litigation in US Courts* (Transnational Publishers, Inc., 1996) (henceforth *Gramajo* Affidavit).

29 *Gramajo* Affidavit, citing US Department of State, *Country Report on Human Rights Practices for 1991* (1992); *International Human Rights Abuses Against Women: Hearings Before the Subcomm. on Human Rights and International Organizations of the House Comm. on Foreign Affairs*, 101st Cong., 2d Sess. 142 (1990) (testimony of Paula Dobriansky, Deputy Assistant Secretary, Bilateral and Multilateral Affairs, Bureau of Human Rights and Humanitarian Affairs).

30 *Gramajo* Affidavit, citing Cable from Secretary of State to All Diplomatic and Consular Posts Re: Instructions for 1991 Country Reports on Human Rights Practices, P 211857Z (August 1991); Statement of the United Nations Special Rapporteur on Torture to the UN Commission on Human Rights, E/CN.4/1992/SR.21 (Summary Record for the 21st meeting, February–March 1992).

31 *Gramajo* Affidavit, citing UN Committee on the Elimination of Discrimination Against Women, *Adoption of Report*, 11th Sess., General Recommendation No. 19, at 2, UN Doc. CEDAW/C/1992/L.1/Add.15 (1992). See also UN Economic and Social Council Commission on the Status of Women, *Physical Violence Against Detained Women That Is Specific to their Sex*, 34th Sess., Agenda item 5, UN Doc. E/CN.6/1990/L.18 (1990).

32 *Xuncax v. Gramajo*, 886 F. Supp. 162, 175 (D. Mass. 1995). See also 886 F. Supp. 173–4 for description of torture inflicted on Sister Diana Ortiz.

33 Jennifer M. Green, *et al.*, "Affecting the Rules for the Prosecution of Rape and Other Gender-Based Violence before the International Criminal Tribunal for the Former Yugoslavia: A Feminist Proposal and Critique," *Hastings Women's Law Journal* Vol. 5, No. 2 (1994): 171–87.

lawyers combined forces and brought two cases against him on behalf of women who had survived rape and other sexual violence as part of the genocide and other atrocities in the former Yugoslavia. These cases were initially dismissed but then appealed to the US Court of Appeals for the Second Circuit. In 1995, the Court of Appeals found that the:

> allegations that Karadžić personally planned and ordered a campaign of murder, rape, forced impregnation, and other forms of torture designed to destroy the religious and ethnic groups of Bosnian Muslims and Bosnian Croats clearly state a violation of the international law norm proscribing genocide [...].[34]

The court also ruled that rape "committed in the course of hostilities, violate[d] the law of war."[35] The court allowed claims under both the ATS and the TVPA.

The case continued to be litigated for the next five years, and in 2000, two jury verdicts were issued on behalf of both women and men victims of the genocide. Karadžić had stopped defending the case, refusing to appear for a deposition and otherwise respond to plaintiffs' allegations; the district court judge found him to be in default. Two juries then issued judgments for $575 million and $4.5 billion.[36]

3. Mehinović v. Vuković: *Rape as Torture and Crimes against Humanity*

In a second case resulting from acts of genocide in Bosnia, Bosnian refugee men living in the United States sued one of their prison guards who had fled to the United States. In 2002, the US federal court for the Northern District of Georgia found that the torture of the plaintiffs included beatings on the genitals.[37] The court also stated rape or sexual assault committed against the refugees to be crimes against humanity.[38]

4. Doe v. Constant: *Rape as Torture and Crimes against Humanity*

Also in the 1990s, a group of Haitian women's organizations and lawyers based in Haiti and in the United States made a series of written communications, and representatives testified before a hearing of the Organization of American States Inter-American Commission on Human Rights (OAS/IACHR) to address violence against women in Haiti during the mid-1990s. At that time, women were subjected to attacks because of their own roles as activists and also as punishment for their husband's activities or to terrorize their families. Rape was a weapon used in particular against women. Systematic documentation lead the IACHR to a finding that the acts committed by military or paramilitary forces were crimes against humanity, and that

---

34 *Kadić v. Karadžić* 70 F.3d 232, 242 (2d Cir. 1995).

35 *Ibid.*, 242.

36 *Doe v. Karadžić*, September 2000 jury verdict, available at <www.ccr-ny.org/humanrightsbook>.

37 *Mehinović v. Vuković*, 198 F. Supp. 2d 1322, 1345 (N.D. Ga. 2002).

38 *Ibid.*, 1353.

"sexual abuse against Haitian women was carried out in various ways, but with a single aim: to create a climate of terror among people supporting Aristide."[39]

Following, two organizations, the Center for Constitutional Rights and the Center for Justice and Accountability, brought a lawsuit against Emmanuel Constant, a paramilitary leader in Haiti who was living in New York. In *Doe v. Constant*, the court issued a default judgment that included a judgment for rape as torture and a crime against humanity.[40]

5. Doe v. Reddy: *Sexual Slavery or Trafficking*

This class action lawsuit was brought on behalf of Indian citizens, including dozens of young women, alleging that a conspiracy of extended family members, in part through their business enterprises, fraudulently induced them to come to the United States from India on false promises that they would be provided education and employment opportunities, but then instead subjected them to forced labor and sexual abuse.[41] In a 2003 decision on defendants' motion to dismiss, sexual slavery and trafficking claims were allowed and the court held that the "defendant reinforced coercive conduct [of forced labor] through threats, physical beatings and sexual battery."[42]

6. Doe v. Bolkiah: *Forced Prostitution*

Two American women who were unknowingly recruited for forced prostitution in Brunei by talent agencies. After plaintiffs arrived in Brunei, they were sent home because they refused to engage in sexual relations with the Sultan of Brunei, defendant palace officials, and their male friends. The women brought suit against the Sultan of Brunei, and the suit was allowed. The court held that no immunity could be applied since these were not official acts of state.[43]

7. Doe v. Liu Qi: *Sexual Assault as Cruel, Inhuman, or Degrading Treatment*

In *Doe v. Liu Qi*, a case brought by Falun Gong supporters against the former mayor of Beijing, China, the court found that one plaintiff's allegations of sexual assault constituted cruel, inhuman, or degrading treatment, citing a report of the Committee Against Torture that "specifically lists sexual abuse as a cruel act." The Court noted that a plaintiff alleged that a police officer attempted to force his hand into her vagina while several other officers pinned her down.[44]

---

39 Organization of American States, Report on the Situation of Human Rights in Haiti (1995), paras 121–2.

40 Available at <www.ccr-ny.org/humanrightsbook>.

41 *Doe v. Reddy*, Civ. No. 02-05570, 2003 US Dist. LEXIS 26120, *12 (N.D. Cal. August 4, 2003).

42 *Ibid.*, *36.

43 *Doe v. Bolkiah*, 74 F. Supp. 2d 969 (D. Haw. 1998).

44 *Doe v. Liu Qi*, 349 F. Supp. 2d 1258 (N.D. Cal. 2004).

Cases against Multinational Corporations

1. Doe v. Unocal*: Rape*

In the early 1990s, increasing information was released about human rights abuses committed in connection with the construction of a natural gas pipeline project in Burma, and the involvement of the California-based oil corporation Unocal in its construction. Unocal participated in a joint venture with the Myanmar Oil and Gas Enterprise (MOGE) and the French company, Total. Abuses committed by forces participating in the pipeline project included forced labor and rape. In 1996, after a series of attempts by activists and the Center for Constitutional Rights to persuade Unocal to stop the violations or cease participation with the Burmese military regime in the pipeline project, two lawsuits were filed in September and October of 1996.

In *Doe v. Unocal*, two women came forward with claims of rape and other sexual abuse. For security reasons, they, along with the other plaintiffs, have never publicly revealed their names,[45] and were known as Jane Doe I and Jane Doe II. After their home village was forcibly relocated as part of the pipeline project, Jane Doe II and her great niece Jane Doe III, were raped when they tried to return to their village to get food.[46] A decision by the United States Court of Appeals for the Ninth Circuit allowed these claims of rape to proceed against the corporation and its officers.[47] The allegations against the company were that it was complicit in the commission of these acts and that it aided and abetted, was the agent of, was a joint venturer in, and conspired with and/or worked in concert with those that physically perpetrated the violations.

This was the first of a series of cases against multinational corporations that recognized that allegations of rape were justiciable in US courts. In their complaint, plaintiffs also charged with "violence against women" and crimes against humanity, but none of the courts considering the case ruled on these claims.

2. Presbyterian Church of Sudan v. Talisman Energy*: Rape as Torture and War Crimes*

Plaintiffs are current and former residents of southern Sudan who alleged that they were victims of genocide, war crimes, crimes against humanity, and other human rights violations committed by the government of Sudan and a Canadian energy company, Talisman Energy, Inc., resulting from oil exploration conducted in Sudan.

---

45 As the litigation proceeded, the names of the plaintiffs had to be revealed to the defendants. Plaintiffs' counsel spent months negotiating a careful protective order to provide the maximum security for the plaintiffs. See <www.ccr-ny.org/humanrightsbook> for a copy of the protective order.

46 Third Amended Complaint, available at <www.ccr-ny.org>.

47 *Doe v. Unocal*, 395 F. 3d 932 (9th Cir. 2002), vacated by, rehearing, *en banc*, granted by *Doe v. Unocal* Corp., 395 F. 3d 978, 2003 US App. LEXIS 2716 (9th Cir. 2003). Shortly after the *en banc* hearing, the *Unocal* cases successfully settled (final settlement entered in 2005), providing the plaintiffs with compensation and a fund for humanitarian relief for other victims from or in the Yadana Project pipeline region.

The court ruled that rape constitutes torture when "plaintiffs can show that these acts were committed for any reason based on discrimination and with the consent or acquiescence of a public official or other person acting in an official capacity."[48]

3. Sarei v. Rio Tinto: *Rape as War Crimes and "Atrocious Human Rights Abuses"*

In this case charging the Rio Tinto Corporation with abuses committed in Papua New Guinea in connection with a gold mine project, the plaintiffs also charged rape against some of the defendants. In its ruling, the US Court of Appeals for the Ninth Circuit included rape when describing plaintiffs' allegations of "atrocious human rights abuses and war crimes."[49]

4. Jama v. INS: *Sexual Assault as Cruel, Inhuman, or Degrading Treatment*

In this case, undocumented foreign citizens brought a case against US officials and a private company that had contracted with the US government to operate a detention center in New Jersey for the US Immigration and Naturalization Service (INS). The plaintiffs alleged that while they were detained, they were beaten and subjected to torture and other cruel, inhuman, or degrading treatment, including sexual assault. In a 1998 ruling, the judge allowed international law claims of cruel, inhuman, or degrading treatment of punishment to proceed. The claims against the INS and the United States government settled on or about October 31, 2001, and in a 2004 ruling, the court dismissed the remaining claims against US officials because of immunity defenses, but allowed international law claims against the private contractor of the prison and its officers to proceed. The court also allowed a state law claim of sexual harassment against an individual guard based on evidence that the female inmate was repeatedly assaulted by the guard.[50] After the beginning of a jury trial, the defendants settled with the majority of the plaintiffs, including those alleging sexual abuse.[51]

5. General Recognition of Rape as War Crimes, Crimes against Humanity, or Human Rights Abuses in Cases against Corporations

In addition to cases in which individual survivors came forward and brought claims of rape and other forms of sexual abuse, a number of courts have listed rape as a crime against humanity when discussing these norms, even in cases in which the plaintiffs were not charging sexual violence. These include cases against Royal

---

48 *Presbyterian Church of Sudan v. Talisman Energy*, 244 F. Supp. 2d 289, 326 n.34 (S.D.N.Y. 2003), dismissed on other grounds, 453 F. Supp. 2d 633 (S.D.N.Y. 2006) (appeal pending).

49 *Sarei v. Rio Tinto*, 456 F. 3d 1069, 1075 (9th Cir. 2006).

50 *Jama v. INS.*, 22 F. Supp. 2d 353 (DNJ, October 1, 1998) 361, 383.

51 Personal communication with trial counsel Penny Venetis.

Dutch Shell for human rights abuses in Nigeria,[52] and a case against manufacturers of Agent Orange.[53]

Limitations: The Problems of Immunity

1. Joo v. Japan*: Political Question*

In 2000, 15 women from China, Taiwan, South Korea, and the Philippines brought an ATS suit against Japan for sexual slavery during World War II. Plaintiffs alleged that they and approximately 200,000 other women were kidnapped or coerced and forced into sexual slavery by the Japanese Army between 1931 and 1945. They were imprisoned at the so-called "comfort stations" and repeatedly raped—often by as many as 30 or 40 men a day—beaten, mutilated, and sometimes murdered. Some of the women were held for years. Plaintiffs estimated that only 25 percent to 35 percent of the "comfort women" survived the war, and those who survived, suffered health effects, including damage to reproductive organs and sexually transmitted diseases.[54] The plaintiffs filed this lawsuit because of the lack of any official apology or payment of reparations to the vast majority of women who were sexual slaves during World War II. The only compensation that was ever provided was to approximately 30 Dutch women living in Indonesia.

The case was dismissed by the US Court of Appeals for the District of Columbia because, "much as we may feel for the plight of the appellants, the courts of the United States simply are not authorized to hear their case."[55] The court held that the case would be more properly heard by one of the "political" branches that it was deferring to the opinion of the US executive branch in its interpretation of the peace treaties signed by Japan and the plaintiffs' countries of origin.[56]

2. In Re Iraqi Detainees*: Immunity for US Officials*

A series of four cases was brought against US officials for their role in torture in detention facilities in Iraq and Afghanistan, and the torture claims included sexual abuse. In a shocking ruling, the court held that torture was committed within the "scope of employment" of US officials and ruled that the US officials would therefore be immune.[57] The ruling is currently on appeal to the US Court of Appeals for the District of Columbia Circuit.

---

52 *Wiwa v. Royal Dutch Petroleum Co.*, Civ. No. 96-8386, 2002 US Dist. LEXIS 3293, *27 (S.D.N.Y. February 22, 2002).

53 *In Re Agent Orange Prod. Liab. Litig.*, 373 F. Supp. 2d 7, 136 (E.D.N.Y. 2005).

54 *Joo v. Japan*, 172 F. Supp. 2d 52, 55 (D.D.C. 2001).

55 *Joo v. Japan*, 413 F.3d 45, 53 (D.C. Cir. 2005), quoting 332 F.3d, 67.

56 *Joo v. Japan*, 413 F.3d 45.

57 *In Re Iraq and Afghanistan Detainees Litigation*, 479 F. Supp. 2d 85 (D.D.C. 2007).

3. Other Possibilities for Suing US Officials

Another, largely untested theory is arguing that US civil rights law incorporates customary international law.[58] To date, no case has included sexual violence.

4. Limitation: Sexual Violence against Women Not Yet Recognized as Justiciable

Claims that have not yet been recognized by the United States courts are claims for violence against women as a separate norm. Plaintiffs have attempted to assert independent claims for "violence against women" and sexual violence, but the only court to address these claims rejected it without analysis. In *Doe v. Exxon Mobil Corp*, the court held that plaintiffs could not bring a claim for sexual violence because "it is not sufficiently recognized under international law." Notably, the court specifically recognized that "claims of sexual violence may be cognizable elements of such illegal conduct as torture." The *Exxon* court simply cross-referenced this discussion in rejecting plaintiffs' claims for "violence against women."[59]

Commentators remain concerned that the particular characteristics of rape and other gender violence not be lost within definitions of broader international torts. The various forms of violence against women and gender violence must be recognized rather than limiting "gender violence" or "violence against women" to sexual violence. Violence against women as a claim is critical to highlight the violence that is targeted specifically at women and gender-based violence to highlight both violence against women, and violence because of other issues of sexual orientation and identity. Numerous international instruments recognize gender-based violence as a violation of fundamental human rights and obligate states to take positive steps to prevent and redress gender-based violence.[60]

A growing literature on sexual violence, including rape and other gender-based violence, is exploring the development of human rights norms dealing specifically

---

58 Sandra Coliver, Jennifer M. Green, and Paul Hoffman, "Holding Human Rights Violators Accountable by Using International Law in US Courts: Advocacy Efforts and Complimentary Strategies," *Emory International Review* Vol. 19, No. 1 (2005): 169–226, see, in particular, 169, n. 103.

59 All quotes, *Doe. v. Exxon Mobil Corp*. 393 F. Supp. 2d 20, 24 (D.D.C. 2005).

60 These sources of the customary international law norm against gender-based violence include, but are not limited to, the International Covenant on Civil and Political Rights (ICCPR), 999 UNTS 171 (1966); Convention Against Torture and Other Cruel, Inhuman, or Degrading Treatment or Punishment, 1465 UNTS 85, (1984); Convention on the Elimination of All Forms of Discrimination Against Women (CEDAW), 1249 UNTS 20378 (1981), *as interpreted by* Committee on the Elimination of Discrimination Against Women, General Recommendation No. 19, UN Doc. A/47/38 (1992); *Vienna Declaration and Programme of Action*, General Assembly, World Conference on Human Rights, UN Doc. A/Conf.157/23 (1993); *Beijing Declaration and the Platform for Action*, General Assembly, Report of the Fourth World Conference on Women, UN Doc. A/Conf.177/20 (1995); *Declaration on the Elimination of Violence Against Women*, GAOR Res. 104, 48th Sess. UN Doc. A/Res/48/104 (1994).

with these issues.[61] Future claims might assert gender violence as an independent human rights violation, in addition to asserting it as a form of one of the other violations, such as torture or a crime against humanity.

Conclusion

In the 1990s, the recognition in US courts that sexual violence constituted a violation of customary international law was tremendous progress in mainstreaming sexual violence claims. This progress resulted from continuing advocacy, including careful legal claims, as well as scholarship demonstrating how these acts of sexual violence could be seen as none other than forms of the most egregious violence condemned in international law—slavery, torture, genocide, crimes against humanity, and war crimes, rather than a "byproduct" of war, a crime against a woman's "honor" or an "outrage on personal dignity." Progress also has been made internationally in recognizing the prohibition against all forms of gender violence, although this norm has not yet received the recognition by a US court.

These developments are steps forward in the world movement against gender violence towards an international legal system in which not only sexual violence, but all gender violence, is prohibited, punished, and deterred.

Bibliography

Cases

Affidavit of International Law Scholars, *Ortiz v. Gramajo*, reproduced in Appendix I to *International Human Rights Litigation in US Courts* (eds), Beth Stephens and Michael Ratner. Transnational Publishers, Inc., 1996.
Doe v. Bolkiah, 74 F. Supp. 2d 969 (D. Haw. 1998).
Doe. v. Exxon Mobil Corp. 393 F. Supp. 2d 20, 24 (D.D.C. 2005).
Doe v. Karadžić, September 2000. Jury verdict: <www.ccr-ny.org/humanrights book>.
Doe v. Liu Qi, 349 F. Supp. 2d 1258 (N.D. Cal. 2004).
Doe v. Reddy, Civ. No. 02-05570, 2003 US Dist. LEXIS 26120 (N.D. Cal. August 4, 2003).
Doe v. Unocal, 395 F.3d 932 (9th Cir. 2002). Vacated by, rehearing, *en banc*, granted by *Doe v. Unocal Corp.*, 395 F.3d 978, 2003 US App. LEXIS 2716 (9th Cir. 2003).
Farmer v. Brennan, 511 US 825 (1994).
Filartiga v. Pena-Irala, 630 F.2d 876 (2d Cir. 1980).
In Re Agent Orange Prod. Liab. Litig., 373 F. Supp. 2d 7, 136 (E.D.N.Y. 2005).
In Re Extradition of Suarez Mason, 694 F. Supp. N.D. Cal. (1988).
In Re Iraq and Afghanistan Detainees Litigation, 479 F. Supp. 2d 85 (D.D.C. 2007).

---

61 See, for example, Rhonda Copelon, "Surfacing Gender: Re-Engraving Crimes against Women in Humanitarian Law," *Hastings Women's Law Journal* No. 5 (1994): 243–65.

Jama v. INS., 22 F. Supp. 2d 353 (DNJ, October 1, 1998).
Joo v. Japan, 172 F. Supp. 2d 52, 55 (D.D.C. 2001).
Joo v. Japan, 413 F.3d 45, 53 (D.C. Cir. 2005).
Kadić v. Karadžić, 70 F.3d 232, 242 (2d Cir. 1995).
Mehinović v. Vuković, 198 F. Supp. 2d 1322, 1345 (N.D. Ga. 2002).
Presbyterian Church of Sudan v. Talisman Energy. 244 F. Supp. 2d 289, 326 n.34
  (S.D.N.Y. 2003). Dismissed on other grounds, 453 F. Supp. 2d 633 (S.D.N.Y.
  2006). Appeal pending.
Sarei v. Rio Tinto, 456 F.3d 1069, 1075 (9th Cir. 2006).
Sosa v. Alvarez-Machain, 542 US 692. (2004).
Wiwa v. Royal Dutch Petroleum Co., Civ. No. 96-8386, 2002 US Dist. LEXIS 3293
  (S.D.N.Y. February 22, 2002).
Xuncax v. Gramajo, 886 F. Supp. 162, 175.
United States v. Bailey, 444 US 394 (1980).
United States v. Smith, 18 US 5 Wheat. (1820).
Zubeda v. Ashcroft, 333 F.3d 463, 472 (3rd Cir. 2002).

Covenants, Documents, Laws, Regulations, and Reports

The Alien Tort Statute, 28 USC Section 1350.
The Torture Victim Protection Act of 1991, Public Law No. 102-256, 106 Stat. 73
  (1992).
"Convention (IV) Respecting the Laws and Customs of War on Land and Its Annex:
  Regulation Concerning the Laws and Customs of War on Land." October 18,
  1907.
"Convention for the Amelioration of the Condition of the Wounded and Sick in
  Armed Forces in the Field." August 12, 1949. 75 UNTS 31.
"Convention Relative to the Protection of Civilian Persons in Time of War." August
  12, 1949. 75 UNTS 187.
"Instructions for the Government of the United States in the Field by Order of the
  Secretary of War." Washington, DC, April 24, 1863.
Office of the Chief of Staff, "Rules of Land Warfare." War Department Document
  No. 467. GPO 1917. Approved April 25, 1914.
Organization of American States. Report on the Situation of Human Rights in Haiti.
  1995.
United Nations. The International Covenant on Civil and Political Rights (ICCPR).
  999 UNTS 171 (1966).
—— UN Office of the High Commissioner for Human Rights. Protocols to the
  Geneva Conventions. 1977.
—— Convention Against Torture and Other Cruel, Inhuman, or Degrading Treatment
  or Punishment. 1465 UNTS 85. 1984.
—— Convention on the Elimination of All Forms of Discrimination Against Women
  (CEDAW). 1249 UNTS 20378 (1981), *as interpreted by* Committee on the
  Elimination of Discrimination Against Women, General Recommendation No.
  19, UN Doc. A/47/38. 1992.

—— *Vienna Declaration and Programme of Action*, General Assembly, World Conference on Human Rights, UN Doc. A/Conf.157/23. 1993.

—— *Beijing Declaration and the Platform for Action*, General Assembly, Report of the Fourth World Conference on Women, UN Doc. A/Conf.177/20. 1995.

—— *Declaration on the Elimination of Violence Against Women*. GAOR Res. 104, 48th Sess. UN Doc. A/Res/48/104. 1994.

Secondary Sources

Aceves, William J. *The Anatomy of Torture*: *A Documentary History of Filartiga v. Pena-Irala* (Washington, DC: Bridge Street Books, 2007).

Askin, Kelly Dawn. *War Crimes against Women*: *Prosecutions in International War Crimes Tribunals*. Leiden: Martinus Nijhoff Publishers, 1997.

—— "Developments in International Criminal Law: Sexual Violence in Decisions and Indictments of the Yugoslav and Rwandan Tribunals: Current Status." *American Journal of International Law*. Vol. 93. No. 1 (1999): 97–123.

Blatt, Deborah. "Recognizing Rape as Method of Torture." *Review of Law and Social Change*. No. 19 (1992): 821–65.

Bunch, Charlotte. "Women's Rights as Human Rights: Toward a Re-Vision of Human Rights." *Human Rights Quarterly*. No. 12 (1990): 486–98.

Coliver, Sandra, Jennifer M. Green, and Paul Hoffman. "Holding Human Rights Violators Accountable by Using International Law in US Courts: Advocacy Efforts and Complimentary Strategies." *Emory International Review*. Vol. 19. No. 1 (2005): 169–226.

Copelon, Rhonda. "Surfacing Gender: Re-Engraving Crimes against Women in Humanitarian Law." *Hastings Women's Law Journal*. No. 5 (1994): 243–65.

—— "Introduction: Bringing Beijing Home." *Brooklyn Journal of International Law* 21/3 (1996): 599–604.

—— "Gender Crimes as War Crimes: Integrating Crimes against Women into International Criminal Law." *McGill Law Journal*. Vol. 46. No. 3 (2000): 217–40.

Green, Jennifer M., *et al.* "Affecting the Rules for the Prosecution of Rape and Other Gender-Based Violence before the International Criminal Tribunal for the Former Yugoslavia: A Feminist Proposal and Critique." *Hastings Women's Law Journal*. Vol. 5, No. 2 (1994): 171–87.

Pritchard, John R. (ed.), *The Tokyo Major War Crimes Trial*: *The Judgment, Separate Opinions, Proceedings in Chambers*. New York: Mellen Press, 2005.

Ruckerl, Adalbert. *The Investigation of Nazi Crimes 1945–1978*. Heidelberg: C.F. Muller, 1979.

Sellers, Patricia Viseur. "Sexual Violence and Peremptory Norms: The Legal Value of Rape." *Case Western Reserve Journal of International Law*. Vol. 34, No. 3 (Fall, 2002): 287–303.

Stephens, Beth. "Humanitarian Law and Gender Violence: An End to Centuries of Neglect?" *Hofstra Law & Policy Symposium*. No. 3 (1999): 87–109.

Chapter 9

The Traffic in "Trafficked Filipinas": Sexual Harm, Violence, and Victims' Voices

Sealing Cheng

Introduction

In the transnational circulation of norms and policies against human trafficking, victims' testimonials serve an important function in making truth claims about trafficking and its harm to individuals. This chapter discusses how the key symbol of anti-trafficking campaigns—the "trafficked woman"—is constructed and deployed in the cultural advocacy of non-government organizations (NGOs). Interrogating "the mediations involved in the discovery and presentation of testimony,"[1] it argues that the focus on sexual harm and the driven pursuit of victimization narratives silence and erase the agency and personhood of individuals. This chapter assesses how the "victim" is framed within the political ideals, ideological commitments, and strategic considerations of the NGO, often removed from the experiences and needs of those for whom they advocate.

NGOs have exerted increasing influence on national policies and international conventions as lobbying groups through networking, consultative meetings, reports, as well as individual communications with policy-makers. Advocates play the role of spokespersons, using the language of human rights to include the disenfranchised and demand due recognition from states and supranational bodies. As Margaret Keck and Kathryn Sikkink demonstrate, the issue of violence against women has functioned crucially as the shared norm for women activists since the late 1980s, giving rise to the growth of transnational feminist networks and advocacy.[2] Yet, such a shared norm does not mean the emergence of a homogenous global feminism—various research has shown that feminist engagement operates on an uneven terrain, contesting scattered hegemonies in different sites while forging cross-border alliances and reshaping norms in the process of these global-local dynamics.[3] These

---

1 Margaret Keck and Kathryn Sikkink, *Activists beyond Borders: Advocacy Networks in International Politics* (Ithaca and London: Cornell University Press, 1998).

2 *Ibid.*

3 See Valentine M. Moghadam, *Globalizing Women: Transnational Feminist Networks* (Baltimore and London: Johns Hopkins University Press, 2005); and, Nancy Naples and Manisha Desai, *Women's Activism and Globalization* (London: Routledge, 2002).

theorizations and empirical studies have helped our understanding of transnational feminist activism as a realm of political, ideological, and strategic negotiations with tremendous potential for collaboration, but also for conflict and division. In recent years, critical assessments of the politics of representation in rights claims helped us further question the ways knowledge is produced in human rights discourses. In transnational feminism, scholars and activists have pointed to the important cultural role which advocacy plays in the shaping of women's activism and policy, and how uncritical use of women's experiences and calls for women's human rights could re-victimize women in different global locations and be deployed for repressive political ends.[4]

Issues of legitimacy and accountability in the NGO production of testimonies are rarely discussed. These are tricky for NGOs that represent stigmatized and migratory groups who are difficult to access and who rarely participate directly in political action. Advocacy for "victims of trafficking" constitutes one such problematic category, where the problem of accessibility justifies the generalization of a few (often the most tragic) testimonials to hundreds of thousands of others who are no more than statistical estimates. This gives NGOs disproportionate power to speak for a largely invisible group. Furthermore, advocates' interpretative framework—informed by their pre-existing political ideals, ideological commitments, and strategic considerations—become the primary lens through which testimonials are produced and labeled. "Giving voice" to women in advocacy may, in effect, reproduce the social, moral, and global divide between white, Western, middle-class women advocates and the passive and sexless "Third World women" for whom they advocate, as a number of critical analyses of anti-trafficking discourses targeted at the elimination of prostitution have shown.[5] Instead of asking what women *want*, victimizing discourses focus on what women *are* and demand protective legislation that ultimately reproduces the authority of the state. Finally, the pragmatic focus of NGOs often renders any discussion of methodology and reflexivity insignificant compared to powerful testimonies—taken as "truth"—which supports urgent calls for action. In other words, NGOs play a critical role in constructing the subject of "victims of trafficking."

How is such knowledge obtained? How do NGOs establish their legitimacy and accountability? How do activists meet and interact with their "clients"? How do they establish their legitimacy and accountability? These questions are particularly important for NGOs that represent stigmatized, criminalized, and migratory groups.

---

4 See Wendy S. Hesford and Wendy Kozol (eds), *Just Advocacy? Women's Human Rights, Transnational Feminism, and the Politics of Representation* (New Brunswick, New Jersey: Rutgers University Press, 2005).

5 Laura Agustin, "Migrants in the Mistress's House: Other Voices in the 'Trafficking' Debate," *Social Politics: International Studies in Gender, State and Society* 12, No. 1 (2005): 96–117; Jo Doezema, "Forced to Choose: Beyond the Voluntary v. Forced Prostitution Dichotomy," in *Global Sex Workers: Rights, Resistance, and Redefinition* (ed.), Kamala Kempadoo and Jo Doezema (London: Routledge, 1998), 34–50; Doezema, "Ouch!: Western Feminists' 'Wounded Attachment' to the 'Third World Prostitute'," *Feminist Review* 67 (2001): 16–38; and Francine Pickup, "Deconstructing Trafficking in Women: The Example of Russia," *Millennium: Journal of International Studies* 27, No. 4 (1998): 995–1021.

Stigma often poses obstacles for direct clients' participation, mobility further undermines their propensity for political actions, and both factors make accessibility to clients difficult—but not impossible.[6] Here I juxtapose ethnographic material with NGO publications and public statements to trace how some trafficking victims are discovered and represented between the local and global in anti-trafficking discourses. Such an analytical project is premised on the understanding that NGOs' discourses are historically produced and that their practices are shaped by a complex sets of relationships with other associations, agencies of the state, and individuals and communities.[7] Therefore, the anti-trafficking NGO operations and discourses will be analyzed here as part of a larger set of processes, with reference to local contexts and regional political economy, the transnational NGO network, and the global anti-trafficking drive in which national governments and supranational bodies, such as the United Nations, have been engaged since the late 1990s. While my analysis draws on one major international anti-trafficking NGO, the issues raised are not unique to the individuals or organization discussed here. My critique is therefore launched at a more general phenomenon of knowledge construction in anti-trafficking activism and discourses in which states, funders, and the media participate.[8] It is not my argument that all narratives of victimization need to be suppressed, but the analysis speaks to the silences and violence incurred by a driven pursuit for victimization narratives.

Defining "Trafficking"—NGO Advocacy and Contestations of Meaning

According to the definition laid down in the 2000 United Nations Protocol to Prevent, Suppress, and Punish Trafficking in Persons, Especially Women and Children:

> "Trafficking in persons" [means] the recruitment, transportation, transfer, harboring or receipt of persons, by means of the threat or use of force or other forms of coercion, of abduction, of fraud, of deception, of the abuse of power or of a position of vulnerability or of the giving or receiving of payments or benefits to achieve the consent of a person having control over another person, for the purpose of exploitation. Exploitation shall include, at a minimum, the exploitation of the prostitution of others or other forms of sexual exploitation, forced labor or services, slavery or practices similar to slavery, servitude or the removal of organs.[9]

---

6 Cf. Erving Goffman, *Stigma: Notes on the Management of Spoiled Identity* (New York: Simon & Schuster, 1963).

7 William Fisher, "Doing Good? The Politics and Antipolitics of NGO Practices," *Annual Review of Anthropology* 26 (1997): 439–64.

8 Carole Vance, "Innocence and Experience: Melodramatic Narratives of Sex Trafficking and Their Consequences for Health and Human Rights," paper presented at the panel "Sex Slaves in Media," Columbia University, April 15, 2004.

9 United Nations, *Protocol to Prevent, Suppress and Punish Trafficking in Persons, Especially Women and Children, Supplementing the United Nations Convention against Transnational Organized Crime*, Article 3(a), <untreaty.un.org/English/notpubl/18-12-a.E.doc> (accessed October 22, 2007).

This definition marks a significant departure from previous definitions of human trafficking that had exclusively focused on prostitution and, instead, importantly recognizes that trafficking in persons affects migrants in all sectors. Yet this definition is also "an unusual mix of compromises" between lobbying groups with distinct ideas about the relationship between prostitution and trafficking, according to the anthropologist Penelope Saunders who participated as a lobbyist in the Protocol's drafting process.[10] Firstly, even as this definition includes a discussion of "forced labor" and "slavery" and, therefore, makes it applicable to all forms of labor, it also singles out prostitution as a distinct form of exploitation in that same context. Secondly, the Protocol leaves undefined the concept of the "exploitation of the prostitution of others" to allow for the adaptation of what constitutes prostitution in national laws. Therefore, although the Protocol departs from the equation of trafficking with prostitution and includes the important notion of "coercion,"[11] it nonetheless resonates with a historical conflation of trafficking, prostitution, and violence that has been circulating since the "White Slave Trade" panic in the late nineteenth century.[12] In effect, while the Protocol sets the parameters within which "trafficking" could be understood, it also allows NGOs and states to deploy customary meanings and prevalent anxieties to shape its local understanding, and the equating of trafficking with prostitution, regardless of the absence of coercion, has persisted with some anti-trafficking NGOs. Furthermore, as an international agreement to combat trafficking, the Protocol also confers moral authority on NGOs that adopt its language and claim to champion the cause.

The trafficking of migrants into forced prostitution should capture the attention not only of women's groups committed to the abolition of prostitution and their opponents, but also of human rights advocates concerned with migrants' rights and labor rights. This has not been the case, however, and the shorthand of "sex trafficking" has resulted in the collapse of multiple issues of gender, migration, labor, and coercion into a debate about the consequences of prostitution. As Laura Agustin argues, some activists' conflation of "prostitution" with "trafficking" conceptually relocates women migrants who sell sex from the category of migrants to that of "victims," leading to "the disappearance of a migration category" and the erasure of these women's agency in instances of trafficking.[13] Broadly speaking, three different "camps" of NGOs can be delineated in this trafficking debate. The

---

10 Penelope Saunders, "Traffic Violations: Determining the Meaning of Violence in Sexual Trafficking Versus Sex Work," *Journal of Interpersonal Violence* (2005): 348.

11 Previous conventions on trafficking either ignored the issue of consent (for example, the 1904 International Agreement for the Suppression of White Slave Trade), or specified its irrelevance to the definition of trafficking (the 1949 Convention for the Suppression of Traffic in Persons and the Exploitation of the Prostitution of Others).

12 Jo Doezema, "Loose Women or Lost Women?: The Re-Emergence of the Myth of 'White Slavery' in Contemporary Discourses of 'Trafficking in Women,'" paper presented at the ISA Convention, Washington, DC, February 17–21, 1999; and Penelope Saunders and Gretchen Soderlund, "Traveling Threats: Trafficking as Discourse," *Canadian Women Studies* 22 (2003): 35–46.

13 Laura Agustin, "The Disappearance of a Migrant Category," *Journal of Ethnic and Migration Studies* 32, No. 1 (2006): 29–47.

abolitionists advocate for the end of all forms of prostitution and trafficking, which categorically constitute violations of women's rights and autonomy. The Coalition Against Trafficking in Women (CATW) is the main body in the abolitionist lobby.[14] A second group makes a distinction between those who have been coerced into prostitution and those who have voluntarily entered into prostitution or who have migrated overseas to engage in sex work. In other words, prostitution in this perspective is not inherently harmful, but coercion into prostitution must be stopped. The Global Alliance Against the Trafficking in Women (GAATW) is a representative of this second camp.[15] A third group proposes a broad human rights framework to understand the harms of trafficking. It argues that the "voluntary/forced" dichotomy in understanding prostitution is untenable as it serves to reproduce the "whore/Madonna" distinction. According to this group, the "harms" of prostitution are caused by moral attitudes towards sex work and the tendency to criminalize it, both of which continue to stigmatize people engaged in sex work. It calls for the decriminalization of prostitution and for the adoption of a migrant and labor rights framework in dealing with trafficking into forced prostitution. The Network of Sex Work Projects is the key organization in this last group.[16]

The subsequent material draws on my ethnographic fieldwork research in South Korea with a focus on Filipina entertainers in US military camp towns from 1998 to 2000, and my subsequent visit to the Philippines in May 2000. Apart from meeting with the Filipinas and their GI friends, the communication and collaboration with NGOs were important parts of my fieldwork. The Korea Church Women United (KCWU) received funding to conduct research on migrant entertainers in Korea and recruited a Korean researcher and myself for the task. Using the material we gathered, the KCWU staff wrote the first research report on migrant entertainers, "Fieldwork Report on Trafficked Women in Korea," which was released in November 1999. Jean Enriquez, a representative of Coalition Against Trafficking in Women–Asia Pacific branch (CATW–AP), was invited by KCWU to give a speech at the press conference for the release of the report. My co-researcher and I had a lunch meeting with Enriquez to brief her on our findings. I further met with Enriquez in Manila with two Filipina returnees from Korea. In addition, I also looked at texts that are produced for the consumption of the general public—both local and global. I include in my analysis below published statements and reports of the CATW–AP, as well as media reports of their work.

---

14 CATW defines sex trafficking as "the transport sale and purchase of women and girls for prostitution, bonded labor and sexual enslavement within the country or abroad" (CATW–AP 1999).

15 Before GAATW adopted the 2000 UN Protocol definition of trafficking, it had defined trafficking as "[a]ll acts involved in the recruitment and/or transport of a woman within and across national borders for sale, work or services by means of direct or indirect violence or threat of violence, abuse of authority or dominant position, debt bondage, deception or other forms of coercion" (GAATW, *Practical Guide to Assisting Trafficked Women* [Bangkok: GAATW, 1997]).

16 For a historical and critical analysis of these three camps, see Pickup, *op. cit.*

Migrant Entertainers and Trafficking in Korea

Migrant entertainers around US military camp towns entered Korea in the late 1990s within the larger context of labor importation. Since 1993, the Korean government introduced the foreign industrial trainees program due to a shortage of labor for "dangerous, dirty, and difficult" jobs abandoned by Korean nationals. Korean women servicing a US military clientele around US military camp towns (*gijichon*) have gained derogatory labels such as "Western whores" and "Western Princesses," referring to the sale not only of their bodies, but also of their nation, to "the West." In the 1990s, Korea's rapid economic advancement led to a shortage of Korean women to serve these American soldiers both because of the stigma assumed by and of the relatively low income of those workers, which in turn necessitated the importation of women from the "Third World."

According to some Korean and international activists such as the CATW, migrant entertainers in *gijichon* were "victims of sex trafficking." This understanding of the Filipinas as "trafficked" became widely shared among the NGOs in 1999. The International Organization for Migration estimated in 2001 that at least 5,000 foreign women have been trafficked into the sex industry in South Korea.[17] Most of these women entered Korea on entertainer (E-6) visas. In September 2002, the Ministry of Justice stated that 4,234 of 4,735 foreign women holding E-6 visas were reported to be working in clubs and bars; Russian women made up the majority with 1,823, followed by 1,471 from the Philippines; and the rest of the women were from Uzbekistan, China, the Ukraine, Bulgaria, Mongolia, the US, and Kazakhstan.[18] The majority of Filipino women worked around US military camp towns.

In the Philippines, overseas employment has been essential to keeping the economy afloat since the mid 1970s. The Philippine government estimated that in 2006, there were about 8.23 million overseas Filipinos in more than 193 countries: 3.8 million were overseas workers, and 874,792 were classified as irregulars.[19] Women became the majority in this outflow of labor since the 1990s: the ratio of women increased from 30 percent in 1975 to 51 percent in 1991, and subsequently to 60 percent in 1994.[20] Filipinas mainly leave their homeland to work as entertainers, domestic helpers, and nurses overseas. Those who end up working in the sex industry have been identified readily as the "victims of sex trafficking" by the media, local NGOs, and international NGOs such as the CATW.

The Filipinas in *gijichon* were between 17 and 35 years of age. They were usually in Korea on one-year contracts. Most of them had a vague idea of their jobs

---

17 IOM, *A Review of Data on Trafficking in the Republic of Korea* (Geneva: International Organization for Migration, 2002).

18 *Korea Times*, "Most Female E-6 Visa Holders Work in Nightspots: Justice Ministry" (September 28, 2002), <http://www.hankooki.com/kt_nation/200209/t2002092717213441110. htm> (accessed February 3, 2003).

19 Philippine Overseas Employment Administration (POEA), "Of Global Presence: A Compendium of Overseas Employment Statistics," <http://www.poea.gov.ph/html/statistics. html 2006> (accessed October 22, 2007).

20 Joaquin L. Gonzalez, *Philippine Labour Migration: Critical Dimensions of Public Policy* (Singapore: Institute of Southeast Asian Studies, 1998).

but rarely understood the exact nature of their working conditions in Korea—both because of the managers' attempt to conceal the truth and the different management in different clubs. The reasons they gave for coming to Korea included wanting to make better money for their family and themselves, to see the world, and to show their independence. While they considered themselves "entertainers," they were frequently assumed to be "prostitutes." In my research, I found that the Filipinas and GIs engaged in a range of emotional, social, and sexual relationships mediated by discourses of romance and friendship. The Filipinas' major complaints about their jobs were arbitrary fines, pressure on selling drinks, verbal abuse, limitation of their movements (and therefore out-of-clubs socialization with GIs), and the lack of redress. These complaints are resoundingly similar to those of migrant workers in manufacturing industries in Korea according to an Amnesty International report.[21] The difference is that the number of these migrants is seven times greater than that of entertainers: 52 percent of an estimated total of 360,000 were "irregular" migrant workers, particularly vulnerable to abuses because of their illegal status.

None of the local or international NGOs, however, consider these problems shared by entertainers and industrial workers collectively within the framework of migrants' rights, or trafficking. Instead, they frame the problems exclusively within the specific issue of "sex trafficking": the workers' migrancy has become overshadowed by their sexuality. And in NGO discourses, they have come to embody the multiple oppressions of neo-colonialism, militarism, capitalism, and patriarchy. In this representation, the state, the military, and capital are the main culprits to these women's demise, and the ultimate solution—apart from stricter immigration control and better protection of women—is the eradication of prostitution. The discourse of Coalition Against Trafficking in Women (CATW) is one such example.

The Coalition Against Trafficking in Women–Asia Pacific (CATW–AP)

In the following discussion the first part outlines CATW's ideological position on prostitution as sexual exploitation that harms all women. It goes on to trace the CATW–AP's production of knowledge about "trafficked women" before any actual encounter with what it defines as a "victim." The second part discusses how the ideological commitments of the NGO and the national context in the Philippines have ensured that claims of trafficking of women into US military camp towns are tied to the colonial experiences of the nation, highlighting the Philippine government's failure to protect its citizens from masculinist US imperialism and militarism and thus paving the ground for the anti-trafficking bill as a rectification. The third and final part of this analysis examines how the pursuit for narratives of victimhood have governed the interactions between CATW–AP activists and two Filipina entertainers who returned from Korea, specifically, how activists "gave voice" to "victims" and erased their personhood.

---

21 Amnesty International, *Report on Migrant Workers in Korea* (Seoul: Amnesty International, 2006).

CATW was founded in 1988 by Kathleen Barry who is renowned for her book *Female Sexual Slavery*.[22] CATW, according to its online statements, is an organization that "promotes women's human rights" and "works internationally to combat sexual exploitation in all its forms, especially prostitution and trafficking in women and children, in particular girls." Its philosophy categorically states that "all prostitution exploits women, regardless of women's consent," and the section on "Harm" is concerned exclusively with "sexual exploitation," epitomized by prostitution: "Prostitution affects all women, justifies the sale of any woman, and reduces all women to sex." CATW's vision for women and girls is that they "have the right to sexual integrity and autonomy." CATW obtained Category II Consultative Status with the United Nations Economic and Social Council in 1989. CATW and its regional branches have been the recipients of significant private and governmental funds for their research, law enforcement training, and awareness-raising program on "human trafficking, especially sex trafficking of women and girls."[23]

The summary above indicates some themes and delineations whose contradictory character will become manifest subsequently. Firstly, prostitution is seen as inherently a form of sexual exploitation, and the link is established between prostitution and trafficking. Secondly, all women, not just women who become prostitutes, are considered to be victims of prostitution. Thirdly, CATW draws a parallel between women with children and girls which dismisses any differential degrees of autonomy between these groups. Finally, CATW's vision for women's human rights and the achievement of sexual integrity and autonomy does not include the recognition of a woman's ability to consent to commercial sex. In other words, this perspective entails a discursive reliance on the construction of women as "innocent victims" and, hence, it mitigates against reading social agency into their entrance into the sex trade.

Transnational Sisterhood?

In November 1999, at a Seoul press conference hosted by the Korean Church Women United (KCWU) for the release of a field research report on Filipina entertainers around US military camp towns in South Korea, Jean Enriquez, a representative from the CATW–AP from the Philippines, gave a speech entitled "Filipinas in Prostitution around US Military Bases in Korea: A Recurring Nightmare."[24] CATW–AP had been advocating in the Philippines for an anti-trafficking bill for four years when they received the invitation to present at the Conference. The proposed bill was soon to be tabled at both the Philippine Senate and the House of Representatives in May 2000,

---

22 Kathleen Barry, *Female Sexual Slavery* (Englewood Cliffs: Prentice-Hall, 1984).

23 All quotes, CATW, <http://www.catwinternational.org/about> (accessed September 14, 2007).

24 The invitation of Enriquez was a serendipitous event. Miss Kim, project manager for migrant women at KCWU, happened to watch an interview with Enriquez in a Korean TV program on migrant Filipina entertainers. Independent of the transnational feminist network, Kim relied on the TV production team's contact to invite Enriquez. Other than the fact that Enriquez worked for an organization that dealt with trafficking of women and children, Kim said she knew very little about her or the CATW–AP.

and therefore CATW–AP's visit to Korea was an opportune moment to highlight their views on the plight of these "trafficked Filipinas" to augment the legitimacy of its cause. Following Enriquez's return to the Philippines, the CATW–AP organized a press conference in Manila for her to speak on the subject of trafficking of Filipinas to Korea. Enriquez also wrote a report entitled "Meeting My Sisters in Korea" in the CATW newsletter.

This abundance of transnational "knowledge" about the Filipina entertainers ("my sisters"?), intriguingly, was produced by Enriquez without her actually meeting any of the Filipina entertainers who had worked in Korea, or conducting any research on the subject in Korea, since she had no time to visit any *gijichon* during her two-day stay in Seoul. However, basing her talk on the Philippine experience with US military, nationalist movement, and gendered relationship to the nation, Enriquez was able to establish rapport with her Korean audience.

In her conference presentations in Seoul and Manila, Enriquez emphatically spoke about both Korea's and Philippine's history of US military presence and the high-profile prostitution of non-Western women. Her speech invoked the anti-American sentiments of her audience and referred to the continued presence of US military bases in Korea as "certainly a magnet for trafficking of Filipinas." She went on to state: "In Korea, the Philippines and elsewhere, the women are viewed as commodities to be bought, and being Asians, they are certainly perceived as less than human."[25] It should be noted first that this assumption of a Pan-Asian identity misses the multiple and contradictory dynamics of power within the present-day Asia–Pacific region.[26] Men from the First World (in this case, the US) are traditionally viewed as exploiters of women in the Third World (here, Filipinas). By relying on the rhetoric of a dichotomous model of domination, Enriquez was able to bypass the complicated network of the actual participants in the "trafficking" of Filipinas into Korea.

The construction of "trafficked women" as young, innocent, poor, and ignorant is central to Enriquez's description of the women's victimhood: "Profiles of women trafficked show that they are mostly young, with high school or less education, coming from the rural areas and from poor families."[27] In her argument, "rural" women came to symbolize the vulnerability of the nation and culture, and hence the fears and anxieties of the dominated. Enriquez told the press that airport officials allegedly received "at least $25,000" from a Korean recruiter for each departing young woman. When questioned about this big amount, Enriquez unconvincingly explained that, in addition to being facilitated to leave the country illegally, the girls chosen to be trafficked "were 'young and innocent.'" This exaggeration of the money involved (my research showed that $300–400 was paid to the immigration for each woman) fits well into the general victimizing formula of the abolitionist

---

25 Jean Enriquez, "Filipinas in Prostitution around US Military Bases: A Recurring Nightmare," CATW–AP, 1999. <http://www.catw-ap.org/filipinas.htm> (accessed September 27, 2007).

26 Vera Mackie, "The Language of Globalization, Transnationality and Feminism," *International Feminist Journal of Politics* 3, No. 2 (2001): 183.

27 Enriquez, *op. cit.*

camp, which states that "if any money is offered to the women or their parents it should be as pitiful as possible, whereas the profits being made from their sexual labor should be as enormous as possible."[28] And when these profits come from the "youth and innocence" of Filipino girls, moral indignation is guaranteed and support for its end rallied.

In her report "Meeting My Sisters in Korea," Enriquez called on "sisters in Asia and other parts of the globe" to engage in a feminist struggle against "the West." In particular, she highlighted the importance of personal testimonials in their crusade, stating that "what would be most important in winning cases [...] is *giving value to the voices* of prostitutes in the courts and other arenas of battle" (my emphasis).[29] In the ethnography below, I extend this concern and ask the question, "Giving *what* value to the voices of women?"

The Value of the Voice

In May 2000, during my visit to the Philippines, Enriquez asked me to introduce some of the Filipina entertainers who had returned to Korea to the CATW–AP, for they had not managed to talk successfully with any of these women. Supposing that meeting the women might give CATW–AP a greater understanding of the phenomenon of women in the sex trade, I went with Katie and Milla to their Manila office one afternoon.[30] Both had worked as entertainers in a *gijichon*. Katie ran away from a club after eight months when she suspected that the club-owners were planning on making the entertainers sell sex by giving them individual rooms. She subsequently lived with her Filipino boyfriend and worked in a factory for a year before returning to the Philippines. Milla went to Korea unwillingly under arrangements between her father and a Filipino manager. In Korea, she soon met a GI who bought her contract and lived with her as a fiancé for three months before Milla returned home. The following conversation is transcribed from the videotape I took of the meeting between Katie, Milla, Enriquez, and myself at CATW–AP in May 2000.[31]

(Milla arrives after the meeting has begun.)

Enriquez (turning to speak to Milla): We are just talking about, as an organization, what we can do to help you. Because we come up with an idea of what happen to women in Korea, what some of you may have gone through, what others have gone through, that's the purpose why women, you included, escape. Did you also escape?

---

28 Alison Murray, "Debt-Bondage and Trafficking: Don't Believe the Hype," in *Global Sex Workers: Rights, Resistance, and Redefinition* (ed.), by Kamala Kempadoo and Jo Doezema (London: Routledge, 1998), 59.

29 Jean Enriquez, "Meeting My Sisters in Korea," in *Coalition Against Trafficking in Women–Asia Pacific*, Report Vol. 3, No. 2 (Manila: CATW, 1999).

30 These are pseudonyms. "Katie" and "Milla" knew nothing about the CATW before they went to meet with Enriquez.

31 The conversation took place in English. This is a verbatim record of the meeting as videotaped.

Milla: No. I met a guy there. He is now my fiancé.

Enriquez: A Filipino?

Milla: Black American.

Enriquez: GI?

Milla: Yes, GI Air Force. He had to buy the contract […].

Enriquez: But you didn't receive a penny […].

Milla: No. I received my six months' salary, but he had to pay $2,500 to buy my contract. And I just received like $700 or 800.

Enriquez (turning away from Milla and speaking to the group): So going back. We were thinking about how to help.

Enriquez's attempt to find an ideal victim in Milla's story failed at every instance in this short exchange. Milla straightforwardly denied each of Enriquez's assumptions: Milla did not escape, she received her pay, and her fiancé who helped her out of the club was not a Filipino, but an American—and a black GI—who embodies foreigners' sexual exploitation in CATW–AP's discourse. Finding Milla to be a misfit in her paradigm of victimhood, Enriquez "went back" to her own agenda and reasserted her position as the one to help the entertainers who would be in need of help, thereby asserting an epistemological hierarchy allowing her to read Milla as a victim. The rhetoric of help was repeated throughout the meeting, in phrases such as the following:[32]

So, basically, the thing that we were saying was that these are the things that we do, and wonder how we can help each other, and how we can help you. So to begin with, if you can tell us your stories. For confidentiality, absolute confidentiality […] OK. So we can talk about this. We will get in touch with you to chat about. (Slowing down and softening her voice) There may be some *sad stories* you have to go back (*sic!*) (my emphasis).[33]

The Interview and the Injury

Katie, not Milla, was contacted by CATW–AP for two interviews. One took place in the city of Pampanga near Katie's hometown, and one in Manila, a three-hour bus ride from Katie's home. The second interview was, according to Katie, conducted by staff from Women's Education, Development, Productivity and Research Organization, Inc. (WEDPRO). Below is the transcript of my first phone conversation with Katie after her interview in Manila in August 2000.

---

32 Though Enriquez did mention at one point that CATW was an advocacy organization and thus was not in a position to offer direct assistance, she emphasized that they could refer them to relevant organizations.

33 Videotaped recording by author (May 9, 2000).

Author: What did they ask you?

Katie: All the worst things. Like if they hit me, or how they treat us […].

Author: Did you tell them that you didn't work as a prostitute?

Katie: Yes. They asked about other girls. I told them everything […]. They said they will have my story in a book and then they will give me one. It's a book on all Asian girls, I think. They are kind. I cried. They made me tell all […]. Things since I was a child [...]. It's kind of difficult to tell. The woman who interviewed me said, "You have something in your heart that you can't tell […]. It seems that you have a real problem."[34]

Upon this prompting in a prolonged interview by an apparently skillful interviewer, Katie revealed that she had been repeatedly raped by her uncle since she was eight years old. After getting this sensational piece of personal history, Katie related, all the interviewer had to say was: "You need a doctor."[35]

Excavating the childhood experiences of sexual abuse in a "victim of (sex) trafficking" may not make immediate sense to the reader, except for the obvious "sexual" connection. (Do abused children have a greater tendency to be "trafficked" as adults into sex industry? If so, this connection remains unexplained in the CATW reports. But prostitution and domestic sexual abuse are mentioned under the same category of "Harm" on the CATW website.) Indeed, one needs to see this framing of trafficking as an issue of "violence against women" in its own right. For, including childhood sexual abuse in the profile of victims of trafficking highlights the sexual vulnerability of women and, by illustrating the extensiveness of violence (that one woman can be the victim of multiple violence) and implicitly suggesting that one form of exploitation leads to the other, this framework reinforces the connection of womanhood with victimhood, while making women's desires and needs irrelevant. My conversation with Katie illustrates this last point:

Author: Did you tell CATW that you want to go back to Korea?

Katie: No, not yet. Why? Shall I? Can they help?

Author: Did they ask you if you have a job?

Katie: No.

Author: Did they ask you if there is anything you need?

Katie: No. They just said keep in touch.[36]

Katie went home with only 460 pesos (1 USD = 43 pesos in August 2000) for bus fare and open wounds to heal. Apart from her sexual victimhood, the interviewers did not express concerns about her current needs, her livelihood or her future. Only

---

34 "Katie," interview by author (August 14, 2000).

35 *Ibid.*

36 *Ibid.*

her heart-rending past had value in her configuration as a "trafficked victim." Neither CATW–AP nor WEDPRO communicated with Katie again, nor did they send her "the book" with her story as promised or provided the "help" that Enriquez pledged in the first meeting. The question arises: What was the value of Katie to CATW–AP after she had given them her "voice"? What was the value of the interviews to Katie? Did Katie see CATW–AP as an organization she could seek help from—in view of Enriquez's alleged commitment to help?

Apparently not. As a single mother in her thirties, without a college degree, Katie eventually left for a job in Japan in November 2000 and ran into worse abuses— 11 months after returning from Korea and three months after her interviews with CATW–AP. She returned from Japan to an even more serious limbo. I suggested in earnest to Katie that maybe she could benefit from visiting the CATW–AP office, since Enriquez promised to help her. But she did not see CATW–AP as a place where she could seek help. Her response was: "You know some people just telling that [*sic*]. They just tell that."[37]

CATW–AP and its member organization's single-minded drive to find the "victim" in Katie turned her personal story into just another "voice" and a statistic in their reports—or maybe not even that, as her story did not fit their narratives. I failed to locate Katie's story in their reports, and they never sent her a copy of the report as promised. By introducing Katie to CATW–AP and indirectly putting her through the emotional ordeal of the intrusive interview process at WEDPRO, I felt myself partly responsible for creating a victim. Katie's life story and its pathos had been appropriated in the process of making the "injured body" required for the advancement of their cause in the international arena, but not necessarily for the betterment of her life. While CATW–AP gained success in their lobby for a new anti-trafficking bill that was passed in 2003, Katie and working-class women like her continued their struggle for an opportunity to go overseas.

Discussion

This analysis captures the process through which an NGO identified, interacted with, and represented Filipina entertainers in *gijichon* to the global anti-trafficking community categorically as "victims of sex trafficking." It is indisputable that the Filipina entertainers in *gijichon* are being subjected to exploitation and abuses. Their lack of control of their employment conditions in Korea is structured by their identity as migrants, as women, and as "entertainers." The privileging of these structural oppressions risks subsuming under the issue the material, social, and legal conditions that made sexual exploitation possible in the first place.

In the context of what Keck and Sikkink refer to as "information politics" in transnational activism, "victims' voices" continue to lend tremendous authenticity and legitimacy to NGO claims. The production of convincing victimization is in fact a necessary step in communication with governments, funders, the media, and other non-state agents. As we know from fairytales and the mass media, stories that

---

37 *Ibid.*

sell best are those that have clearly identified villains and innocent victims—stories that are simple, unambiguous, and emotionally appealing. Anti-trafficking NGOs like the CATW have their own needs and agendas formulated *independently* of the women they try to help. This single-mindedness effectively flattens the complexity of women's lives and desires, and unwittingly re-victimizes the women by ignoring their agency and needs expressed in their migratory journeys.

This brings us to the larger context of the revival of global trafficking panic at the turn of the twenty-first century. Concerns about trafficking arose in the context of burgeoning migration—both legal and illegal—across borders. That climate gave rise to critical questions such as: What are the political implications of this anti-trafficking discourse that frequently conflate trafficking with prostitution and with violence against women? What are the unintended consequences of state powers over migration and sexuality? In line with the advocacy studied here, state anti-trafficking initiatives construct "victims of sex trafficking" as victims *par excellence*. The US Trafficking Victims Protection Act 2000 (TVPA), for instance, defines "sex trafficking" as a distinct category aimed at "the recruitment, harboring, transportation, provision, or obtaining of a person for the purpose of a commercial sex act" as inherently exploitative regardless of the absence of abuse or coercion (Section 3[9]).[38] As we have learnt from the panic over the White Slave Trade, measures against "sex trafficking" have often led to greater regulation and policing of women who transgress their ideal gender roles and realms. A century later, a similar set of dynamics set in train by the UN Protocol and the TVPA generated a political opportunity for the triumph of abolitionists in different regional and national contexts.

The preoccupation with sexual harm in the globalization of anti-trafficking representations effectively constitutes a new global knowledge/power regime around sex, creating "victims of trafficking" as subjects in need of state protection and justifying greater state regulation on mobile populations and sexuality. Despite the rhetoric of human rights, states' anti-trafficking discourse constructs women's migration as a suspicious form of globalization. We are witnessing the development of a global network of NGOs collaborating with states to intensify the policing of mobile subjects as objects of knowledge while engendering the benevolent state. Capitalizing on the unequivocal moral repugnance that "sexual harm" commands, the laws, policies, and high-profile arrests to combat "sex trafficking" and protect its victims confer moral authority upon the state. It leaves relatively untouched the structures that have generated gendered disadvantages, capitalist exploitation of migrant labor, restrictive immigration policies, lack of inter-government collaboration for the protection of human rights, and global economic and political disparities. A particular political order is thus "normalized" through anti-trafficking policies.

---

38 *The US Trafficking Victims Protection Act*, <www.state.gov/documents/organization/10492.pdf>, 8 (accessed October 22, 2007). As Wendy Chapkis argues, the TVPA conflates migrant abuse with sex slavery and relies on extreme sexual violence as the premise of victimhood while strengthening prosecution and immigration control against illegal migration. In effect, it criminalizes prostitution and masquerades "as a good cop to anti-immigration policies' bad cop" (Wendy Chapkis, "Trafficking, Migration, and the Law: Protecting Innocents, Punishing Immigrants," *Gender and Society* 17, No. 6 [2003]: 932).

Are anti-trafficking advocates uncannily facilitating the aggrandizement of state powers and reproducing a particular gender order? The formation of a transnational activist network that would pool together the perspectives, experiences, and strategies at different locations can be a critical force in social transformation on a global scale. However, if this transnational network operates to impose a particular sexual morality, feminist ideology, and nationalist ideals on the working classes, obliterating the voices and visions of the individuals they claim to serve, whatever their successes on the stage of international politics, they will become just another disciplinary regime with which individuals have to contend.

Bibliography

Agustin, Laura. "Migrants in the Mistress's House: Other Voices in the 'Trafficking' Debate." *Social Politics: International Studies in Gender, State and Society* 12, No. 1 (2005): 96–117.

—— "The Disappearance of a Migrant Category." *Journal of Ethnic and Migration Studies* 32, No. 1 (2006): 29–47.

Amnesty International. *Report on Migrant Workers in Korea*. Seoul: Amnesty International, 2006.

Barry, Kathleen. *Female Sexual Slavery*. Englewood Cliffs, NJ: Prentice-Hall, 1984.

Chapkis, Wendy. "Trafficking, Migration, and the Law: Protecting Innocents, Punishing Immigrants." *Gender and Society* 17, No. 6 (2003): 923–37.

Doezema, Jo. "Forced to Choose: Beyond the Voluntary v. Forced Prostitution Dichotomy." In *Global Sex Workers: Rights, Resistance, and Redefinition*. Edited by Kamala Kempadoo and Jo Doezema, 34–50. London: Routledge, 1998.

—— "Loose Women or Lost Women? The Re-Emergence of the Myth of 'White Slavery' in Contemporary Discourses of 'Trafficking in Women'." Paper presented at the ISA Convention, Washington, DC, February 17–21 1999.

—— "Ouch!: Western Feminists' 'Wounded Attachment' to the 'Third World Prostitute'." *Feminist Review* 67 (2001): 16–38.

Enriquez, Jean. "Filipinas in Prostitution around US Military Bases: A Recurring Nightmare." CATW–Asia Pacific, 1999. <http://www.catw-ap.org/filipinas.htm>.

—— "Meeting My Sisters in Korea." In *Coalition Against Trafficking in Women–Asia Pacific Report*. Vol. 3. No. 2 (Manila: CATW, 1999).

Fisher, William. "Doing Good? The Politics and Antipolitics of NGO Practices." *Annual Review of Anthropology* 26 (1997): 439–64.

Goffman, Erving. *Stigma: Notes on the Management of Spoiled Identity*. New York: Simon & Schuster, 1963.

Gonzalez, Joaquin L. *Philippine Labour Migration: Critical Dimensions of Public Policy*. Singapore: Institute of Southeast Asian Studies, 1998.

Hesford, Wendy S. and Wendy Kozol (eds), *Just Advocacy? Women's Human Rights, Transnational Feminism, and the Politics of Representation*. New Brunswick, New Jersey: Rutgers University Press, 2005.

International Organization for Migration. *A Review of Data on Trafficking in the Republic of Korea*. Geneva: International Organization for Migration, 2002.

"Katie." Interview by Sealing Cheng. August 14, 2000.

Keck, Margaret, and Kathryn Sikkink. *Activists beyond Borders: Advocacy Networks in International Politics*. Ithaca and London: Cornell University Press, 1998.

Korea Times. "Most Female E-6 Visa Holders Work in Nightspots: Justice Ministry." September 28, 2002. <http://www.hankooki.com/kt_nation/200209/t2002092717213441110.htm>.

Mackie, Vera. "The Language of Globalization, Transnationality and Feminism." *International Feminist Journal of Politics* 3, No. 2 (2001): 180–206.

Moghadam, Valentine M. *Globalizing Women: Transnational Feminist Networks*. Baltimore and London: Johns Hopkins University Press, 2005.

Murray, Alison. "Debt-Bondage and Trafficking: Don't Believe the Hype." In *Global Sex Workers: Rights, Resistance, and Redefinition*. Edited by Kamala Kempadoo and Jo Doezema. 51–64. London: Routledge, 1998.

Naples, Nancy, and Manisha Desai. *Women's Activism and Globalization*. London: Routledge, 2002.

Pickup, Francine. "Deconstructing Trafficking in Women: The Example of Russia." *Millennium: Journal of International Studies* 27, No. 4 (1998): 995–1021.

Philippine Overseas Employment Administration. "Of Global Presence: A Compendium of Overseas Employment Statistics." 2006. <http://www.poea.gov.ph/html/statistics.html>.

Saunders, Penelope. "Traffic Violations: Determining the Meaning of Violence in Sexual Trafficking Versus Sex Work." *Journal of Interpersonal Violence* 20, No. 3 (2005): 343–60.

Saunders, Penelope, and Gretchen Soderlund. "Traveling Threats: Trafficking as Discourse." *Canadian Women Studies* 22 (2003): 35–46.

Vance, Carole. "Innocence and Experience: Melodramatic Narratives of Sex Trafficking and Their Consequences for Health and Human Rights." Paper presented at panel "Sex Slaves in the Media." Columbia University, April 15, 2004.

United Nations, *Protocol to Prevent, Suppress and Punish Trafficking in Persons, Especially Women and Children, Supplementing the United Nations Convention against Transnational Organized Crime*, Article 3(a), 2000, <untreaty.un.org/English/notpubl/18-12-a.E.doc>.

The US Government, *The US Trafficking Victims Protection Act*, 2000, <www.state.gov/documents/organization/10492.pdf>.

Chapter 10
Victims, Villains, Saviors:
On the Discursive Constructions
of Trafficking in Women

Loretta Ihme

What is in general called "trafficking in women"—the involuntary displacement and forced prostitution of women—constitutes a serious form of violence against women bound to the issues of sex work and migration.[1] Indeed, it is considered one of the most serious forms of violence against women. Yet, there is an additional aspect of this dynamics which has been frequently neglected in scholarly and practical work: the very discourse on trafficking reveals traces of "othering"—the representation of both victims and perpetrators through class, racial and gender stereotypes.

Whereas the range of violence explored in talking about trafficking constitutes a social reality, the phenomenon of "trafficking in women" can also be read as a culturally constructed category. Cultural narratives on trafficking become interesting from this perspective in a twofold sense—as narratives with specific content and as narratives with specific aims. The most prominent tendencies observed in representations of trafficking are the constitution of the perpetrator, the victim, and her customers as ("racial" or sexual) *others*, as well as the construction of the imagined place of trafficking as an imaginary *elsewhere*, outside of a particular national context. The discursive functionalities of this *othering* are various, but its most important consequence is that trafficking is pictured as a problem caused by *others*, coming from *elsewhere*, having nothing to do with "us."

This chapter analyzes European, more precisely, German, discourses on trafficking, particularly their racist, sexist, and classist elements. Using mainly the material from German print media that emerged during the discussions about the reform of penal justice on trafficking in human beings that took place between 2000 and 2004,[2] I examine how trafficking and the violence connected to trafficking are

---

1 I would like to thank Andrea Rick, Leigh Swancott, and Daniel Mang for their support in proofreading and discussing this chapter as well as for their patience with my "creative" English and sometimes stubborn nature.

2 The reform of penal justice concerning the facts constituting trafficking in human beings implemented the basic aspects of the UN *Protocol To Prevent, Suppress and Punish Trafficking In Persons, Especially Women and Children, Supplementing The United Nations Convention Against Transnational Organized Crime* (2000). Now the legal definition includes the possibility of trafficking into forms of exploitation other than prostitution. By contrast, the public image of "trafficking" remains connected to forced prostitution and female victims.

represented in cultural narratives and I argue that this form of representation itself constitutes a form of violence. In conclusion I will argue for a discursive practice that does justice to the actual victims of violence within sex work and/or the process of migration—one that would avoid the reinforcement of racist, sexist, and classist stereotypes.

Significant Narratives: What Is at Stake in the Discourse on Trafficking?

Trafficking in women has been primarily discussed as a problem of security—a lack of control over irregular migration and organized crime; it has also, therefore, been posited as a violation of law and, due to its cross-border characteristics, of national sovereignty. In addition, trafficking in women has been discussed as a violation of victims' human rights. The *United Nations Protocol to prevent, suppress and punish trafficking in persons, especially women and children, supplementing the United Nations convention against transnational organized crime* (2000) defines trafficking as:

> [... the] recruitment, transportation, transfer, harbouring or receipt of persons, by means of the threat or use of force or other forms of coercion, of abduction, of fraud, of deception, of the abuse of power or of a position of vulnerability or of the giving or receiving of payments or benefits to achieve the consent of a person having control over another person, for the purpose of exploitation. Exploitation shall include, at a minimum, the exploitation of the prostitution of others or other forms of sexual exploitation, forced labour or services, slavery or practices similar to slavery, servitude or the removal of organs.[3]

In this document, the consent of a victim of trafficking is regarded as irrelevant. Therefore, the trafficked persons may have been forced into migration or may have migrated of their own will, they may have made the decision to work in the sex industry or they may have been forced into prostitution—or any other slavery-like working contexts. They also can be either male or female. The representation of trafficking in human beings, however, is dominated by portraying "victims" as young and innocent women who have been forced into prostitution. Discourses on trafficking rarely mention other forms of trafficking in women, such as forced marriages or various forms of exploitation and violence connected to migration, and when they do it, their descriptions tend to stay bland and technical.

The need to fight trafficking in women may seem obvious. The perpetrators of sexual trafficking and the violence they exert on women are usually represented in an evil light, one that leaves no space for any other response but a merciless battle against it. Yet, at second glance, one may observe interferences that lead to a disturbance both in the representation of trafficking and in the eye of the (willing) observer. If one is prepared to take this second look, one may be struck by the prominence of racist, sexist, and classist elements in the cultural narratives on trafficking in women; in turn, one may observe how those perceptions have

---

3 United Nations. *Protocol To Prevent, Suppress and Punish Trafficking In Persons, Especially Women and Children, Supplementing The United Nations Convention Against Transnational Organized Crime* (2000), <www.uncjin.org/Documents/Conventions/dcatoc/final_documents_2/convention_%20traff_eng.pdf> (accessed March 20, 2007), Article 3(a).

guided—and frequently misguided—reactions to trafficking in women. What is more, the consequences of these discourses are ambivalent. Policies regarding the protection of victims and law enforcement are subject to criticism because of their negative impact on the already-precarious life situation of migrants and sex workers, for example when the existence of forced prostitution is used as a justification for criminalizing all forms of prostitution or for an increasing number of police raids and other repressive measures within the affected area.[4] As such, prevention campaigns against trafficking are criticized as instruments to control the mobility of women.[5] Furthermore, the discursive field of trafficking in women has been criticized as an arena where, as the scholar Rutvica Andrijasevic states, the fear of the current transformation of European citizenship is revealed. The proliferation of trafficking in Europe indicates a boundary crisis;[6] hence, debates on trafficking do not only address the protection of victims but also negotiate questions of the European "sense of belonging" in the context of multiple and competing national projects.[7]

On the other hand, trafficking in women is discursively explosive. In as much as women are significant for the constitution of national identities—for reasons of biological and cultural reproduction, and as the bearers and sustainers of community and "honor"—their seemingly increased dislocation, rape, and forced prostitution necessarily produce irritations in the myth–symbol complex of the national communities involved.[8] Finally, trafficking does not only unsettle identities, it also helps their constitution. Specific cultural narratives on trafficking simultaneously strengthen national identities and support the development of a supranational European identity. Particularly active in the corroboration of national identities is the process of *othering* due to the racist, sexist, and classist elements within a nation's culture. In *Gender and Nation* Nira Yuval-Davis argues that identities, as "cultural

---

4 See for example Laura Agustin, "Forget Victimization: Granting Agency to Migrants," *Development* 46, No. 3 (2003): 30–6; Jo Doezema, "Loose Women or Lost Women? The Re-Emergence of the Myth of 'White Slavery' in Contemporary Discourses of 'Trafficking in Women,'" (2000), <www.walnet.org/csis/papers/doezema-loose.html> (accessed November 8, 2005); and Penelope Saunders, "Migration, Sex Work, and Trafficking in Persons," (2000), <www.walnet.org/csis/papers/saunders-migration.html> (accessed December 8, 2005).

5 See Rutvica Andrijasevic, "Trafficking in Women and the Politics of Mobility in Europe" (2004), <http://igitur-archive.library.uu.nl/dissertations/2005-0314-013009/index.htm> (accessed December 8, 2005).

6 See Jacqueline Berman, "(Un)Popular Strangers and Crises (Un)Bounded: Discourses of Sex-Trafficking, the European Political Community and the Panicked State of the Modern State," *European Journal of International Relations* 9, No. 1 (2003): 37–86.

7 See Loretta Ihme, "Europas Gespenster. Frauenhandel, Nation und Supranation." In *Perspektiven für ein neues Europa—Die neue Öffnung?* (ed.), by Marcin Witkowski and Joanna Dlugosz (Berlin: Peter Lang, 2006), 197–207.

8 The term "myth–symbol complex" refers to a combination of myths, symbols, values, and memories which (ethnic/national) collectives use to sustain themselves. The myth–symbol complex serves both to bind together groups and to enable them to distinguish themselves from "others," thereby establishing collective "identities." See Anthony Smith, *Nations and Nationalism in a Global Era* (Cambridge: Polity, 1995).

narratives," serve to (re)produce the ground of difference between "us" and "others" within a national context.[9] In the context of national projects, to refer to this kind of "narrative of identities" allows for the constant negotiation of borders and for the arbitration of the access to relevant social, cultural, and economic resources. The *other* in these narratives is always a stranger and a danger to "our" national and cultural identity. Speaking about trafficking in women (re)produces those others as *significant others*, in which the difference between "us" and "them" is more pronounced in terms of the violence "they" can initiate against "us." Hence, victims and perpetrators represent internal and external strangers that contribute both to the constitution of shared European identity and the re-invention of old national identities. Moreover: in so far as the imaginary place where the act of trafficking supposedly happens is constructed as a significant *other* place, debating trafficking supports European negotiations of the inside and the outside.

Young Girls Jeopardized by Monsters: Cultural Narratives on Trafficking in Women

The cultural narratives on trafficking, its victims, and its perpetrators, are suffused with endlessly repeated stereotypes. These stereotypes stem from assumptions of trafficked women as innocent, white, and naive victims who are lured into migration and prostitution by an uncontrollable number of creepy, dark, and monstrous villains. What is understood to be the actual performance of trafficking is imagined to take place in desperate, soulless locations. Although these stereotypes of the victim, perpetrator, and the space of trafficking are visible in more or less all debates on trafficking in women, the degree of their manifestation depends on the particular social actor that engages this type of discourse.

Different actors articulate trafficking in different ways. Politicians and political institutions refer to trafficking as an issue of the political and legal framework and policymaking in the nation; as such, they use trafficking as a rhetorical figure in negotiating policies and legal framework regarding borders, migration, the European Union enlargement, and organized crime. Furthermore, political parties use the discursive figure of trafficking to reinforce national beliefs in it as a symbol of the danger and evil coming from outside (border and migration policies) and inside (prostitution policies). Finally, politicians and political institutions influence research on trafficking by making money available for it. Politicians' reinforcement of stereotypes in trafficking may be illustrated by the example of the International Organization for Migration (IOM), which both organizes and conducts intergovernmental research on trafficking.[10] The IOM's core-interest lies

---

9 Nira Yuval-Davis, *Gender and Nation* (London: Sage, 1997), 43.

10 With 120 member states, the International Organization for Migration (IOM) is the most important intergovernmental organization in the field of migration. Cooperating with governmental and non-governmental actors, they aim at the promotion of human and orderly migration by implementing trans- and international strategies of migration management. The IOM's attitude toward both migration and deportation has been criticized by various human rights organizations.

in "managing" (mainly cross-border) migration, and thus this organization is closely affiliated with nation-states and their migration policies; "managing migration" here becomes predominantly the hindering of migration and the organization of repatriation. The IOM also participates in prevention campaigns and different kinds of support for "victims" by cooperating with various non-governmental organizations (NGOs) within nations.

In addition to their actual psycho-social work with women who have been trafficked, NGOs work on awareness-raising, and, more generally, public relations. To accomplish those goals, NGOs organize public discussions on trafficking and conduct awareness-raising campaigns; they are present at bigger socio-political events such as church congresses and on the Internet; and they publish articles and books. By participating in round tables and expert hearings and groups, NGOs insert their own, client-centered perspectives into political debates; in this way, they aim to influence legal and political frameworks concerning their clients. Nongovernmental organizations also conduct trainings (so-called sensitization-measures) for the police and other co-actors in the field. From the scope of their activity, one may infer that NGOs are responsible for the main part of the research on trafficking, either alone or in cooperation with mostly non-academic researchers.[11]

Taking NGOs' good intentions for granted, one may distinguish between two sets of aims in their work. First and foremost, NGOs purport to fight trafficking in women on every level. Secondly, and crucially to their work, NGOs secure their future existence by ensuring access to their clients: a solid client base means also secure funds for their own work. Most German NGOs offering psycho-social care and counseling for the trafficked women have developed out of organizations working on issues such as domestic violence or counseling female migrants. Supporting the trafficked women, they are confronted with the situation in which the majority of their clients are deported within a short timeframe. To advocate regulations which would allow the trafficked women to stay in Germany for at least a couple of weeks (despite their "illegal" status) is, therefore, not only a humanitarian concern but also a crucial existential issue for the NGOs. For nongovernmental organizations, another important aspect of their work is cooperation with the police, as women subjected to trafficking usually do not recognize themselves as victims but have to be recognized as such by others.[12] Finally, the raising of general awareness of the phenomenon of trafficking has been recognized as a quintessential project. In this effort NGOs cooperate with the media. The media, on the other hand, have their own motives for report on this subject. Without denying that the media is sincerely

---

11 Most research done in this area has to be characterized as methodologically weak and tendentious, although helpful for policymaking processes. See Liz Kelly, "'You Can Find Anything You Want': A Critical Reflection on Research on Trafficking in Persons within and into Europe," *International Migration* 43, No. 1–2 (2005): 235–65.

12 Women who have been trafficked mostly understand themselves as "perpetrators," since they often have made a decision to work in the sex sector (if often only under pressure), have migrated illegally, and have been told repeatedly by the traffickers that they will go to jail and then be deported if found by the police. For those reasons, some of the more recent awareness raising campaigns focus on encouraging women in the sex business to learn more about and to exercise their rights.

concerned about trafficking in women as a violation of victims' human rights, it is clear that one central motive for dealing with trafficking informs their interest: sex sells. It can be observed that what is implicit in alternative discourses on the issue may become explicit in media coverage, so that what is represented in media reflects the ideologies of the majority populace.

At the beginning of the twentieth century, the American suffragette, Harriet Laidlaw, emphasized in the debate on the so-called "white slavery"—what we would today call trafficking—that "[i]t is more important to be aroused than to be accurate. Apathy is more of a crime than exaggeration in dealing with this subject."[13] It is this attitude that is curiously replicated in the contemporary media coverage of trafficking in women. In order to arouse strong feelings on the issue of trafficking, culturally specific representations of perpetrators, victims, and trafficking itself are drawn. First of all, in media coverage the imagined places where trafficking supposedly starts are described as backward, boring, and neglected villages, or morally degenerate and fallow industrial cities. The inhabitants are corrupted, devious, primitive, ignorant, greedy, and, apart from a small number of "braves," cowardly. Appalling conditions inform family life: social neglect, violence, incest, alcoholism. In the German weekly journal *Der Spiegel*, the journalist Walter Mayr paints a rich tableau of one of these places, Moldova's largest village Costeşti:

> For in Costeşti, where the dead souls are barricaded alongside endless streets of sand, behind gates of wood and metal, between geese, donkeys and dogs, between draw wells and iconostas, where civil society died a picturesque death and even the few braves talk about a "village of monsters"—in Costeşti only money matters.[14]

Whether or not these descriptions correspond to truth is of little significance at present. Much more decisive is the question of what implications such representations may have. In discourses on trafficking, these representations relegate the location of trafficking in women to an imaginary space that is outside of the nation, and therefore, that is the realm of *others*. The quintessence of such representational discourses seems to be the idea that trafficking in women is, after all, not a European problem, but a problem for Europe.

Locating trafficking in women in an imaginary outside space absolves the countries of destination from taking responsibility for being involved in the phenomenon. Hence, to explore the economic interests of the countries to which women are trafficked is usually deemed an unnecessary or even cynical activity.[15] "Our" participation in trafficking is one of the things difficult to express. The inevitability of this position is endorsed by the representations of trafficking as an

---

13 Quoted in Ruth Rosen, *The Lost Sisterhood: Prostitution in America, 1900–1918* (Baltimore: Johns Hopkins University Press, 1982), 114.

14 Walter Mayr, "Das Dorf der toten Seelen," *Der Spiegel* 26 (June 23, 2003). All excerpts from newspapers have been translated by Loretta Ihme, if not mentioned otherwise.

15 Studies that focus on economical interests of states in this field are rare, and if existing, they typically address the economical interest of the countries of origin (see, for one, Petra Streiber, *Internationaler Frauenhandel. Funktionsweisen, soziale und ökonomische Ursachen und Gegenmaßnahmen* [Berlin: Das Arabische Buch, 1998]).

activity wicked beyond imagination, of perpetrators as evil past comprehension, and of victims as thoroughly innocent. The amount of violence exerted by perpetrators is inconceivable—at least, for "us." For example, the daily newspaper *Süddeutsche Zeitung* renders the case story of "Anna P." as follows:

> For two days she [Anna P.] was beaten, ducked in a tub with ice-cold water, thrown into a windowless cellar. Then she was told to put on some make-up to disguise the black eyes and the bruises, and to go to the customer. Again she screamed, refused. Again there was beating, and she was raped brutally. They had taken her passport; she was guarded round the clock.[16]

Every aspect of Anna P.'s capture is described in extremes: not only was Anna P. beaten, she was beaten for two days; not only was she ducked, but the water was "cold," even ice-cold; not only was she thrown into a cellar, but the cellar was "window-less"; not only was she told to work after that, but she was also forced to masquerade, to disguise what had happened. And when she was raped, she was not only raped, but raped "brutally"—as if it were possible to rape somebody in any other way but brutally. This description not only excludes any possibility of social agency on the part of the women subject to trafficking (for example, the woman voluntarily working as a sex worker)—a fact that I will discuss later in this chapter—but it also shows perpetrators in a specific light.[17] The descriptions surrounding Anna P. reflect the media's representations of perpetrators: they are ice-cold (as the water in the tub) and calculating: they break Anna P.'s will with physical, psychological, and sexual means. Both the way they lure the women into prostitution and their strategies to get and keep them under control are perfidious. Aside from being cold and calculating, however, perpetrators are first and foremost foreign to "us." In media "victims" as well as "perpetrators" are usually described as citizens of countries other than the countries of destination. At the same time, "perpetrators" are often described as even more of a foreigner than the "victims": whereas the "victims" are usually pictured as citizens of the countries where they were recruited—which indicates their "orderly" status before they became victims—perpetrators are often discursively allocated a citizenship of a country different from both the country of destination and that of recruitment. They appear displaced, shifting, homeless, or to use the German, symbolically laden word, *heimatlos*.

All of this allows that the perpetrator be persistently figured as a significant external *other*. In Germany, most perpetrators represented in public debates, particularly in media depictions, are pictured as Poles, Turks, "Gypsies," Uzbeks, Ukrainians, or Greeks; the irony of these representations lies in that fact that according to criminal statistics, about 40 percent of the alleged perpetrators in Germany are German,

---

16 Thomas Urban, "Hinter tausend Fenstern," *Süddeutsche Zeitung* (March 15, 2005).

17 The constant reference to perpetrators' effort to force victims into sex work feeds an image of victims as women who have *not* consented to work as prostitutes. This imaging, however, does not correspond to the reality where the majority of victims that have become visible actually have consented to this type of work.

not foreign.[18] The only media report located so far that explicitly names a German perpetrator significantly gives him the name "Malik," a name which does not "sound" German.[19] The decision to use this foreign-sounding name arouses suspicions among the broader German public that the perpetrator might be "less German." He might be foreign-born or an *Aussiedler*.[20] Finally, this perception of agents in trafficking as mainly foreign applies also to the customers of trafficked women. Customers are considered alternatively as potential saviors of the trafficked women (then they have a Western European nationality) or perpetrators (then they are mostly foreigners). In the German media imagination, the incarnation of the worst type of customer is the Turkish "john." This representation of the Turks is evidenced in the story of "Natalja," a Ukrainian woman who was trafficked. "Natalja" is in the focus of an extended biographical report in the German weekly *Die Zeit*. In that report, "Natalja" notes that she reached the most horrible point of her "career" when she was sold into a brothel where all johns were Turks. She notes: "They stank."[21] Another report by Harald Martenstein in Berlin's daily *Der Tagesspiegel* informs us that: "The most popular means of exerting pressure [on the trafficked women, L.I.] is the Turks' brothel. The Turks' brothel is the punishment for misbehavior."[22]

This discursive constitution of perpetrators (or customers-turned-perpetrators) in the media reflects a widespread racist representation of Turks as involved in trafficking. This image pictures the male Turk as the racialized *other* who is both inferior and uncivilized, but who possesses an overpowering, irrepressible sexuality. It is not by chance that the perpetrators are characterized as being "dark" (as "gypsies" or Arabs)—in contrast to the representation of their "white" victims. Even less accidental is the association of perpetrators with nations that are often regarded as significant in current discussions about the expansion of the European Union (EU) to include Muslim-dominated countries, such as Turkey, and or in discussions concerning European heritage and belonging, such as the case of Ukraine. Political scientist Jacqueline Berman points out that this racialized representation of the perpetrator evidenced in political discussions surrounding the EU feeds into the virtually panic-stricken perception of the widespread "criminal networks" that threaten to infect the nations involved in the EU:

> Traffickers are discursively positioned as responsible for everything from illegal immigration to moral chaos, a dangerous "law unto themselves," infecting "our"

---

18 Bundeskriminalamt, "Bundeslagebild Menschenhandel 2005" (Karlsruhe, Wiesbaden: BKA, 2006), <www.bka.de/lageberichte/mh/2005/mh2005.pdf> (7) (accessed November 24, 2006).

19 Frauke Hunfeld, "Lina und die FRAUENHÄNDLER—Mitten unter uns," *Stern* 49 (November 30, 2005).

20 *Aussiedler* is a German word attached mainly to Russian- and Polish-born Germans who came to Germany as immigrants of German origin as re-settlers. The attitude of German majority society toward these immigrants is highly ambivalent. On the one hand, they are perceived as Germans; on the other hand, they are exposed to anti-Slavic prejudice and are suspected to be criminal and lazy beneficiaries of the German welfare system.

21 Michael Schwelien, "Das Paradies im Roten Licht," *Die Zeit* 41 (October 2, 2003).

22 Harald Martenstein, "Die Zeugin der Anklage," *Der Tagesspiegel* (March 8, 2004).

community with violence and disease. They strike at the institutions of the state and the market—hallmarks of Western rule of law—with their immoral sexuality and rampant criminality.[23]

European racialized representations of perpetrators engender the characterization of all perpetrators as external *others* who penetrate European borders, endanger European reality, and contaminate European moral foundations. That characterization can also be found in visual materials, particularly in the so-called "awareness-raising and information campaigns" that have been conducted since the late 1990s by European NGOs and intergovernmental organizations. Particularly the IOM has been conducting several campaigns to encourage potential migrant women to make informed decisions when migrating and to warn them of the dangers of trafficking.[24] Indoor and outdoor posters, leaflets, brochures, flyers, postcards, stickers, pocket-calendars, and fact-sheets constitute the main part of those campaigns; in some cases, those campaigns involve conducting informational workshops for special target groups, for example, young female high school graduates, using brochures and posters. Other campaigns engage radio and television advertisements and documentaries.[25] Most of these campaigns are financed and produced by large, intergovernmental organizations such as the IOM or the UN. NGOs often participate in conceptual preparations of these campaigns, but the aesthetic and dramatic aspects are often determined by advertising experts who are involved in the realization of larger campaigns.[26] The pictures used in these campaigns usually focus on the victim, but exclude the perpetrator. The offender, if at all, appears in fragments: dismembered hands taking money, usually shown with gold bracelets, rings, and expensive watches. Sometimes one can see the torso of a procurer, either dressed in an expensive suit, worn lasciviously, or with a leather jacket, implying that the perpetrator is a "Mafioso" and/or a pimp. This fragmentation, the display of overly dismembered parts of "perpetrator's" body, allows for his objectification as the other. This ambivalent representation is further reinforced in more recent campaigns where the "perpetrator" is rather symbolized than shown. Although one can still find the "fragmented perpetrator" that was visible in the campaigns of the 1990s, perpetrators in campaigns conducted within the last seven years seem even less

---

23 Berman, *op. cit.*, 54f.

24 It should be mentioned here, that an "informed decision" in the eyes of the IOM seems nearly always to be a decision against migration.

25 The UN has produced a number of awareness-rising ads (see <www.unodc.org/unodc/multimedia_video.html>), and the IOM has produced several documentaries, for example, *Women Sold into Slavery* (IOM, *Women Sold into Slavery*, Lithuania, 2002) and *Prey of Silence* (IOM, *Prey of Silence*, Ukraine, 2001).

26 As small campaigns conducted by NGOs alone and realized by graphic and/or advertisement experts who are in close discussion with the NGOs are different in the way they show both "perpetrators" and trafficked women, I will focus on larger international campaigns for my argument. Suffice it to mention that in NGO campaigns trafficked women are more frequently endowed with social agency.

visible.[27] Instead of being represented by human body parts, perpetrators are glossed by "objects of violence," for example, hooks or ropes. The employment of objects to represent "otherness" allows an exaggeration of the culpability and immorality of the perpetrator. The implied anonymity is amplified by the representation of the perpetrator by violent, estranged objects; the latter reinforces direct correlations between the perpetrator and violence in the space of "otherness."

Such images connote the trafficker as a faceless threat to populaces within the EU. The trafficker could be anybody—a passer-by, a neighbor, a friend, a brother. No one can be trusted. This message is supported by statements such as that appearing on the homepage accompanying an IOM prevention campaign directed at potential victims of trafficking. Under the English headline "Lies and Realities [*sic*!] About Job Abroad," the campaign lists a number of "lies" and "truths" about trafficking in women. One of the lies is that "traffickers always look like criminals, you can recognize them by their appearance." The "reality" according to this website is that one "can meet various traffickers," including those who "will not resemble criminals at all" and might even "look very decent and reliable. They may have a nice family, children, even a daughter—like you."[28]

Thus, recent representations of traffickers in campaigns aim to warn women of the dangers of trafficking imply that they resemble just "anybody"; in turn, "anybody" can be regarded as a potential perpetrator. Rutvica Andrijasevic has analyzed this image as follows:

> [T]he recent IOM campaigns uncouple the concept of traffickers from its narrow identification with "Mafiosi" and/or pimps and consequently imply a quite ample characterization of eastern European nationals as traffickers. While IOM's intent is to warn women about possible (hidden) dangers, the representational practices and concepts used to convey this message constitute fertile ground for myth making and stereotyping. In fact, they foster common assumptions about large scale criminalization of eastern European societies in the post 1989 period and fuel the fear of a westward expansion of criminal networks.[29]

It is interesting to reflect on how the "absent representation" of the perpetrator in certain campaigns manages to depict perpetrators as both "(any-)one of *us*"—from the perspective of the general public in the countries the prevention campaigns are mainly aiming at—and as "(any-)one of *them*"—from the perspective of the general public in the countries of destination. Whereas young women in Eastern and Central Europe are encouraged to mistrust just anybody, or, more precisely, any man who encourages them or wants to help them to migrate, "we" (in this chapter: the Germans) are led to mistrust just anybody (particularly any man) from Eastern and Central Europe. To depict the perpetrator in fragments or to represent him by objects

---

27 This tendency is particularly visible in IOM campaigns. Recent TV spots produced by the United Nations Office of Drugs and Crime (UNODC) in contrast still show the fragmented perpetrator. See UNODC, "Trafficking in Women," n.d., <www.unodc.org/unodc/multimedia_video.html> (accessed November 26, 2006).

28 <www.refocusbaltic.net/en/main/advice/myths> (accessed November 25, 2006).

29 Andrijasevic, *op. cit.*, 168.

allows space for the play of imagination that is contingent on who is reading, who is watching.

If one can ascribe any characteristic to the "elusive" trafficker, it is that the trafficker is a male subject. Even though German criminal statistics indicates that female traffickers comprise 22 percent of the registered traffickers,[30] female offenders are rarely represented in German discourses on trafficking. If they are mentioned, they are represented only in so far as they can gain the confidence of female victims, necessary to recruit and lure them into prostitution. Moreover, when they are mentioned, they are depicted in association with narratives of their own former victimization within trafficking. Hence, female offenders in trafficking are pictured with a traumatic history that has caused them to remain involved in situations of trafficking against other women. In comparison with the (non-)depiction of male traffickers and their motives, the specific depiction of female perpetrators renders their criminal and inhuman involvement in trafficking comprehensible, if not acceptable. In contrast to the male perpetrator who is not represented by any such history of victimization himself and is granted no background that would justify his involvement in trafficking, the female offender, in the end, becomes just another victim in the cycle of trafficking. A social worker in the specialized psycho-social care center of the international human rights organization *La Strada* in Warsaw has related this story:

> A young woman had found a job as a "dishwasher" in a hotel in Spain, near the border. When she told this to her mother, her mother, a woman of forty, suggested coming with her daughter. [...] When they arrived in Spain, both mother and daughter were forced to work as street prostitutes, standing right next to each other. After a couple of weeks the mother was sent home, alone. The pimps told her that if she sent them two new girls, they would let her daughter go. The mother, however, decided to call *La Strada*, and with the help of the Spanish police it was possible to rescue the girl and bring her home.[31]

As in many other narratives, one can perceive two aspects of the potential victimization of a female trafficker/potential perpetrator in this story. Firstly, the mother is rendered a victim of trafficking and forced into prostitution herself; her victimization is intensified by the fact that she has to stand next to her daughter and watch her perform sex work without being able to help her. Secondly, even when she is freed from trafficking, the mother remains in the hands of the perpetrators who demand from her to recruit more women in order to free her daughter. Under these specific circumstances, it would have been easy to understand if she had decided to become a perpetrator herself. That she did not choose this path makes the social worker's narrative a pedagogical one; the testimony aims to encourage other concerned women to call *La Strada*. This story contributes to a discourse which tries to establish social agency for women in general and demonstrates that resistance is possible, both for victims and (potential) female perpetrators. While we do not have any reason to question the validity of this story, it is obvious that the account

---

30 Bundeskriminalamt, *op. cit.*, 6.

31 Interview by author, *La Strada*, Warsaw, April 2004, anonymity of the source protected.

occludes the subjectivities and motivations of male perpetrators, while, at the same time, the motives of the female offenders/victims are overemphasized.

The same scenario applies to the victim. In current newspaper reports one will frequently find the motives behind future victims' desires to migrate illuminated in depth. Here the women are frequently depicted as having a certain amount of social agency. Yet, to show the motives or how women themselves engage in being trafficked does not presuppose a fair depiction of trafficked women as subjects with social agency; rather, it establishes the difference between morally acceptable and unacceptable behavior within this area. Female victims of trafficking may become engaged "(semi)-voluntarily" in trafficking to flee poverty or to search for a better life, as did the mother and her daughter mentioned above. In and of themselves, these and other motives (such as poverty, desperation, restricted perspectives, greed, foolishness, and so on) are comprehensible. Yet, while victims' motives are often explicitly addressed in German media accounts of trafficking, that discussion is always immediately followed by a discursive emphasis on how uninformed their choice has been. Hence, even as their motives are elaborated, these women are ultimately pictured as naïve, gullible, and, moreover, addicted to luxury and amusement. This is evidenced in the story of "Ljudmila" from St Petersburg, Russia. A report about "Ljudmila's" case claims that she came to Germany "because her monthly salary of 75 Euro (converted) was not enough for her to enjoy the boutiques, the perfumeries and tanning salons along the Newa."[32]

Finally, representations of female "victims" tend to be voyeuristic. These are usually representations showing women naked or in sexually compromising situations, or "case-stories" elaborating at length on the victimization of the affected women, stories that emphasize details of their violation. The body of the victim—and thus the female body as such—is constituted as a "spectacle,"[33] as aptly exemplified by Thomas Urban's report in *Süddeutsche Zeitung* noted earlier. Within the well-established cultural codes clarifying who is—and who is not—a "proper woman," the patriarchal voyeuristic gaze that is directed on women limits readings of women in general and those of the victims of trafficking in particular. Improper women can thus be represented only as stupid, dangerous, impure, and a potential danger to the collective—"us," or the national community.[34]

This danger is particularly woven in certain representations of the female "victims" that tend to construct the "victims" as just "anybody." This might seem, at first glance, to contradict the representation of the victim as "other," but in fact these representations form part of an ambivalent, contextualized representation of the "victim." Whereas the representations of victims in the countries of destination in the EU connote the ethnic "other," representations in the countries of origin are characterized by an ambiguity of generalization. Particularly the so-called prevention campaigns often imply that it is "anybody" who risks becoming a victim.[35] Regarding

---

32 Andrea Brandt *et al.*, "Verkauft wie eine Kuh," *Der Spiegel* 26 (June 23, 2003).

33 See Andrijasevic, *op. cit.*, 168.

34 Yuval-Davis, *op. cit.*, 47.

35 Loretta Ihme, "Huren, Mädchenhändler und Perverse: Zur Reproduktion von Differenz im Reden über Frauenhandel," *diskus* 1.06 (2006): 31ff.

the gendering of trafficking, the campaigns emphasize the risk of being a woman in the first place. Thus the risk of becoming sexually victimized within a nation is paralleled with (but also exceeded by) the dangers women face outside of the family, outside of the home village, and therefore, in spaces outside of the country of origin. If we agree with Nira Yuval-Davis's theory of the symbolic significance of women for a nation's myth–symbol complex, as discussed earlier, then we can assume that there is something more at stake when a woman is exposed to a risk of trafficking; one could argue that, on a symbolic level, it is the nation itself that is at risk.

While stoking the fears of violence against women in this way is primarily an attempt to control female sexuality,[36] it is, in my opinion, the control of female mobility that is also at stake here. Marc Warr has argued that the fear of being raped prompts women to choose a certain lifestyle, for example, that of not going out alone.[37] If the latent danger of sexual victimization is present in the entire public space, many women will restrict their mobility to avoid danger. It is of interest in this context that, according to criminal statistics, the chances of being raped by a stranger tend towards zero, while the danger of being abused, raped, or otherwise sexually harmed by family members, colleagues, friends, or acquaintances is much higher. Similarly, the percentage of victims of trafficking who did not know the perpetrator is comparatively low; traffickers are frequently friends, partners, or acquaintances of the future victim, and thus a high number of victims have been recruited personally.[38]

This discursive constitution of victims in media and artistic renderings can be read as justification for the decisions made about the life of victims after they have been "rescued." First and most urgently, in the view of rescuers—NGOs, police officers, less often, "johns," and less directly involved, politicians—victims are in need of help. Support for that view is bolstered by the information given about the physical and psychological condition of those victims; while well-intended, these reports are often simplified in order to give a more vivid account of the situation. These simplified accounts are most frequently taken for granted by those who reproduce these narratives—the media and the politicians. Consequently, the representations created by such narratives fail to acknowledge the complex life situations of trafficked women. Instead, women victims are read mainly in terms of violence, objectification, and helplessness, whereas their strength, survival strategies, and scope of action in their stories are neglected. Female victims are, thus, discursively

---

36 One can relate discourses on trafficking to recent discourses on rape and the connected fear of sexual victimization. References can be made to the relationship between the fear of sexual victimization and female identity, particularly in times of economical and political transition. Cf., Joan M. McDermott and Sarah J. Blackstone, "White Slavery Plays of the 1910s: Fear of Victimisation and the Social Control of Sexuality," *Theatre History Studies* 16 (1996): 154.

37 Marc Warr, "Public Perceptions of Crime and Punishment," in *Criminology: A Contemporary Handbook* (ed.), by Joseph F. Sheley (Belmont: Wadswoth, 1995), 15–31.

38 A European study claims that for about 58 percent of the victims the perpetrator was a stranger; 42 percent were friends, acquaintances, family members, and partners. Only 6.4 percent were recruited through an advertisement (European Commission, *Research Based on Case Studies of Victims of Trafficking in Human Beings in 3 EU Member States.*, n.d., 37f.).

inscribed in the role of objects. As such, limited descriptions of their life situations are often voyeuristic, as evidenced in the *Stern* report "Lina and the TRAFFICKERS amongst us." This report opens with the following paragraph, leaving a lot of space for the readers' imagination—maybe even for their/our own voyeuristic pleasure:

> The johns tortured her [Lina] with objects she had never seen before. One of the men whipped her for hours in his apartment, another tied her to a pillar, beat and kicked her and bellowed at her: "Smile!" [English in the original]—Smile! One fastened metal clamps to her nipples and chains to her legs; one jammed his whole hand into her vagina and balled it into a fist there, and when she screamed he said laughingly: "I can do anything with you, I paid."[39]

From such descriptions, the reader learns that what happens in sex work is perverted and far removed from "normal" and "healthy" sexuality. It is significant that the practices described here are not part of commonly accepted sexual practice—it would of course be possible as well to picture "normal" heterosexual practices as violent and brutal, but in most cases journalists, politicians and NGOs choose not to do so. As a consequence, "deviant" sexual practices are discredited as violent and distorted.

Judging by the account quoted above, the only solution to the problem of the future life of these women could be their repatriation. In this context, repatriation does not mean just a geographical relocation of the women back to their original home spaces, but also a "homecoming" to traditional life forms, such as marriage and family. Deportation, as Jacqueline Berman wrote, returns "women 'home,' where, it is assumed, they properly belong."[40] As Berman further explains, this "return" also presupposes that the trafficked women will find their way back to their proper place as women within the national community—both on individual and symbolic planes. Thus, the journalists writing about trafficking do not fail to mention that some women who have been repatriated have found a new husband.

Yet some women cannot fit back into society: either they do not believe in love anymore or they are terminally ill. This is illustrated by "Anna K.'s" story presented in *Der Spiegel*: "A charitable customer, a police officer by profession, helped [Anna K.] to escape [from being trafficked]. Too late, she now has AIDS."[41] Although "Anna K." was saved and (as far as the reader is informed) brought "home" safely, she will be ill for the rest of her life, and, what seems to be even worse, it will be hard for her to have a "normal" family life. "Anna K." is "lost" to her home nation as a bearer of the biological reproduction, one of the traditional symbolic functions of women in national ideologies. By contrast, "Jana," protagonist in Monika Maier-Albang's report in the *Süddeutsche Zeitung*, still has "some wishes: to work where she can help people; an apartment, where she can be undisturbed. And a husband whom she can smile at in the morning."[42] Likewise "Anna P.," a figure that appeared

---

39 Hunfeld, *op. cit.*
40 Berman, *op. cit.*, 43.
41 Brandt *et al.*, *op. cit.*
42 Monika Maier-Albang, "Raus aus dem Elend, Rein in die Hölle," *Süddeutsche Zeitung* (March 10, 2004).

in another report featured by the *Süddeutsche Zeitung*, has hopes "for a 'good life,' a respectable husband, children."[43] Others are less lucky: "'love,' proclaims the blond girl, 'I have never thought about that. I hate men.'"[44] Another "blond girl," one might remark sarcastically, is lost to family life and biological reproduction. From this perspective, it comes as no surprise that the *La Strada* office in Kiev has, as rumor has it, an awards certificate for the services to the family that is signed by the former head of government, Viktor Janukowitsch.[45] For, *La Strada* is actively involved in both preventing trafficking (as well as migration, one might add) and in supporting women to repatriate and re-integrate in their home societies. The return of a victim to her family has a symbolic meaning that is particularly strong in the context of post-socialist countries. Engaged in societal transition, these countries have become the main region of origin for the victims of trafficking. It is particularly against this background of social transformation and globalization within a nation that preserving traditions—fetishizing and essentializing identities—may take on a defensive character and become more ingrained.

Finally, it is important to note that the migration of some women constitutes a greater problem for symbolic representation than that of others. National and international anti-trafficking campaigns are predominantly focused on young women who have recently finished their education. The representation of women without educational achievement, women of ethnic minorities, and women who are already working in prostitution is significantly less prominent in campaigns—and it is precisely these women who constitute the greater part of victims. Not all women, it seems, are able to act as the bearers of national traditions; the "non-exemplary" are not given visibility in campaigns that seek to repatriate women. Thus, the concern of national campaigns seems to be mobility and the victimization only of those women who are symbolically relevant to the nation, namely, young and educated.

Conclusion: Not Just Fairy Tales

The violence described under the term "trafficking in women" constitutes a serious violation of victims' human rights. At the same time, trafficking is discursively exploited. The meta-discourse implicitly engaged when debating trafficking in Germany and Europe implies questions of belonging, and of European and national identities. Actors debating trafficking refer to and (re-)produce certain representations of the act of trafficking, as well as the stereotypes of perpetrators, victims, and their customers. These representations have been found to be interwoven with racist, sexist, and classist stereotypes which reinforce the notion of the *other* as a threat to "our" society and culture.[46] The violence described under the term trafficking is

---

43 Urban, *op. cit.*

44 Mayr, *op. cit.*

45 Urban, *op. cit.*

46 An important line of inquiry opens here: it remains to be analyzed exactly how cultural narratives on trafficking have changed the way in which specifically non-Caucasian migrants and sex workers are perceived in Europe and what impact this perception has on their everyday lives.

seen not as "our" problem but as a problem *for* "us." "Our" responsibility for the violence that is exerted on women, migrants, and sex workers is externalized and displaced because the place where the crime supposedly takes place is constructed as *elsewhere* and the involved persons are constituted as significant *others* in relation to the nation in question.

In discussions about cultural *narratives* on trafficking in women, we have to realize that these narratives are not just gloomy fairy tales. The assumptions made of both victims and perpetrators produce specific legislative decisions. If perpetrators are considered to come from or to be based "elsewhere," the hindering of women's cross-border movement is easily understood to be a valid strategy to prevent trafficking in women. If the decision of a later victim to migrate is considered to be the core problem leading to her becoming a victim, repatriation will be believed to be a reasonable way to help her, as it will restore her to her rightful nation-space. If potential and actual victims are considered to be helpless, naïve, and even foolish, their incapacitation might seem to be an acceptable strategy to "save them from themselves." Institutional decisions on life-choices, lifestyle, migration, and witnessing are influenced by ambivalent representations of the women concerned. Within this logic, women are easily repatriated, their choice of work and education is limited and other fundamental decisions are made—often rather *for* than *with* the affected women. Some decisions by NGOs are even made against the explicit and implicit wishes of the victims, a behavior that, in some cases at least, could be considered true violence against women. In an "impressive" case which I witnessed in my own fieldwork, the employees of an NGO decided actively to obtain the deportation of one of their clients for "pedagogical" reasons: the women was not conforming to the rules of the NGO in question. Disturbingly, it was considered that the women would "learn" her lesson from being deported. I would like to emphasize that this is an extreme example, which fortunately does not reflect the general practice, but it is nevertheless revelatory of the dynamics in question.

Discourse is, I would like to conclude, always a practice. The vice versa is true, too: the way we talk about trafficking shapes the way we (counter-)act this phenomenon. To analyze the way trafficking is debated is crucial if "we" want to develop (institutional) practices and legal frameworks that do justice to victims without harming other women, migrants and sex workers, and without adding to the discursive violation of people who are already in a precarious position.

Bibliography

Agustin, Laura. "Forget Victimization: Granting Agency to Migrants." *Development* 46, No. 3 (2003): 30–36.

Andrijasevic, Rutvica. "Trafficking in Women and the Politics of Mobility in Europe." <http://igitur-archive.library.uu.nl/dissertations/2005-0314-013009/index.htm>.

Berman, Jacqueline. "(Un)Popular Strangers and Crises (Un)Bounded: Discourses of Sex-Trafficking, the European Political Community and the Panicked State of the Modern State." *European Journal of International Relations* 9, No. 1 (2003): 37–86.

Brandt, Andrea, *et al.* "Verkauft wie eine Kuh," *Der Spiegel* 26 (June 23, 2003).

Bundeskriminalamt, "Bundeslagebild Menschenhandel 2005." Karlsruhe, Wiesbaden: BKA, 2006. <www.bka.de/lageberichte/mh/2005/mh2005.pdf>.

Doezema, Jo. "Loose Women or Lost Women? The Re-Emergence of the Myth of 'White Slavery' in Contemporary Discourses of 'Trafficking in Women'." <http://www.walnet.org/csis/papers/doezema-loose.html>.

European Commission. *Research Based on Case Studies of Victims of Trafficking in Human Beings in 3 EU Member States.* n.d.

Ihme, Loretta. "Europas Gespenster. Frauenhandel, Nation und Supranation." In *Perspektiven für ein neues Europa—die neue Öffnung?* Edited by M. Witkowski and J. Dlugosz. 197–207. Berlin: Peter Lang, 2006.

—— "Huren, Mädchenhändler und Perverse: Zur Reproduktion von Differenz im Reden über Frauenhandel." *diskus* 1.06 (2006): 29–35.

International Organization for Migration. *Women Sold into Slavery.* Lithuania (2002).

—— *Prey of Silence.* Ukraine (2001).

—— *Lies and Realities about Job Abroad.* <http://www.refocusbaltic.net/en/main/advice/myths> Accessed November 25, 2006.

Hunfeld, Frauke. "Lina und die FRAUENHÄNDLER—Mitten unter uns." *Stern* 49, (November 30, 2005).

Kelly, Liz. "'You Can Find Anything You Want': A Critical Reflection on Research on Trafficking in Persons within and into Europe." *International Migration* 43, No. 1–2 (2005): 235–65.

Martenstein, Harald. "Die Zeugin der Anklage." *Der Tagesspiegel* (March 8, 2004).

Maier-Albang, Monika. "Raus aus dem Elend, Rein in die Hölle." *Süddeutsche Zeitung* (March 10, 2004).

Mayr, Walter. "Das Dorf der toten Seelen." *Der Spiegel* 26 (June 23, 2003).

McDermott, M. Joan, and Sarah J. Blackstone. "White Slavery Plays of the 1910s: Fear of Victimisation and the Social Control of Sexuality." *Theatre History Studies* 16 (1996): 141–56.

Rosen, Ruth. *The Lost Sisterhood: Prostitution in America, 1900–1918.* Baltimore: Johns Hopkins University Press, 1982.

Saunders, Penelope. "Migration, Sex Work, and Trafficking in Persons." <www.walnet.org/csis/papers/saunders-migration.html>.

Schwelien, Michael. "Das Paradies im Roten Licht." *Die Zeit* 41 (October 2, 2003).

Smith, Anthony. *Nations and Nationalism in a Global Era.* Cambridge: Polity, 1995.

Streiber, Petra. *Internationaler Frauenhandel. Funktionsweisen, soziale und ökonomische Ursachen und Gegenmaßnahmen.* Berlin: Das Arabische Buch, 1998.

United Nations. *Protocol To Prevent, Suppress and Punish Trafficking In Persons, Especially Women and Children, Supplementing The United Nations Convention Against Transnational Organized Crime.* <www.uncjin.org/Documents/Conventions/dcatoc/final_documents_2/convention_%20traff_eng.pdf>.

United Nations Office on Drugs and Crime. "Trafficking in Women." <http://www.unodc.org/unodc/multimedia_video.html>.

Urban, Thomas. "Hinter tausend Fenstern." *Süddeutsche Zeitung* (March 15, 2005).

Warr, Marc. "Public Perceptions of Crime and Punishment." In *Criminology: A Contemporary Handbook*. Edited by J.F. Sheley. 15–31. Belmont: Wadsworth, 1995.

Yuval-Davis, Nira. *Gender and Nation*. London: Sage, 1997.

Chapter 11

Ethnicity and Gender in the Politics of Roma Identity in the Post-Communist Countries

Angéla Kóczé

Introduction

The Roma or "gypsies" are considered to be the largest minority group in Europe.[1] The estimates of the size of the Roma population differ widely. According to the World Bank, about seven to nine million Roma live in Europe; approximately 70 percent of Roma in Europe live in the countries of Central and Eastern Europe.[2]

Over the centuries, in all nations in Europe, the Roma have suffered from persecution, discrimination, and social and economic marginalization and exclusion. Most of academic studies characterize the Roma as a unique minority in Europe perhaps because they have no historical motherland and live in nearly all countries in Europe as well as in North and South America. While Roma are known in Western countries as a nomadic group, most Roma in Central and Eastern Europe settled there centuries ago.[3] The origins of the Roma are widely debated, but linguistic evidence indicate that they migrated in waves from northern India into Europe between the ninth and fourteenth centuries. The Roma are extremely diverse and are divided into multiple sub-ethnic groups based on language, history, religion, and economic occupations within their culture. The term "Roma" is a politically constructed category which evolved as an attempt to produce a name that would not be related to the pervasive negative and romantic images of the group, as generated by terms such as gypsy, *ziguener*, and *tsigane*—all of which engender various negative connotations

---

1 Note on terminology: "gypsy" is an English term used to denote ethnic groups formed by the dispersal of commercial, nomadic, and other groups rooted in northern India beginning in the tenth century and subsequently mixing with European and other groups in diasporic contexts. Throughout the chapter, I use the term "Romani women." This study also employs the word "Roma" as an umbrella category, which is politically constructed and used by politicians, activists, and academics to refer to a wide variety of communities including Lovari, Romungro, Beas, Kaldreashi, Rudari, Kale, Sinti, Manush, and so on. Romani is mostly used as an adjective in the chapter.

2 Dena Ringold, Mitchell A. Orenstein, and Erika Wilkens, *Roma in an Expanding Europe*: *Breaking the Poverty Cycle* (Washington: The World Bank, 2003), 3.

3 See, Judith Okley, *The Traveller Gypsies* (Cambridge: Cambridge University Press, 1983); and Angus Fraser, *The Gypsies* (Oxford: Blackwell Publishing, 1995).

in every European language. Conversely, the term "Roma" is tightly connected with the group's political participation and visibility on an international level.

The transnational political awareness of the Roma emerged in the 1970s and led to the foundation of the International Romani Congress (RIC), which held its first conference in London in 1971. Although there were Romani delegates from 14 countries at this meeting, only a few Romani women were present. The RIC requested the use of the term "Roma" instead of "gypsy" in all official documents in order to create a new identity constructed by the Roma people themselves and not by the non-Roma majority.[4] In this context, one of the most important by-products of the post-communist transition globally was the emergence of identity-based Roma politics and the development of minority political participation in Central and Eastern Europe. The conceptualization of Romani identity has been approached by scholars such as Will Guy, Judith Okley and Peter Vermeersch, who seek to understand the Romani identity not as objective category based on biological characteristics, lifestyles, and historical diasporas, but rather as "the product of classification struggles involving both classifiers and those classified as Roma."[5]

Until recently, most political scientists and historians who have written about the Romani "movement" and its political mobilization eschewed a consideration of the conjunction of ethnic and gender identity in their analyses—in part as a result of the traditional emphasis on forms of political struggle in which men have taken a leading part. As described by Peter Vermeersch, the "Romani movement in Central and Eastern Europe is complex and diffuse," thus necessitating a more nuanced understanding of the concept of a "movement" itself: "[a movement] must not be understood as a clearly defined and bounded collection of officially recognized organizations, but as a conceptual term denoting the totality of activities carried out in the context of defending and cultivating shared identity."[6]

The main characteristic of the Romani "movement," in comparison to other social justice movements, is that the movement is embedded in a human rights discourse based on the wholesale adoption of a neo-liberal rule-of-law and "democratization" principles, as formulated by influential international agencies dealing with the question of the Roma, such as the World Bank, and the George Soros-funded Open Society Institute (OSI). The imported discursive trend of those agencies has marked the theoretical and ideological terrain of the Romani political activism. However, as Nidhi Trehan and I have recently argued, viewing the Romani "movement" as similar to the Black civil rights movement in the United States, or to that of the anti-apartheid movement in South Africa can be misleading, due to the different nature

---

4 Nicolae Gheorghe and Andrzej Mirga were the first scholars to write extensively about the development of the Roma political participation. They drafted the policy paper *The Roma in the Twenty-First Century: A Policy Paper*, PER Report (New Jersey: Project on Ethnic Relations, 1997), available at <http://www.per-usa.org/21st_c.htm>.

5 Peter Vermeersch, *The Romani Movement: Minority Politics & Ethnic Mobilization in Contemporary Central Europe* (New York and Oxford: Begrhahn Books, 2006), 13. See, also, Will Guy, "Romani Identity and Post-Communist Policy," in *Between Past and Future: The Roma of Central and Eastern Europe* (ed.), by Will Guy (Hertfordshire: University of Hertfordshire Press, 2001), 3–32; and Okley, *op. cit.*, 28–37.

6 Vermeersch, *op. cit.*, 9.

of power and political organization in contemporary Europe, particularly in post-socialist countries, and their connections with global structural forces that impinge upon the current trajectory of the transnational "Roma rights" movement.[7]

Notwithstanding the contextual distinctions, however, the Roma movement does share one important trait with social movements in other parts of the globe: the centrality of gender activism as a progressive force. In the Roma activism, the gender equality discourse became a new political leverage and has been adopted by key international Romani women activists. Yet, the transnationally imposed rights-based ideas have been locally translated and adopted in a contentious mode by women activists of different generations, and, in the next section of this chapter, I will briefly outline the evolvement of the transnational Romani women activism as a force always assisted by and organized around different international organizations' political agendas. The implications of this state of affairs on the trajectory of Romani projects and initiatives throughout Central and Eastern Europe will be my concern as I proceed to explore the roots of the ideological approach toward ethnic and gender identity, and how this discursive politics informs/shapes the work of old and young generations of Roma activists. Thus, a more comprehensive purpose of my present analysis is to examine, in socio-anthropological terms, how ethnicized and gendered discourse influences the social life of a subaltern group such as the Roma, and what types of frameworks offered by human rights discourse could allow for activists to claim gender equality in Romani context. It is still not obvious how the international spread of human rights institutions and discourses are reshaping the specific local structural inequalities of Romani women. Questions remain, for example, as to whether human rights law is simply a strategic weapon used internationally and nationally by powerful groups to legitimize their power grabs—a window dressing for real politics—or whether it provides a practical emancipatory tool for Romani women in their struggle to contest the structures of patriarchy that govern their life. Clearly, there are no simple answers to these pressing questions.

The Emergence of the Transnational Romani Women's Activism

A considerable number of political leaders, political parties, and interest groups turned to ethnicity as a predominant frame of reference for political mobilization and identification after the breakdown of the communist regimes in Central and Eastern Europe in the early 1990s. In the case of the Roma, identity-based politics offered them the sites for political action and made it possible for them to maintain their political struggle against ethnic-based marginalization, discrimination, and maltreatment. One way in which activists hoped to find public support for their claims was by establishing ethnically based political parties.[8] Thus, Romani political parties gained a forefront position in the Romani "movement"; some of these parties

---

7 Angéla Kóczé and Nidhi Trehan, "Postcolonial Racism and Social Justice: The Struggle for the Soul of the Romani Civil Rights Movement in the 'New Europe,'" in *Racism, Post-colonialism, Europe* (ed.), by G. Huggan (Liverpool: Liverpool University Press, 2007; forthcoming).

8 Vermeersch, *op. cit.*, 102.

also had aspirations to play a role in mainstream electoral systems. As a result of strong political lobbying, several Romani activists got an individual party ticket to be a member of the national or the European Parliament based solely on their ethnic identity. These deputies became a strategic alliance for the international Roma activism. Romani candidates who participated in the national or European electoral system had access to one of the most visible channels to promote political recognition and mainstream Roma issues in the national and the international political discourse. The effect of the Romani participation in electoral politics is, however, questioned by the fact that these members favor the ethnic basis for their political organization.

In that context, Romani women's participation in electoral politics deserves much more academic and political attention than it had previously acquired. From 1990 to 2004, several women Romani candidates contested for political office. In the 1990 elections of Czechoslovakia, two women were elected who were identified as Roma: one was Klara Samkova, a human rights lawyer, who was elected as a Civiv Forum (OF) representative. Although Samkova is non-Roma, she is the wife of a well-known Roma activist, Ivan Vesely, and, as such, she was perceived as a Romani representative. Furthermore, Samkova publicly associated herself with the biggest Romani party, Romani Civiv Initiative (ROI). The other woman was Anna Koptova who was elected in 1990 for the People against Violence (VPN). Koptova is known as Director of the Legal Defense Bureau for Ethnic Minorities of the Good Romany Fairy Kesaj Foundation and also as Director of the High School for Roma of Kosice. After the collapse of Czechoslovakia in 1993, only one Roma representative and representative of the Freedom Union, Monika Horakova, was elected to the Czech Chamber of Deputies. She was considered a representative of the new generation of Roma politics at the international level. In 2000, Monika Horakova, Rumyan Russinov, and the author of this chapter, Angéla Kóczé, organized a Romani political leadership training in Czech Republic, Bulgaria, and Hungary with a specific attention to women's representation.

In Hungary, on the other hand, Romani women became one of the most progressive forces in mainstream politics. There were three Roma MPs in the Hungarian National Parliament between 1990 and 1994. One of them is a woman, Antonia Haga, who had been elected from the list of the liberal party, Alliance of Free Democrats (SzDSz), and was able to keep her seat until 1998. As interpreted by Vermeersch, Hungary gained international headlines for being a country with the first two female Romani MEPs in 2004.[9] Livia Jaroka, who was elected directly from the list of the right-wing liberal party FIDESZ to the European Parliament, has been playing the most decisive role on the international level to shape the discourse on Romani women. She is a member of the Women Rights Committee in the European Parliament, where she initiated a public hearing by several Romani women activists, experts and representatives of the European Commission in November 2005 to explore the situation of Romani women. That hearing provided a forum to discuss public policies concerning multiple forms of discrimination against Romani women. But the second Romani MEP who took the place of Gabor Demszky, Viktoria Mohacsi, has slightly different views on Romani women. Mohacsi believes in working against

---

9 *Ibid.*, 114.

domestic violence and in family planning, arguing that no one should intervene in the family affairs. With their different approaches to Romani women's issues, these two female Romani MEPs made some undeniable changes, the most notable of which is making the presence of Romani female politicians a norm, rather than an exception, in European politics.

Romani women are less visible in the mainstream politics and in Roma political parties, which are organized around the concept of ethnicity. While the Roma have no traditional geographical corroboration (the land) for their national identity, recently there has been a proliferation of Roma political parties that base their agenda on the idea of ethnicity. They are particularly prominent in Bulgaria and Romania where there is a strong legacy of ethnic political parties. For example, in Romania there is an ethnically based Roma political party (*Partida Romilor*) which has existed for more than ten years. In the last election, they changed their strategy: instead of relying alone on the Roma constituency, they made an alliance with the Social Democrats. In some countries, this form of political strategizing can be construed as a form of political empowerment rather than marginalization. In the case of Macedonia, where there has always been a large Roma constituency especially in the Suto Orizari municipality in Skopje, the MP, the local council, and mayor are all Roma. The need to establish a Roma-based political party in this particular neighborhood was obvious to all the political constituents.[10]

Romani politics in the movement became further diversified when English-speaking, highly qualified Romani individuals started to work at high-paid NGOs, organizations supported by Western donors, such as the OSI and European Roma Rights Center or in intergovernmental organizations, such as the Council of Europe. This group has been severely criticized by the older generation of Roma for being favored by non-Roma constituents: they were characterized as traitors of their communities. Despite that criticism, these English-speaking, highly qualified Roma have much more influence in shaping Roma politics than the older generation. Nicolae Gheorghe notes: "[T]here is a crisis now in Romani politics: the bright ones are drawn into work in NGOs; they are better paid, they are self-appointed, they are less accountable to the people—they are less democratic."[11]

Since the end of the Cold War era in 1989, post-communist countries have hosted a number of Western NGOs and donors, from the United States to the United Kingdom, Germany and other European countries, all working on various aspects of democratic institutional development, independent media, civic and human rights advocacy, as well as the reduction of ethnic conflict. Examining the impact of the assistance of Western organizations on the Roma movement, Sarah E. Mendelson and John K. Glenn have found that Western NGOs working in post-communist countries employ status-raising strategy to improve the situation of Roma; this means that, on a programmatic level, they purport to improve the education level of the Roma and decrease human rights violation against them. As Mendelson and Glenn

---

10 For the discussion of the productiveness of Romani political parties, see the interview with Nicolae Gheorghe, "In Search of a New Deal for Roma," *Roma Rights Quarterly*, No. 4 (2001): 14–17.

11 *Ibid.*, 14.

emphasize, "Western funding for Roma programs in the 1990s increased. Funding has shifted from material assistance to education, and human rights work."[12] Yet, that funding strategy has been criticized by scholars such as Kathy Pinnock, Balázs Wizner, and Nidhi Trehan, mostly because it enforces Western popular concepts such as "empowerment," "human rights," and "sustainability" onto the Romani population, without addressing the real needs of local communities.[13] In her study on the subject, Trehan quoted Chidi Odinkalu, human rights lawyer of the London-based Interrights: "A number of NGOs financed directly by Western donors do not enjoy grass-roots constituency support [...], thus they are not required to be accountable to any constituency, apart from a limited number of donors."[14] Odinkalu's assessment parallels that of Nicolae Gheorghe, who also cites the unaccountability to a constituency as an anomaly of Western-supported NGOs.

In post-communist countries, most of the Roma NGOs, civic organizations, and activists still heavily depend upon the political and financial support of Western organizations, such as the Open Society Institutions and the Mott Foundation. Before the post-communist countries joined the European Union, almost all the Roma NGOs activities in these societies had been financed by these Western organizations. In his 1995 book *After Liberalism*, Immanuel Wallerstein connects philanthropic activity to the "democratization" of the post-Soviet bloc by international organizations. He notices that liberal international donors opted not to talk about human rights in their own countries, but instead started a struggle for human rights in other countries, most notably in those that were emerging out of the dismantled Soviet bloc. According to his analysis, those philanthropic organizations were looking for new "peoples" whose rights, they thought, needed to be affirmed in the emerging "new democracies." The Roma people, being one of the most discriminated and marginalized groups, became a target group for which Western liberals felt they needed to ensure human rights. As a consequence, nowadays a host of organizations originating in Western Europe (Amnesty International, Human Rights Watch, Medicines du Monde, and others) do not heed similar discriminations and violence "at home," but focus on the political change in the post-Soviet countries and the plight of the Roma who live in Central and South-Eastern Europe. Introduced by the Western countries, human rights based discourse created a new political leverage by which the Roma could present their issues as a serious form of discrimination—in specific, as perpetrated against them by the state. The language of human rights is governed by intergovernmental organizations such as the Council of Europe (COE), UN, Organizations for Security

---

12 Sarah Mendelson and John K. Glenn, "Democracy Assistance and NGO Strategies in Post-Communist Societies," *Carnegie Endowment Working Papers*, No. 8: *Democracy Assistance and NGO Strategies in Post-Communist Societies* (February 2000), <http://www. carnegieendowment.org/files/final.pdf>, 62.

13 Kathy Pinnock, "'Social Exclusion' and Resistance: A Study of Gypsies and the Non-Governmental Sector in Bulgaria 1989–1997" (PhD diss., University of Wolverhampton, 1999); Balázs Wizner, "The Development of the Romany National Movement in Hungary" (MA thesis, Central European University, 1999); Nidhi Trehan, "In the Name of Roma," in *Between Past and Future* (ed.), by Will Guy (Hertfordshire: University of Hertfordshire Press, 2001), 134–57.

14 Trehan, *op. cit.*, 138.

and Cooperation in Europe (OSCE), and European Union (EU), and it pressurizes the EU-acceding countries to emphasize the respect for the human rights of the Roma population and to provide an adequate legal remedy that would guard the Roma against additional levels of violation. The framing of violence against the broader Roma population within a specific rights-based discourse has helped to create a receptive audience for the more specific issues of gender equality and gender-based violence in the Roma communities. The issues of gender-based discrimination became a priority for certain donors, such as the OSI, EU, and COE, all of which are still supporting and conceptualizing Romani women's rights activism in Europe.

The specific Romani women's issues have been gradually identified by activists and connected to significant public discourses, such as those concerning gender, ethnicity, and public policy. Initially, Romani women's issues were framed in correspondence to the general Roma problems, such as the low level of education, high unemployment rate, lack of health protection and family planning programs, lack of enforcement of existing legislation, and problems of racism and violence. This approach did cast some light on the precarious situation of Romani women: it was recognized that Romani women face double discrimination, one based on both their ethnicity and their gender. Nowadays, Romani women's issues are most often elaborated in terms of the uniqueness of their experience, that is as an experience of the forms of discrimination that are different from those suffered by Romani men and non-Romani women. Indeed, Romani women's subject-positions are forged by variables at the intersection of specific ethnicity, gender, and class identities, rendering them different from the subjectivities of both their Romani-male and non-Romani fellows.

Romani women's issues first gained visibility in public discourse at the Congress on the EU Roma/Gypsies organized by the European Commission Against Racism and Intolerance in Seville, Spain, in 1994. One of the most striking results of the Congress was the publication of the "Manifesto of Roma/Gypsy Women," the first publicly printed material that specifically referred to the situation of Romani women in Europe. One year later, in September 1995, the Council of Europe in Strasbourg organized the "Hearing of Roma/Gypsy Women" as part of the Steering Committee for Equality between Women and Men. The purpose of the hearing was to identify the problems and conflicts concerning equality and human rights that Romani women encounter. Although it was the first attempt by intergovernmental organizations to invite Romani women activists and to bring visibility to their issues, the report of the European Commission Against Racism and Intolerance notes that the hearing emphasized the economic hardship and educational discrimination against Roma in general (that is, it paid less attention to the specific concerns of Romani women).[15] Nevertheless, it was the first political recognition of Romani women's issues on the international level, and, as such, it allowed them to set up a network through which to exchange information and foster contacts with other women activists.

---

15 European Commission against Racism and Intolerance, *Activities of the Council of Europe with Relevance to Combating Racism and Intolerance* (2004/7) (Strasbourg: ECRI, February 2004), 58.

In 1998, the OSI organized an International Conference of Romani Women in Budapest, Hungary, attended particularly by delegates from Central and Eastern Europe. The meeting was unique because it focused on sensitive issues such the tradition of the Roma culture versus women rights. It is noteworthy that, at the conference, some Romani women challenged the existing male dominated power structure in the Roma movement itself. In 1999, the OSI established the Romani Women Initiative (RWI), which has since worked to develop, link, and catalyze a core group of committed young Romani women leaders, in an effort to improve the human rights of Romani women. In 2003, with the assistance of the Council of Europe, Romani women activists from 18 European countries launched the International Romani Women's Network (IRWN). The leadership of this organization is older and more traditional than that of the RWI. The main focus of the IRWN activities is Romani women's health, and that focus has been consistently encouraged by the Council of Europe. Under the auspices of the COW, the IRWN has produced the important report entitled "Romani Women and Access to Public Health Care" in 2002. Even though all that external assistance has not substantially changed the material well-being of Romani women, it has brought political visibility to their issues (both within Europe and internationally), in turn allowing them to develop a gender-based discourse within the Romani movement itself.

Dialogical Character of Romani Women's Activism

The foundational inequalities of Romani women's participation in various political forms are linked to their gender, social and ethnic oppression. The progressive Romani women activists' discourses do not only address contentious issues such as the forced sterilization of Romani women, forced marriages, prostitution, trafficking, and lack of political representation of Romani women, but they also constitute a challenge to the broader patriarchal power structure of Romani communities and to societal hierarchy in general. Each of these discourses produces a different subject position for Romani women in the interest of broader and complex strategies of empowerment.

Until recently, most political scientists and historians who have written about the Roma movement and the political mobilization of Roma eschewed a consideration of gender in their analysis—arguably as a result of the traditional emphasis on the forms of struggle in which men have taken a leading part. However, the "gender equality" discourse concerning Romani women is much more appreciated, at least in rhetoric, by donors and international organizations. According to postcolonial feminist scholars such as Gayatri Spivak and Chandra Mohanty, this kind of interest is informed by a Western urge to civilize the "savage" population (here the Romas), while the interested party pursues its own economic and political interests.[16] Hence this interest in the problems of the Romani women resonates with dominant Western

---

16 Gayatri Chakravorty Spivak, "French Feminism in an International Frame," in *Other Worlds: Essay in Cultural Politics* (New York and London: Routledge, 1988), 134–53; and Chandra Talpade Mohanty, "Under Western Eyes: Feminist Scholarship and Colonial Discourses," in *Third World Women and the Politics of Feminism* (ed.), by Chandra Talpade

attitudes to historically subaltern groups and indigenous peoples; its effect is an occlusion of Romani women's identity and activity.

In his essay "The Politics of Recognition," Charles Taylor examines the recent emergence of political movements galvanized by the need for recognition. The recognition of the importance of equality has given rise to the idea of universal human rights; simultaneously, the new importance attached to (ethnic and gender) identity has generated the politics of difference. Taylor explains the connection between identity and recognition through the notion of dialogue, claiming that the latter is "the crucial feature of human life."[17] Identity is affirmed when others signify recognition; thus recognition struggles are characteristically discursive in nature and conducted in the dialogue-based domains of civil society such as the media or politics. I would propose a view of Romani women's struggle for recognition in this light.[18] The Romani women's recognition struggle has "dialogical character" because its visibility and expression of resistance is influenced by both its interaction with the global human rights regime and its interdependence with the male-led Roma movement.

While this "dialogical character" is critical for the actualization of ethnic and gender identities, scholarly treatments of recognition struggles usually discuss feminist and anti-racist movements as autonomous or, at best, parallel dynamics. Thus it should not come as a surprise that even a highly educated Roma leader could make the following statement: "Romani women have to choose between their ethnicity and their gender."[19] This example shows the lack of intersectional thinking: instead of analyzing the dialogical relationship between gender and ethnicity, the male-dominated leadership of the movement argues for the separation of these categories. Feminist intersectional theories highlight the dangers of this static approach and emphasize that racial/ethnic, gender, and class subordination do not exclude, but reinforce, each other. The divisional or additive approaches have been particularly critiqued by scholars and activists working within the context of other movements concerning women of color. Critical race theorist Kimberlé Crenshaw thus deploys the concept of political intersectionality in a context highly relevant to my discussion. In her essay "Mapping the Margins: Intersectionality, Identity Politics, and Violence against Women of Color," Crenshaw argues that "racism as experienced by people of color who are of a particular gender—male—tends to determine the parameters of antiracist strategies, just as sexism as experienced by women who are of a particular

---

Mohanty, Ann Russo, and Lourdes Torres (Bloomington: Indiana University Press, 1991), 51–80.

17 Charles Taylor, "The Politics of Recognition," in *Multiculturalism: Examining the Politics of Recognition* (ed.), by Amy Gutmann, (Princeton: Princeton University Press, 1994), 32.

18 A similar line of argumentation has been pursued with respect to the gender issues concerning Aboriginal women in Marylin Lake's "Women, Black, Indigenous: Recognition Struggles in Dialogue," in *Recognition Struggle and Social Movements: Contested Identities, Agency and Power* (ed.), by Barbara Hobson (Cambridge: Cambridge University Press, 2003), 145–60.

19 Iulius Rostas, at the meeting of the Open Society Institute, Budapest, September 2005.

race—white—tends to ground the women's movement."[20] The solution, according to Crenshaw, is not to examine race and gender oppressions separately and then put them together (an "additive" approach), but to recognize precisely the inadequacy of these discourses when taken discretely and pursue an "intersectional" approach. In this vein, feminist intersectional theories have been recently enhanced to include class as a third category; the intertwine "race-class-gender" has become a decisive concept in gender equality discourse.

Applied to the Romani context, this line of enquiry recognizes that the ideologies of racial violence and discrimination do not affect Romani men and women in the same way. For example, when Romani women were raped during the Kosovo crisis, the abuse was predominantly and even officially regarded *not* primarily as an attack against a woman's human rights, but against her identity as a Roma.[21] Furthermore, the plethora of testimonies collected by the European Roma Rights Center evidences that Romani girls in particular face verbal, physical, and sometimes sexual harassment by classmates and teachers, harassment based on ethnic and sexist premises at the same time. Whereas these experiences influence negatively education and personal development of Romani girls, the reports state that teachers rarely punish these practices, and that these events elicit substantially less media attention and communal support than when they happen to white girls in the same society.

Positioned at the intersection of at least two subordinate groups (to which one may easily add the third—class), Romani women not only confront more issues quantitatively when they suffer violations of their human rights (for example, less media attention, lack of support in both the judicial system and their community, and so on), but their experience is also qualitatively different from that of white women. The political recognition and participation-related violence is a good example here. Romani women activists face multiple scales of resistance and contempt, from patriarchal attitudes within their own communities to the contempt of majority groups, from issues such as early childbearing to the broad problem of deeply rooted poverty. These are issues that rarely affect white, middle-class feminists. More importantly, however, it is the dominant human rights framework that offers Romani women legal and political tools with which to articulate their struggle and translate the ideas of political and social rights into their socially and culturally determined context. If they want to gain visibility and political recognition through the human rights "machines," Romani activists must use the human rights discourse, a conceptual language most frequently rendered in English and most confidently used by English-speaking activists.

---

20 Kimberlé Crenshaw, "Mapping the Margins: Intersectionality, Identity Politics, and Violence against Women of Color," *Stanford Law Review* 43 (July 1991): 1252. This article extends the discussion of political intersectionality initiated in Crenshaw's influential article "Demarginalizing the Intersection of Race and Sex: A Black Feminist Critique of Antidiscrimination Doctrine, Feminist Theory and Antiracist Politics," *University of Chicago Legal Forum* (1989): 139–67.

21 Human Rights Watch, Report "Kosovo: Rape as a Weapon of 'Ethnic cleansing,'" <http://www.hrw.org/reports/2000/fry/Kosov003.htm> (accessed October 31, 2007).

Romani women still have room to resist and polarize this discourse: for this to happen, they should investigate and analyze ethnographically the process by which human rights are translated and contextualized in local actions. It is then that the proper translation of the discourse will not be exhausted in a simple act of linguistic translation, but it will reach the social, cultural, and gender experiences of Romani women. The call for such a "politics of translation" highlights Romani women's need to articulate their own experience and their own struggle in indigenous terms, specifically in terms that are distinct from those proposed by the Western human and gender rights discourse. In this context, it is interesting to note that Romani women who resist the universality of feminist theory and politics sometimes develop alternative dialogues with other women of color who have already challenged Western feminism. This emphasis on sisterhood of women of color discloses the failure of the largely white and middle-class feminist movement globally to recognize factors of classism, racism, and modern-day imperialism as fundamental forms of *gender* oppression. There are groups such as the Black and "Third World" feminists who are excluded from an analysis of how patriarchy functions in the development of new historical and cultural canons; these marginalized feminist groups and other feminists of color endeavor to recover their lost histories and their cultural production, and in this recovery, they resist the totalizing norms of broader feminist movements. By establishing dialogues with these marginalized groups, Romani women gain a useful basis to develop strategies for contesting the specific forms of oppression that affect them. At the same time, it is important to be aware that creating an alliance solely with women of color would reinforce the marginalization of women of color and generate an "additional discourse" instead of creating diversity or "dialogicity" within the feminist discourse.

Finally, while challenging racism, sexism, and the universality of human rights discourse, Roma women also have to contest and deconstruct patriarchal power structures within the Roma "movement" itself. The "dialogical character" of Romani women's activism implies interdependence with the male-constituted leadership. If Romani leadership makes a statement or any intervention without paying attention to the gender dimension of the issue, then that leadership needs to be scrutinized and interrogated by Romani women. Male power—not just in the Roma community— is always dependent on the intensification of gender-based resistances. The key institutions and organizations at the international level, which are part of the Romani "movement," are led by Roma men. For instance, the President of the European Roma and Travellers Forum (ERTF), an international organization which brings together diverse Roma groups with the aim "to promote the effective exercise of [their] human rights and fundamental freedoms" and to "struggle against racism and discrimination" is a male Roma leader from Germany.[22] The most significant project for bringing visibility to Romani issues *Decade of Roma Inclusion (2005–2015)*, a project initiated by the Open Society Institute and the World Bank with a political commitment from several Central and South-Eastern European countries, such as Bulgaria, Croatia, Czech Republic, Hungary, Macedonia, Montenegro, Romania,

---

22 The Statutes of the European Roma and Travellers Forum can be found at <http://www.ertf.org/en/statutes.html> (accessed October 31, 2007).

Serbia and Slovakia, is also male-led.[23] As an appendage to the Decade structure, there are two key institutions: the Roma Education Fund (REF), which finances governmental educational and policy initiatives and programs for the integration of Roma in the educational system, whose president is Costel Bercus, a Roma male from Romania, and whose Deputy Director is Rumyan Russinov, a Roma male from Bulgaria, and the Roma Initiative Office (RIO), which is led by Iulius Rostas, a Roma male from Romania.[24] These examples show that the political representations of Roma in key international organizations are dominated by Roma men without any gender balance. Individual stories indicate that those Romani women who challenge the existing male power structure or compete with them are marginalized, discouraged, or betrayed by male activists. Andrea Bučková, the President of the Cultural Association of Roma in Slovakia, was a delegate in the Roma group attending the 2001 UN World Conference Against Racism. She subsequently recalled that, even though the Romani women had identified three issues for the agenda—namely, involuntary sterilization, unemployment, and domestic violence—the Romani leaders (all male) allowed them to discuss solely the issue of forced sterilization, and that only because an effort to control the Roma population is seen as a violation of general Roma rights and not necessarily that of women's human rights.[25] This type of gender-sensitive discourse has been considered rebellious by many Romani activists, both men and women.

Conclusion

The emergence of Romani women's transnational activism has been assisted by international organizations that advocate human rights, particularly women's rights. These organizations uphold Romani women who have been victimized by ethnicity, gender, and class oppression, in order to expand the human rights and gender equality regime. However, the same view of Romani women offers a contradictory site for the Romani women themselves: on one hand, they can use human rights language as a progressive tool to further their own feminist agendas; on the other hand, they must contend with the universalizing idea of "gender equality" underscoring that language and ignoring the structurally unequal power relations specific to Romani women in the post-communist countries. In order to gain political space and recognition and to find alliances on the international level, Romani women have been forced to allow their own agendas to be influenced by certain political factors above and outside of their immediate work. Simultaneously, Romani women's position can be identified

---

23 Cf., <http://www.romadecade.org/index.php?content=1> (accessed August 28, 2007).

24 At the moment, the Executive Director position is fulfilled by a non-Roma man. Read more about the Roma Education Fund at <http://romaeducationfund.hu> (accessed August 28, 2007). Read more about the Roma Office Initiative at <http://www.soros.org/initiatives/roma/about> (accessed August 28, 2007).

25 Andrea Bučková, qtd. in: Isabela Mihalache, "Romani Women's Participation in Public Life," *Roma Rights Quarterly*, No. 4 (2003) <http://www.errc.org/rr_nr4_2003/womens2.shtml> (accessed June 10, 2007).

through their continuous resistance against male-dominated leadership within their own movement. The specific "dialogical character" of Romani women's activism is informed by the movement's peculiar position between the external and internal hierarchies and by the major modes of its activity: contest and subordination.

To address candidly the multiple levels of domination faced by Romani women along the axes of ethnicity, gender, and social class, one would need to explore Romani women's experiences and resistance against oppression on at least three levels: the level of personal testimony; the group or community level (the social and cultural context shaped by ethnicity, class, and gender); and, the systemic level of social institutions. These levels can be extended with the transnational level to examine how neo-liberal human rights institutions have dominated and influenced Romani women's activism and what structure of resistance has been developed during the last decade. Mindful of Michel Foucault's central proposition, "where there is a power, there is resistance," we can assert that all these levels function as both sites of domination and potential sites of resistance.[26] The "dialogical character" of Romani women's activism can be made more transparent and visible through the matrix of domination where axes of oppression can be most easily observed and contextualized, and where the reinforcing or contradictory relationships between various levels can be detected.

Bibliography

Acton, Thomas. *Scholarship and the Gypsy Struggle Commitment in Romani Studies.* Hertfordshire: University of Hertfordshire Press, 2000.

Crenshaw, Kimberlé. "Demarginalizing the Intersection of Race and Sex: A Black Feminist Critique of Antidiscrimination Doctrine, Feminist Theory and Antiracist Politics." *University of Chicago Legal Forum* (1989): 139–67.

—— "Mapping the Margins: Intersectionality, Identity Politics, and Violence against Women of Color." *Stanford Law Review* 43 (July 1991): 1241–98.

European Commission. *The Situation of Roma in an Enlarged European Union.* Report, Directorate-General for Employment and Social Affairs, 2004.

European Commission against Racism and Intolerance. *Activities of the Council of Europe with Relevance to Combating Racism and Intolerance* (2004/7). Strasbourg: ECRI, February 2004.

European Monitoring Centre on Racism and Xenophobia. *Breaking the Barriers: Romani Women and Access to Public Health Care.* Vienna, 2003.

Foucault, Michel. *The History of Sexuality*, Vol. I: An Introduction. Translated by Robert Hurley. New York: Pantheon, 1978.

Fraser, Angus. *The Gypsies.* Oxford: Blackwell Publishing, 1992.

Gheorghe, Nicolae. Interview: "In Search of a New Deal for Roma." *Roma Rights Quarterly*, No. 4 (2001): 14–17.

---

26 Michel Foucault, *The History of Sexuality*, Vol. I, translated by Robert Hurley (New York: Pantheon, 1978), 95–6.

Gheorghe, Nicolae, and Andrzej Mirga. *The Roma in the Twenty-First Century: A Policy Paper*. PER Report. Princeton: Project on Ethnic Relations, 1997. <http://www.per-usa.org/21st_c.htm>.

Guy, Will. "Romani Identity and Post-Communist Policy." In *Between Past and Future: The Roma of Central and Eastern Europe*. Edited by Will Guy. 3–32. Hertfordshire: University of Hertfordshire Press, 2001.

Human Rights Watch. Report "Kosovo: Rape as a Weapon of 'Ethnic cleansing.'" <http://www.hrw.org/reports/2000/fry/Kosov003.htm>.

Kóczé, Angéla and Nidhi Trehan. "Postcolonial Racism and Social Justice: The Struggle for the Soul of the Romani Civil Rights Movement in the 'New Europe.'" In *Racism, Post-colonialism, Europe*. Edited by G. Huggan. Liverpool: Liverpool University Press, 2007; forthcoming.

Lake, Marylin. "Women, Black, Indigenous: Recognition Struggles in Dialogue." In *Recognition Struggle and Social Movements: Contested Identities, Agency and Power*. Edited by Barbara Hobson. 145–60. Cambridge: Cambridge University Press, 2003.

Mendelson, Sarah, and John K. Glenn, "Democracy Assistance and NGO Strategies in Post-Communist Societies." *Carnegie Endowment Working Papers*. No. 8: *Democracy Assistance and NGO Strategies in Post-Communist Societies* (February 2000). <http://www.carnegieendowment.org/files/final.pdf>.

Mihalache, Isabela. "Romani Women's Participation in Public Life." *Roma Rights Quarterly*. No. 4 (2003). <http://www.errc.org/rr_nr4_2003/womens2.shtml>.

Mohanty, Chandra Talpade. "Under Western Eyes: Feminist Scholarship and Colonial Discourses." In *Third World Women and the Politics of Feminism*. Edited by Chandra Talpade Mohanty, Ann Russo, and Lourdes Torres. 51–80. Bloomington and Indianapolis: Indiana University Press, 1991.

Okley, Judith. 1983. *The Traveller Gypsies*. Cambridge: Cambridge University Press, 1983.

Pinnock, Katherine. "'Social Exclusion' and Resistance: A Study of Gypsies and the Non-Governmental Sector in Bulgaria 1989–1997," PhD diss., University of Wolverhampton, 1999.

Ringold, Dena, Mitchell A. Orenstein, and Erika Wilkens. *Roma in an Expanding Europe: Breaking the Poverty Cycle*. The World Bank, 2003.

Spivak, Gayatri Chakravorty. "French Feminism in an International Frame." In *Other Worlds: Essay in Cultural Politics*. 134–53. New York and London: Routledge, 1988.

Taylor, Charles. 'The Politics of Recognition." In *Multiculturalism: Examining the Politics of Recognition*. Edited by Amy Gutmann. 25–73. Princeton: Princeton University Press, 1994.

Trehan, Nidhi. "In the Name of Roma." In *Between Past and Future: The Roma of Central and Eastern Europe*. 134–57.

Vermeersch, Peter. *The Romani Movement: Minority Politics & Ethnic Mobilization in Contemporary Central Europe*. New York and Oxford: Berghahn Books, 2006.

Wizner, Balázs. "The Development of the Romany National Movement in Hungary." MA thesis, Central European University, 1999.

PART IV
Aesthetic and Gendered Transformations

In recent years, there has been a renewed and growing interest in feminine artistic production as an alternative transformative practice that may aid in the processes of discernment, representation, and exposure in the discourse of gender and violence. The editors have chosen the chapters in this part to highlight the dual societal function of contemporary artistic production, as a set of activities that propel a cathartic reconsideration of the hegemonic representations of personal and historical experiences, and an aesthetic move toward the active "healing" of the feminine self and the redressing of society.

Emphasizing the participatory aspect in the production-distribution of a work of art, Deborah L. Madsen juxtaposes recent Chicano feminine literature with factual material about various forms of gender violence to which women and teenage girls of Chihuahua have been subjected in the last decade. She argues that the activity of "lending an ear" to the frequently disquieting stories of gender violence should be understood as equally important as articulating the physical facts of a violent event. Suitably, then, this collection closes with a transnational case of gender agency that is as reliant on facts as it is on artistic (re)configuration: V-Day. Marta Fernández-Morales's chapter treats V-Day, the global women's movement associated with the writer Eve Ensler and the photographer Joyce Tenneson, as a unique fusion of social agency and aesthetics in the globalized world. Relating the V-Day project's treatment of gender violence through an artistic coalescence of facts—from Ensler's personal account of battering and rape, through the testimonies of Bosnian women in a war-zone, to the interviews of women who have transformed their body for aesthetic, cultural, health, or ideological reasons—Fernández-Morales argues that, by touring internationally and endeavoring to reach even the most remote and underprivileged audience, the V-Day project promotes the positive potentials of globalization and the possibilities of a global transformation in mentalities and practices.

Chapter 12

Over Her Dead Body:
Talking About Violence against Women
in Recent Chicana Writing

Deborah L. Madsen

The following extracts are taken from the 2003 Amnesty International report, "Intolerable Killings: 10 years of abductions and murders of women in Ciudad Juárez and Chihuahua":

> Over 370 women murdered, at least 137 of them after being sexually assaulted—this is the harsh reality of the violence which women and teenage girls of Chihuahua state have been subjected to since 1993, according to reports received by Amnesty International. In addition, over 70 young women are still missing, according to the authorities, though Mexican non-governmental organizations say the figure is over 400. The response of the authorities over the past ten years has been to treat the different offences as ordinary acts of violence committed within the private domain, without recognizing the existence of a continuing pattern of violence against women, the origins of which are more deeply rooted in discrimination. The fact that the authorities, both within the state of Chihuahua and at the federal level, have been unwilling to recognize the extent of the pattern of violence against women and to implement effective policies for dealing with it, has meant that Chihuahuan society has been left without the protection it deserves while the families who have lost daughters, mothers and sisters have been left without an effective judicial remedy. [...]

> [...] "Women who have a night life, go out late at night and come into contact with drinkers are at risk. It's hard to go out on the street when it's raining and not get wet" (Arturo González Rascón, Former Procurador de Justicia del Estado, *El Diario de Juárez*, February 24, 1999). [1]

Introduction

Much has been written about the issue of "voice" and feminine social agency in Chicana literature. In this chapter I address the complementary issue of audience

---

1 Amnesty International, "Intolerable Killings: 10 years of abductions and murders of women in Ciudad Juárez and Chihuahua" (August 2003). <http://www.amnestyusa.org/ countries/mexico/document.do?id=1829EE5E27AF155F80256D75005CCB07> (accessed June 12, 2006).

by emphasizing the importance of gaining an "ear" as well as a voice. This issue is key to the reception of Chicana representations of violence against women because the reception of such representations, and especially the interpretation of these representations, depends upon how they are heard. Survivor narratives always risk appropriation by conservative cultural mythologies that seek to naturalize representations of violence in order to reinstate the values that are threatened by the concepts of domestic and sexual violence. To battle such conservative patriarchal mythologies by simply rewriting them is to remain within the domain of mythology— the function of which is to naturalize all threats to the status quo. The authors under discussion include the Mexico-based Chicana Alma Villanueva, Gloria Anzaldúa who grounds her work in the experience of the Texas borderlands, and the US-based writers Sandra Cisneros and Ana Castillo. This range of work offers a variety of perspectives upon the transnational issue of violence against Mexican-American women. Texts such as Gloria Anzaldúa's poem "We Call Them Greasers" (1987), Ana Castillo's novel *Sapagonia* (1994), Alma Villanueva's novel *Naked Ladies* (1994), and Sandra Cisneros's story "Woman Hollering Creek" (1992), are introduced in the context of recent theorizations of trauma, agency, and voice, in order to argue that it is necessary to shift register from the mythological. In this way we attend to the brutal facts of violence against women and listen to these stories of suffering that we would prefer not to hear.

My subject is the transformation of violence into novels, into narratives—not just any narratives but cultural narratives with the power to make violence normal; narratives that permit the former State Governor of Chihuahua, Francisco Barrio, to claim that the number of women murdered "is no greater than that in other parts of the state or country, on the contrary, it's a percentage that can be seen as normal" (Amnesty International, 2003): as if the rape and mutilation of women ever "can be seen as normal." I am referring to cultural narratives that recuperate the physical act of violence as an abstract meaning or the signified divorced from its brutal signifier. Such narratives enable the State Public Prosecutor of Chihuahua to compare becoming wet in a rainstorm to the experience of abduction, torture, rape, and death. The common term in the comparison is the woman who will risk herself—in the face of rain, in the face of masculine brutality. In either case, as these comparisons dictate, the victim, *la chingada*, can only blame herself. These deeply misogynistic discourses, which include Octavio Paz's well-known formulation in *Labyrinth of Solitude* discussed below, normalize masculine sexual violence by prescribing passivity as the normative mode of femininity.

An important focus of Chicana feminist energies has been the reinterpretation of these oppressive masculine discourses, so as to give back voice and agency to the women who are silenced by them. But along with feminine empowerment what is also altered by the "normalizing" narratives of masculine violence is the horrifying reality of violence against women, represented in stories we do not want to hear because they tell of unbearable suffering and pain.[2] In what follows, I want to explore

---

2 The Amnesty International report includes a chronology of the ten years of abductions and murders of women in Ciudad Juarez and Chihuahua, which is unflinching in its representation. The chronology begins: "12 May 1993. The body of an unidentified woman

this dynamic between speaking and hearing, gaining voice and gaining audience, in the work of contemporary Chicana writers who engage with the issues of silence and sexual violence against women.

Violence and (Post)Coloniality

Octavio Paz places sexual violence against women at the center of Mexican cultural identity. In *Labyrinth of Solitude* (1959) Paz makes an emphatic connection between colonization, machismo, and sexual violence against women.[3] In the essay "The Sons of La Malinche" Paz identifies the historical figure of Malinche, the Aztec woman raped (or seduced) by Cortés, as the mother of the hybrid Mexican race and her offspring as the children of *la chingada* (the raped one). Paz describes the word *chingar* as:

> [...] masculine, active, cruel: it stings, wounds, gashes, stains. And it provokes a bitter, resentful satisfaction. The person who suffers this action is passive, inert and open, in contrast to the active, aggressive and closed person who inflicts it. The *chigon* is the *macho*, the male; he rips open the *chingada*, the female, who is pure passivity, defenceless against the exterior world."[4]

With this description, or rather prescription, Paz identifies Mexicans with the consequence of sexual violence, as victims, emasculated, compelled to resort to sexual violence as a means to restore an active and powerful sense of identity that is both cultural and personal. However, that assertion of Mexican masculinity comes at the expense of Mexican femininity, which is identified with the traitor Malinche who betrayed her people to the conquistadors. The degraded Mother and absent Father define the parameters of a powerful cultural symbolism that recuperates the act of rape to represent a cultural mythology that naturalizes and normalizes sexual violence, even as it reinforces stereotypes grounded in masculine privilege. Alma Villanueva, Gloria Anzaldúa, Ana Castillo and Sandra Cisneros are among the

---

found [...] on the slopes of Cerro Bola [...] in a supine position and wearing denim trousers with the zipper open, the said garment pulled down around her knees [...] penetrating puncture wound to the left breast, abrasions on the left arm, blunt force injury with bruising at the level of the jaw and the right cheek, abrasion on the chin, bleeding in the mouth and nose, linear abrasion near the neck, light brown skin, 1.75 cm., brown hair, large coffee-coloured eyes, 24 years old, white brassière pulled up above the breasts. Cause of death asphyxia resulting from strangulation." Office of the Assistant State Public Prosecutor, Northern Area, Office for Preliminary Investigations, *Murders of Women Which Have Caused Indignation at Various Social Levels of the Community 1993–1998—Preliminary Investigation 9883/93-0604* (Ciudad Juárez, Chihuahua, February 1998). In Amnesty International, August 2003.

3 Ana Castillo explores a similar cultural mythology in her analysis of the roots of machismo in "The Ancient Roots of Machismo," *Massacre of the Dreamers: Essays on Xicanisma* (New York: Plume, 1994), 63–84.

4 Octavio Paz, "The Sons of La Malinche," trans. Lysander Kemp, rpt. in *Goddess of the Americas: Writings on the Virgin of Guadalupe* (ed.), by Ana Castillo (New York: Riverhead Books, 1996), 201.

writers who offer revisionary accounts of La Malinche, La Llorona, and La Virgen de Guadalupe, the mythical women who prescribe the possibilities for Chicana femininity. This revisionary effort is an important means to rearticulate the terms in which violence against women is recuperated and normalized. But these writers also understand that the effort to "revision" a passive femininity and to redefine the terms of violence against women must be met with an equal effort to resist the normalization of violence by shifting the discursive register, by moving away from the domain of cultural mythology and normalizing narratives to listen to the stories of victims and by attending to the physical reality of sexualized violence.

One Chicana writer who has achieved a balance between listening to the victims and representing the ideological narrative of their victimization is Gloria Anzaldúa. She creates a clear link between the physical reality of violence and the ideology of colonialism to subvert the narrative of manifest destiny, which justifies and legitimates American colonialist ambitions. A poem that dramatically connects the reality of rape with the violence of colonization is Anzaldúa's "We Call Them Greasers."[5] In this poem, Anzaldúa uses the binary oppositions between center and margin, colonizer and colonized, masculine and feminine, civilization and nature, to deconstruct the sanitized history of American westward expansion. In the poem, the American frontier version of the European myth of *translatio imperii*—the inexorably westward drift of empires into uninhabited "virgin" territory—is exposed as a lie that masks a history of violent conquest. Annette Kolodny, in *The Lay of the Land*, has examined extensively this troping in exploration-narratives: as a general rule, the land is represented as female and the explorer as male and as a rapist.[6] The subject position which these narratives offer their readers is masculine; by contrast, narratives like Anzaldúa's articulate the feminine position. Her poem depicts a mythical "rape of the land" but within the anti-recuperative and de-naturalizing context of the physical rape of an individual woman.

In "We Call Them Greasers" Anzaldúa enacts a feminist appropriation of the traditional views of women associating white colonizer not only with the values of civilization, law, and masculinity, but also with injustice, violence, rape, and death. The colonized are passive, feminine, and close to nature: the poem juxtaposes "chickens children wives and pigs" without even punctuation to set the human apart from the animal. The colonized are indigenous (the speaker claims, "I found them here when I came") of the landscape waiting to be possessed. Through that dynamic, Anzaldúa enacts the moment of colonial possession, which is simultaneously territorial, sexual, and ideological. Her adoption of the voice of the colonizer radically disrupts official representations of the colonialist enterprise. The title of the poem announces that it is written by a woman of color, using the abusive term "greasers," although it articulates the racial values of United States colonialism through the point of view of a white man. Here the story of western settlement, which is based on the concepts of virgin territory and the civilizing mission, is appropriated for a Chicana historical

---

5 Gloria Anzaldúa, *Borderlands/La Frontera: The New Mestiza* (San Francisco: Aunt Lute, 1987).

6 Annette Kolodny, *The Lay of the Land: Metaphor as Experience and History in American Life and Letters* (Chapel Hill: University of North Carolina Press, 1984).

perspective: Anzaldúa tells the story as a part of the Mexican history of annexation, dispossession, and colonization which is grounded in violence against women.

The legacy of sexual violence, as Paz conceptualizes it and as Anzaldúa represents it, informs Ana Castillo's novel *Sapagonia* (1990). The latter narrates the inherited compulsion to rape, which is understood as a key element of the protagonist's mestizo legacy.[7] His grandmother, Mamá Grande, tells Máximo that he has an "old soul" by which she means that he has inherited the sexual compulsion that brought about her rape by the man who would then become her husband and Máximo's grandfather. Sexual violence forces Mamá Grande into the passive subject position that Paz describes as characteristic of *la chingada*. Castillo's narrative problematizes this passivity through the figure of Pastora who chooses to play Máximo's fantasy role of the passive woman.

For, Pastora makes a choice. She performs the part of the sexually passive woman and the very fact that she plays this role, from which she still maintains a self-conscious distance, fuels Máximo's obsession with her. Máximo can view Pastora only in his own terms, never in hers, and always in sexual terms. It is his need for her that empowers Pastora. This dynamics lends her the illusion that she can use her sexuality to gain agency in her life. That this sense of empowerment is an illusion—like the illusion of control over her that she lends Máximo—is starkly revealed when Máximo asserts ultimate dominance over Pastora by murdering her. It is when Pastora attempts to take control of this relationship through the performance of feminine passivity that Máximo reacts with aggressive force. He has inherited from his family and cultural history an understanding of sexual relations as power relations, inseparable from violent domination, and so he cannot surrender control to Pastora, cannot admit that his need is greater than hers and that she is the controlling partner in this relationship. Death dominates the narrative, which opens with Pastora's murder and circles back while telling the history of Máximo's family and of his life, with and without Pastora. It is death that Pastora chooses, when she chooses to play to Máximo's fantasies, as Mamá Grande chooses survival by adopting the feminine passivity that Pastora only plays. Mamá Grande allows herself to become the passive "virgin land" possessed by the white colonizer; Pastora attempts to revise this stereotype by taking control of it. But in this way, Pastora betrays the extent to which she is already a victim of this mythology. She overlooks, to her mortal peril, the physical violence that underpins the cultural mythology. She forgets that men like Máximo, like his grandfather before him, will use physical violence as their masculine prerogative in order to assert control and possession. If Máximo cannot possess and control Pastora while she is alive, then he will take control over her life by ending it. Pastora is complicit in her own destruction by failing to listen to and to credit the stories of the victimized women who preceded her. Pastora's death symbolizes an ultimate tragedy, for it ends the life of a woman who, though conscious of and continually testing the limits of her agency, still cannot escape the violence executed against her by men.

---

7 Ana Castillo, *Sapogonia (An Anti-Romance in 3/8 Meter)* (Tempe: Bilingual Press, 1990).

Violence and the Feminine: Domestic Violence

The violence of colonialism, loss of land, and loss of sovereignty are frequently conceptualized as the loss of masculinity: the Absent Father of machismo. But the loss of women as the sexual property of men, which underpins these connections, produces the counterpart to the Absent Father as the degraded, Raped Mother. In much of the work of Alma Villanueva this violent cultural dynamics is played out in the domestic context in terms of the sexual abuse of children and wife battering. While Villanueva seeks a "deep" cultural explanation for this violence, neither her narrators nor her characters repeat the mistake of Castillo's Pastora: they never forget the reality of violence.

The definition of domestic violence offered by the National Coalition Against Domestic Violence includes elements that render women vulnerable to forms of abuse that are represented powerfully in Villanueva's work.[8] The distinction between domestic violence and stranger-to-stranger violence is particularly significant here: Villanueva's novel *Naked Ladies* (1994) is structured broadly along this divide, with the first part addressing the issue of domestic violence and the latter dealing with violence inflicted by strangers.[9] In her depiction of Alta and her women friends—Katie, Jackie, Rita—Villanueva represents the gamut of abusive strategies to which these women's husbands subject them: from physical battering and rape, to psychological intimidation, and control through economic dependency. Alta is sickened with fear every night before her husband Hugh's payday because of the threat that he will spend the money on a drinking binge leaving nothing with which to feed the children. Her fear is represented in the context of helplessness born of his derision whenever she mentions her ambition to complete her education and find employment in the professions. Hugh's sexual abusiveness, physical violence, and verbal insults eventually lead her to attempt suicide.

Alta survives, because the friend whom she telephones listens to her and responds appropriately. But for most of the victims of domestic abuse represented in Villanueva's novel, the greatest suffering is inflicted by those who refuse to listen to or to credit their stories. That all of the women in this peer group face domestic abuse works to normalize the presence of this kind of violent behavior in society—an effect that is underlined by the fact that only one woman is saved. Rita, the friend who rescues Alta from her suicide attempt, suffers not from her husband's physical violence but from a sustained campaign of psychological abuse. Although Rita's husband's constant infidelity is a torture to her, it is also a secret which Rita keeps with him. Rita's silence sustains Carl's abusive attitude and normalizes his behavior, until one of Carl's mistresses breaks the terms of this unspoken agreement and telephones him at home. This breaking of the pact of silence brings to a sudden

---

8 See, the National Coalition Against Domestic Violence website, <www.ncadv.org>, for relevant definitions of domestic violence and US-based legislative resources. The United Nations Development Fund for Women website provides information about the range of international efforts to counter domestic violence: <http://www.unifem.org/gender_issues/violence_against_women/>. Information about efforts in Mexico may be found at <http://www.unifem.org.mx/site/documentacion.htm>.

9 Alma Villanueva, *Naked Ladies* (Tempe: Bilingual Press, 1994).

end Rita's willingness to continue in a relationship where she is complicit both in her own destruction and the objectification of women like Carl's mistress, who is known only in her sexual connection to Carl. At first, Carl cannot believe that Rita is challenging his authority, that she is taking control of their relationship. But once Rita's silence has been broken she reveals all her secrets, not only those she has kept with Carl: she speaks for the first time of her father's abuse of her, of the molestation that turned to rape, as she grew older. This revelation shocks, excites, and frightens Carl, all at once; and then he betrays Rita's revelation by negating her words, and reducing her again to silence: he refuses to believe her. He calls her insane and, like the doctor whom he telephones for help, Carl blames Rita's recent mastectomy for this unexpected "craziness." Just as Carl denies the continual psychological violence inflicted upon Rita by his infidelity so, together with the doctor, he denies the reality of Rita's childhood sexual abuse. He refuses to listen; he refuses to believe. Rather, he readily embraces the symbolic vocabulary offered by the doctor, which normalizes Rita's traumatic childhood experience. The doctor's recuperative narrative of hysterical femininity reinforces and legitimates the privileged masculine position of both men. Carl's lies are validated as the greater gender truth: Rita's truth is denied along with her ability to control her articulation of the narrative of her life. First her father, and then her husband, assume control over what can be said—over what can be heard—of the story of Rita's life. Her voice is lost and her narrative is appropriated by the social narrative of patriarchy.

This pattern of silence and denial is repeated in the experiences of other female characters in Villanueva's *Naked Ladies*. After she has been battered by Hugh, Alta finds herself falling into a pattern of blaming herself for being beaten. Alta entertains competing narratives of the violence she experiences, one of resistance and one of acceptance. This makes Alta's character different from Rita, whose narrative appears more as a singular account of acceptance and normalization of masculine violence. Alta is reminded of her stepfather's abuse of her mother, the threat of physical violence to Alta herself, and the blame her mother attributed to Alta when Alta had tried to fight back on behalf of her mother, who would not defend herself. Although Alta has a narrative of resistance, it is one that is ambivalent because of its origination in the experiences of her battered mother. Subsequently, her own narrative as a wife is affected by both her mother's narrative of acceptance, and by her own resistance to that abuse when she was a child.

Alta's silent battered mother represents a figure who returns in her friend Jackie's memories, memories of her own father who beat his wife until his daughter grew big enough to hit. Villanueva appears to make a generational distinction between the reactions to male violence of accepting mothers and resisting daughters. Like Alta, Jackie is a poor victim: she screams and refuses to accept this violence silently. She insists that her pain be heard. Villanueva writes: "She [Jackie] screamed loud and long and bloodcurdling, and he hated her for it, and she hated him. He went back to hitting her mother, who remained silent."[10] Only by breaking silence, by refusing complicity, can Jackie escape domestic violence.

---

10 *Ibid.*, 80.

In her text, Villanueva does not evade the issue of women who stay with abusive partners; rather, she confronts head-on the economic and emotional dependencies that bind these individuals together into dysfunctional relationships. Alta attempts suicide because she can envision no other exit from the misery of her life. When Alta's friends counsel her to leave Hugh, she replies that she can imagine neither how she would survive without Hugh to pay for food and the rent, nor how she would survive without the only lover she has ever known. Finally, it is the revelation of Hugh's homosexual infidelity that breaks the bonds of Alta's dependency. This is perhaps the most significant point that Villanueva makes regarding Alta: for it is Hugh's potential homosexuality (not his infidelity, which only increases his masculine authority over her) that diminishes his masculinity in her eyes. This situation places them on an equal standing and breaks the gender dynamic between them, which had allowed both his violation of her and her acceptance of that violence. The loss of Hugh's masculinity coincides with an increase in Alta's feminine agency. His homosexuality renders his gendered narrative now a "false" masculinity to her. The perspective that Villanueva offers here, where Alta's and Carl's agencies are inversely proportional, may be construed as another patriarchal trap, based on a gendered hierarchy. Yet, this revelation coincides with the therapy that has helped Alta to construct alternative narratives of her life. Only with her therapist's guidance is Alta able to break the silence that has shrouded the violence of her own family past and accept the reality both of her suffering and of her survival. However, this new narrative of survival is one guided by the normalizing influence of patriarchy, figured by the continued presence of the doctor/therapist. This represents, then, a compromised form of feminine agency.

The discovery of a woman, even a therapist, who will listen to, and credit the truth of the narratives of sexual abuse and domestic violence is the turning point in Alta's story. Even this, however, is something for which she must struggle. The initial meeting between the therapist, Cheryl, and Alta evolves into a confrontation when Alta realizes that Cheryl's normalizing assumption is that she enjoys her abuse: "Alta stood up. 'Well, I, for one, don't have to pay to be abused. I can get beat up for free, thank you.'"[11] After she has thought about the abuse implicit in this therapeutic situation, which has placed Alta unthinkingly in the subject position of the victim deserving of blame, Cheryl attempts to retrieve a relationship with Alta by introducing into their conversation her own experience of sexual and domestic violence. Cheryl knowingly transgresses the professional and socially-prescribed boundaries that separate therapist from patient: she shares her own personal narrative that resonates with that of Alta, bringing them closer together as women. Even the support of her therapist is something that Alta must fight for, against the deeply embedded assumption that women are somehow to blame, are somehow responsible, for their own suffering.

Whereas Villanueva's heroine, Alta, is an educated woman who is represented as possessing the resources, both personal and social, to fight back against those who would blame her for the violence to which she is victim, Cleófilas, the protagonist in Sandra Cisneros's story "Woman Hollering Creek" (1991), is placed in a passive

---

11 *Ibid.*, 106.

position in respect to her abusive husband. However, unlike Alta, Cleófilas has a stable and loving family to which she can escape. The story opens with Cleófilas's recollection of her father's words on her wedding day: "*I am your father, I will never abandon you.*"[12] That statement, which can be seen as ambivalent in the context of Cleófilas's gender positioning, sets the tone for her particular struggle, which represents the plight of many women who have been placed in the neo-colonial political position of a woman who has been taken as a bride from Mexico to the United States by her Chicano husband. In the United States, Cleófilas speaks no English and finds herself isolated in a small town, without the network of family and community that offered her emotional support back in Mexico. Economically and socially dependent on her husband, she becomes his possession and refers to him as "this keeper, this lord, this master."[13] Cleófilas's passivity is emphasized by Cisneros's clever use of the narrative point of view: the action is focalized through Cleófilas until the closing episodes, in which the narrative shifts to that of a third-person voice. As a consequence, the inconsistency of what is noted in the disparate narratives renders the entire narrative unreliable: the narrative voice articulates only that which Cleófilas can articulate—and Cleófilas cannot understand the significance of her husband's brutality.

It is only in the final sections of the text, narrated through a third-person voice, when Cleófilas asks her husband to take her to the hospital for a routine pre-natal check that we begin to know the extent of his violence against her. In the previous sections, as narrated by Cleófilas, we are told only Cleófilas's responses to his questions and remarks; the reader must fill in the silenced when Cleófilas says, "No, she won't mention it. She promises. If the doctor asks she can say she fell down the front steps or slipped when she was out in the backyard, slipped out back, she could tell him that."[14] But Cleófilas's lies and silences, her acceptance of her husband's brutality, and her complicity in her own brutalizing, are broken by the nurse, Graciela, whom she meets during that hospital visit. Graciela's third-person description of Cleófilas is the first objective indication we have of the abuse that Cleófilas has endured through the course of the story. Graciela telephones her friend Felice to arrange Cleófilas's escape back to her family in Mexico and tells how Cleófilas's body is covered with bruises. This confrontation with the reality of Cleófilas's situation is disturbing to the reader, who has been subject to her silence and only partial disclosure of her husband's violence. However, Cleófilas remains entirely passive throughout the story, permitting the nurse Graciela and her friend Felice to return her to her father's protection. Cleófilas herself never steps outside the normalizing discourse of masculine authority.

The reason for Cleófilas's silence, and Cisneros's primary concern in this story, is the influence of romantic stereotypes on young women who are deeply reluctant to let go of these ideals, even when they are contradicted by the brutal reality of domestic violence. As Felice's alternative narrative of feminine agency comes to dominate the

---

12 Sandra Cisneros, *"Woman Hollering Creek" and Other Stories* (London: Bloomsbury, 1993 [1991]), 43.

13 *Ibid.*, 49.

14 *Ibid.*, 53.

closing section of the story, we see Cleófilas's projection of her own life narrative as a romantic fantasy that supports patriarchal structures. Initially, Cleófilas sees her life as structured by love, by passion: she believes in self-sacrifice, if it is "for love." This adds irony to Graciela's explanation of the significance of Cleófilas's name: "One of those Mexican saints, I guess. A martyr or something."[15]

As her narrative progresses, however, Cleófilas finds her ideals increasingly alienated from reality and specifically the reality of violence against women, incidents of which enclose and encompass her. She looks at one of her husband's friends, who is rumored to have killed his wife and the narrator asks:

> Was Cleófilas just exaggerating as her husband always said? It seemed the newspapers were full of such stories. This woman found on the side of the interstate. This one pushed from a moving car. This one's cadaver, this one unconscious, this one beaten blue. Her ex-husband, her husband, her lover, her father, her brother, her uncle, her friend, her co-worker. Always. The same grisly news in the pages of the dailies. She dunked a glass under the soapy water for a moment—and shivered.[16]

The narrative reveals in indirect ways that Cleófilas is living in a culture that condones violence against women, a culture in which the murder of women is regarded as normal and, when remarked upon, "exaggerated." This positioning in the concrete societal dynamic causes Cleófilas finally to abandon her ideals of romantic love, and with them her abusive husband, to turn back to the love of family instead.

At the beginning of the narrative, juxtaposed with Cleófilas's recollection of her father's words, is the character's thought that "when a man and a woman love each other, sometimes that love sours. But a parent's love for a child, a child's for its parents, is another thing entirely."[17] Cleófilas's past as a child, and her positive relationship with her father, affect her narrative and her ability eventually to leave her marriage. This is significant, in terms of the contrast that Cisneros offers to the different histories of Villanueva's female characters: the family in Cisneros's story acts as a foil against domestic abuse. (While it is noteworthy that both patriarchal paternal and husband figures operate within the same narrative of masculine authority, and Cleófilas has no options that are not prescribed by her male relatives.) The character of Cleófilas is fortunate in several ways: she has a loving and non-violent Mexican family to which she can escape, but, perhaps even more than this, she is fortunate to encounter individuals who are willing to read the signs of domestic violence for the story they really tell (despite her silence and her lies) and they are willing to believe and to act on the meanings they hear in Cleófilas's tears and her physical injuries.

Her body becomes a text that reveals her life story; she is fortunate to encounter sympathetic readers of that life-text. However, although Cleófilas is passive throughout the story, her final insistence that she visit the hospital is revealed as an act of "passive agency." There, the private text of her body becomes public. The decision to go to the hospital construes a form of agency, because Cleófilas shows her body

---

15 *Ibid.*, 54.
16 *Ibid.*, 52.
17 *Ibid.*, 43.

and its marks uncover and add to the language of her otherwise silenced narrative. Like Villanueva's abused characters Alta and Rita, Cisneros's protagonist is heard when she speaks—or when her abused body speaks for her when her conscious voice is rendered mute—because these characters are able in one way or another to break the taboo against speaking out about the reality of domestic violence. Cleófilas survives because she revises the figure of La Llorona whom she imagines haunting the arroyo named "Woman Hollering Creek," subsequently transforming the cries of sadness and rage into defiant laughter.

Violence, Trauma, and the Normalization of Violence

Cisneros and Anzaldúa are among the recent Chicana writers who offer a revised mythology of La Llorona. La Llorona is the "weeping woman" of Chicano mythology: abandoned by her lover, she kills their children in a desperate act of vengeance. She then hides their bodies, so she can confront her lover with the evidence of his misdeeds. When she tries to retrieve the bodies, she cannot find them; and thus she haunts the possible hiding places, weeping and crying for her terrible loss. The transformation of such cultural figures from images of feminine oppression into icons of feminine empowerment operates at a level of abstraction that obscures the necessity not only to speak but also to be heard: to find not only a mouth but an ear. The difference between hearing a myth and listening to the myth is what allows for the transformation of mythical feminine figures from oppression to empowerment. Yet, this transformation of myths is enacted by the characters, not the readers of the texts, who must listen to the eclipsed messages in the myth. In the absence of discourses of hearing, this revised image of women's empowerment through voice can serve rather than challenge the cultural normalization of violence, which is the function of so much mythologizing even when it belongs to revisionary mythologizing. Wendy S. Hesford acknowledges that among the risks of telling a survivor story is the danger of its reappropriation by conservative cultural forces.[18] The risk of survivor testimony lies not so much in the telling but in the appropriation of survivor discourses by dominant gender paradigms and ideologies that "pre-script" such discourse.

The memorialization of the trauma of domestic violence, among the many forms of personal trauma, is described by Jeffrey Olick and others as the disruption of "the legitimating narrative[s] that we as individuals produce for us as a collectivity."[19] In other words, the ongoing nature of trauma lies in the events that cannot be integrated into the constitutive narratives of the communities of memory. This challenge to deeply-held values is managed by the deployment of recuperative narratives that normalize violence and reinstate accepted beliefs: so, for example, acts of domestic and sexual violence against women are represented as "crimes of passion." The romanticization of domestic violence through descriptive words such as "passion" is

---

18 Wendy S. Hesford, "Reading Rape Stories: Material Rhetoric and the Trauma of Representation," *College English* 62, No. 2 (November 1999): 192–221.

19 Jeffrey K. Olick, "Collective Memory: The Two Cultures," *Sociological Theory* 17, No. 3 (November 1999): 345.

what makes this form of violence acceptable in patriarchal discourse, for it enacts a slippage between sexual excitement and violence against women. This recuperation of traumatic stories and the "normalization" of the violence that they expose is the risk of telling survivor narratives. Kalí Tal refers to the "mythologization" of trauma that "works by reducing a traumatic event to a set of standardized narratives [...] turning it from a frightening and uncontrollable event into a contained and predictable narrative. [...]," emphasizing that "[o]nce codified, the traumatic experience becomes a weapon in another battle, the struggle for political power."[20] In this way, survivor discourses become revised or censored narratives of traumatic experiences. The myth becomes an almost tangible way to comprehend the normalization of violence, because it is seen as the residue of many generations of violence against women.

The theoretical "untranslatability" of trauma makes survivor discourse especially reliant upon cultural scripting for the conditions of its own meaning, even when it resists these cultural ideologies. This becomes emphatic in the context of women's inability to express themselves through the phallocentric codes of a patriarchal language. The figurative nature of literary language, together with the representational nature of literature, functions for the articulation of a trauma that does not need to be apprehended and codified in order to be present in the text.[21] In other words, literature preserves the authenticity of trauma as an experience that takes place in a liminal space outside the normal contexts of experience and meaning. This is the place where Anzaldúa takes us by violating convention and adopting the voice of the rapist, the violent colonizer in "We Call Them Greasers." In this text which, granted, is not a survivor narrative in any but the grandest historical sense, Anzaldúa refuses the abstract mythology of "the rape of the land," of "virgin territory," by representing as her subject the sexual violence that grounds all acts of colonial conquest. The possession of women's bodies, like the possession of the land itself, is an act of masculine aggression from which Anzaldúa refuses to flinch. Rather than transforming violence against women into a normalizing narrative by locating the significance of violence somewhere outside the language of the text, Anzaldúa turns upon its head the cultural narrative of westward progress. She brings to visibility the brutal acts of violence that underpin the narrative: hers is an anti-normalizing gesture that exposes the mechanics of cultural normalization.

It seems to me that it is in Anzaldúa's artistic gesture that we can find the seeds of a genuine healing of the trauma of violence against women. In a 1991 speech delivered to the Canadian Mental Health Association, Andrea Dworkin recommends a similar strategy for healing the wounds inflicted by sexual violence. She says:

> I want you to talk about the violence against women and you're here to talk about healing. I wish that you could raise the dead. That is what I would like to see. This is a political point. One of the reasons that the Right reaches so many women is that the Right has a transcendent god that says I will heal all your hurt and all your pain and all your wounds.

20 Kali Tal, *Worlds of Hurt: Reading the Literatures of Trauma* (Cambridge: Cambridge University Press, 1996), 6.

21 Petar Ramadanovic, "Introduction: Trauma and Crisis," *Postmodern Culture* 101 (2001), n.p. para. 2. <www.iath.virginia.edu/pmc/text-only/issue101/11.2introduction.txt> (accessed June 12, 2006).

I died for you. I will heal you. Feminists do not have a transcendent god who can heal that way. We have ideas about fairness and justice and equality. And we have to find ways to make them real. We don't have magic. We don't have supernatural powers. And we can't keep sticking women together who have been broken up into little pieces. So what I think is that fighting back is as close to healing as we are going to come. And I think that it is important to understand that we will live with a fair amount of pain for most of our lives.[22]

Only by telling and *listening* to the horrifying reality that is sexual violence and, indeed, all forms of violence against women, can we begin to understand and to heal. The normalizing of violence, transforming violence into something we can live with, does not constitute healing: it is evasion and self-deception. Normalizing mythologies that reinstate accepted cultural values are blinders that collude in the violence, much like the myth of America's manifest destiny that Anzualdúa so effectively dismantles. We need more Gloria Anzaldúas and Alma Villanuevas and Sandra Cisneroses and Ana Castillos to bring us to a world in which it is impossible for a public official to talk about "normal" numbers of sexually-motivated murders and a world where going out into the rain may make a woman wet—but that is all that she risks.

Bibliography

Amnesty International. "Intolerable Killings: 10 years of abductions and murders of women in Ciudad Juárez and Chihuahua." August 2003. <http://www.amnestyusa. org/countries/mexico/document.do?id=1829EE5E27AF155F80256D75005CCB 07>.

Anzaldúa, Gloria. *Borderlands/La Frontera: The New Mestiza*. San Francisco: Aunt Lute, 1987.

Castillo, Ana. "The Ancient Roots of Machismo." In *Massacre of the Dreamers: Essays on Xicanisma*. 63–84. New York: Plume, 1994.

—— *Sapogonia (An Anti-Romance in 3/8 Meter)*. Tempe: Bilingual Press, 1990.

Cisneros, Sandra. *"Woman Hollering Creek" and Other Stories*. London: Bloomsbury, 1993 [1991].

Dworkin, Andrea. "Terror, Torture, and Resistance." Speech delivered at the Canadian Mental Health Association's "Women and Mental Health Conference—Women in a Violent Society." Banff, Alberta, May 1991. <http://www.nostatusquo.com/ ACLU/dworkin/TerrorTortureandResistance.html>.

Hesford, Wendy S. "Reading Rape Stories: Material Rhetoric and the Trauma of Representation." *College English* 62, No. 2 (November 1999): 192–221.

Kolodny, Annette. *The Lay of the Land: Metaphor as Experience and History in American Life and Letters*. Chapel Hill: University of North Carolina Press, 1984.

---

22 Andrea Dworkin, "Terror, Torture, and Resistance," speech delivered at the Canadian Mental Health Association's conference "Women and Mental Health Conference—Women in a Violent Society," Banff, Alberta (May 1991) <http://www.nostatusquo.com/ACLU/dworkin/ TerrorTortureandResistance.html> (accessed June 12, 2006).

Kozol, Wendy. "Fracturing Domesticity: Media, Nationalism, and the Question of Feminist Influence." *Signs* 20, No. 3 (Spring 1995): 646–67.

National Coalition Against Domestic Violence. <http://www.ncadv.org>.

Olick, Jeffrey K. "Collective Memory: The Two Cultures." *Sociological Theory* 17, No. 3 (November 1999): 333–48.

Paz, Octavio. "The Sons of La Malinche." Trans. Lysander Kemp. Rpt. in *Goddess of the Americas: Writings on the Virgin of Guadalupe*. Edited by Ana Castillo. New York: Riverhead Books, 1996.

Ramadanovic, Petar. "Introduction: Trauma and Crisis." *Postmodern Culture* 101 (2001). <www.iath.virginia.edu/pmc/text-only/issue101/11.2introduction.txt>

Tal, Kali. *Worlds of Hurt: Reading the Literatures of Trauma*. Cambridge: Cambridge University Press, 1996.

Villaneuva, Alma. *Naked Ladies*. Tempe: Bilingual Press, 1994.

Chapter 13

When Theater Becomes
a Crusade against Violence:
The Case of V-Day

Marta Fernández-Morales

Introduction

In the late 1990s, the playwright and performer Eve Ensler published *The Vagina Monologues*. Created from a series of interviews with women on the subject of their bodies and their experiences of violence, the *Monologues* achieved immediate success and won an Obie Award. The play's agenda is premised on Ensler and her team's observation that "bad things are happening to women's vaginas everywhere: 500,000 women are raped every year in the United States; 100 million women have been genitally mutilated worldwide; and the list goes on."[1] As of today, the play has been translated into over forty languages, performed in hundreds of spaces around the world, and it has become the basis of a global movement against gender violence. Born out of Ensler's personal experience with battering and rape, and her theatrical and grassroots feminist activism, V-Day is a transformational movement supported by drama. Every year, communities around the globe join the project, becoming, as the actor Glenn Close has termed it, "part of [Eve's] crusade."[2] On the artistic side, V-Day spawned other plays, such as *Necessary Targets* (2001) and *The Good Body* (2004), and it has also generated a book of photographs entitled *Vagina Warriors* (2005).[3] This chapter examines Ensler's career and her dramatic production. By looking at both branches of the V-Day movement—the political and the artistic—through the lenses of theories such as those of Michel Foucault and Hélène Cixous, this

---

1 Eve Ensler, *The Vagina Monologues* (New York: Villard, 1998), xxii. For updated statistics about gender violence that reveal the everyday occurrence of these and other forms of sexist aggression, see: <www.ojp.usdoj.gov/bjs/welcome.html>; <www.vday.org/contents/violence/statistics>; <www.ndaa.org/links/violence_against_women_links.html#Anchor-VIOLENC-9902>; and elsewhere.

2 Quoted in Dinitia Smith, "Eve Ensler: Today the Anatomy, Tomorrow the World," *The New York Times* (September 26, 1999) <http://talentdevelop.com/EveEnsler.html> (accessed May 16, 2001).

3 Eve Ensler applies the term "Vagina Warriors" to all the women involved in V-Day and committed to fighting gender violence, be they community leaders, celebrities, writers, students, or any other type of female citizen wishing to raise consciousness about this problem.

chapter demonstrates how theater can become a weapon for consciousness-raising, denunciation of abuse, and transformation of mentalities and everyday practices, such that can bring real-life benefits to women around the world.

Eve Ensler: A Political Playwright Building Community

In her public life, Ensler defines herself as a playwright, performer, and activist. In her private life, she is also a survivor: while being raised in a middle-class neighborhood in New York, she underwent abuse at the hands of her own father. In an interview with the theater critic Alexis Greene she reflected on this experience: "[H]e brutalized me on a regular basis until I left home at sixteen. I left my body then, too."[4] This detachment from one's body is one of the most enduring traces of incest and childhood abuse. The phenomenon is part of a specific manifestation of Post-Traumatic Stress Disorder (PTSD), which may be displayed years after the mistreatment stopped, especially when the process has been silenced; such as the case of Ensler, who was unable to verbalize her plight until she became a writer. Other symptoms of this subclass of PTSD include depression, hypersexualized behavior not in accordance with the person's age, nightmares, flashbacks to the abusive episodes, problems with socialization and/or sexual relationships, emotional disturbance, low self-esteem, eating disorders, and addiction to alcohol and/or drugs.[5]

The abuse of minors usually entails a hidden type of violent interaction.[6] Perpetrators tend to exert their violence in subtle ways because they know that they risk rejection and penalty measures, since their crimes are perceived as being among the worst imaginable. They also impose silence on their victims, making them believe that something bad can happen to them or to their family if they reveal the harassment.[7] This violent initiation into sexuality provokes deep suffering in the victims, who tend to feel confused and guilty about their apparent complicity in the relationship. The trauma wrought by molestation often remains concealed for years because, contrary to more "public" traumatic episodes, like war or natural disasters, the abuse of minors has traditionally been perceived as a private, dirty thing; a sort of event that people often do not want to hear about. Mexican scholar Marta Torres elaborates on the correlation between abuse and silence, providing real-life examples and testimonies in her essay *La violencia en casa* ("Violence at Home"), where she concludes that many victims become adults without verbalizing their problem. This tendency to minimize and deny the issue leads to fear, shame, ongoing sleep and eating disorders, difficulty to establish and maintain relationships, and other symptoms related to PTSD. Socially and legally speaking, silence is the

---

4 Quoted in Alexis Greene, *Women Who Write Plays: Interviews with American Dramatists* (Hanover: Smith and Kraus, 2001), 156.

5 Mercedes de la Rosa, "Abusos imperdonables," *Magazine* (November 17, 2002), 72.

6 There is one abused boy for every two abused girls in Americas (Marta Torres Falcón, *La violencia en casa* [México: Paidós, 2001], 84). In Spain, Félix López concluded in a 2002 study that 23 percent of women and 15 percent of men are victims of abuse before they reach the age of 17 (de la Rosa, 67).

7 Torres Falcón, *op. cit.*, 84.

shield that protects the perpetrator, and many abusers spend their whole lives without punishment for their actions, sometimes even with the complicity of other adult members of the family who refuse to acknowledge the abuse.[8]

For Eve Ensler, writing became a way to break the silence and to re-member her psyche, identity, and body. As literary critic María José Navarro explains, bearing testimony of the violence suffered opens a path towards personal reconstruction, and in the case of women, it can become a tool to revise the common experience of coercion in order to turn it into a healing process that restores dignity.[9] Ensler's theatrical activity started in the 1970s with *When I Call My Voices*, a one-woman show followed by *Coming from Nothing*, a testimonial piece about her experience with abuse that she was unable to finish. She then moved on to less personal— although just as political—issues like anti-nuclear activism (*The Depot*, 1987) or the denunciation of the plight of homeless women, who are also frequently victimized (*Ladies*, 1988). Gender violence was again made present in *Floating Rhoda and the Glue Man* (1993), where the main protagonists split in two (Rhoda/Rhoda's stand-in; Barn/Barn's stand-in) as a strategy to stage the plight of their damaged, battered identities. As I have stated elsewhere, the great importance of this text is that it makes evident for the first time Ensler's obsession with words, with naming violence and verbalizing trauma.[10]

Floating Rhoda can be considered the key that opened the door to Ensler's "crusade against violence," which is based on two major pillars: 1) making the abuse of women in all its forms visible to theater audiences and communities around the world; and 2) building a creative and safe environment for female citizens everywhere. Due to her personal history, Ensler acknowledges that she is "obsessed with women being violated and raped, and with incest," and conversely, with the possibilities of empowerment that a more positive relationship to their bodies and sexualities may bring about.[11] This is the basis of what she describes as her mission: to devote the rest of her life to ending violence toward women.[12] Since 1996, when *The Vagina Monologues* was first performed, this commitment has borne several theatrical fruits: the *Monologues* have been published, translated, and staged in many countries, and other plays have grown out of the same effort to denounce sexist abuse.

Necessary Targets (2001) stems from "My Vagina Was My Village," one of the pieces included in the *Monologues*. In it, the audience faces the testimony of a victim of genocidal rape in the former Yugoslavia, where sexual aggression became an integral part of the military strategy during the war, with an estimated 20,000 to 50,000 women and girls being attacked, according to the European Community

---

8 *Ibid.*, 89.

9 María José Navarro Mateo, "La narración de la violencia," *Asparkía. Investigació Feminista* 8 (1997): 17.

10 Marta Fernández-Morales, "'Bits. Fragments. Particles.' Split Identities and Theatricality in Eve Ensler's *Floating Rhoda and the Glue Man*," The 7th International Conference of the Spanish Association of American Studies (University of Jaén, 2005).

11 Julia Bourland, "*The Vagina Monologues* Creator Opens Up" (December 2000), <www.women.com/entertainment/interviews/ensler/ensler.html> (accessed May 15, 2001).

12 Quoted in Bourland, 2.

and the Bosnian Ministry of Interior.[13] In the 1990s in Bosnia, rape was practiced as a form of ethnic cleansing, and since then, it has been conceptualized as a weapon of war in specialized literature and institutional analyses.[14] In a 2004 report on war crimes against women, Amnesty International (AI) explained that rape is implemented tactically to attain specific objectives in many armed conflicts. It is used to conquer, expel, or control women and their communities; as a gender-marked form of torture, it is exerted to obtain information, punish, intimidate, and humiliate. Rape, AI concludes, is a universal weapon employed to rob women of their dignity and to destroy their sense of identity.[15]

In "My Vagina Was My Village" Ensler opposes scenes of a peaceful past to the painful war and post-war times in Bosnia, where thousands of women of all the ethnic groups had to come to terms with terrifying episodes of violence like the one described in the monologue: "the soldiers put a long thick rifle inside me. So cold, the steel rod canceling my heart. Don't know whether they're going to fire it or shove it through my spinning brain."[16] The experience of rape is juxtaposed with other traumatic episodes: husbands coming back from the battlefield and turning into batterers at home; daughters lost during the conflict; friendships broken by fratricidal hatred; identities conflicting due to ethnic nationalism; and the experience of becoming refugees. Using a polyphonic structure, Ensler inscribes the voices of women of all origins and ages in her play, and thereby confronts the audience with a moral dilemma: knowing what we now know about Bosnia, can we still maintain the "us" vs. "them" fallacy that keeps us safe in our world of inaction and neglect? As the playwright suggests in the introduction to the play, the text is a critique of those who are unable to understand that violence is a continuum that cannot be hidden behind the labels such as "us" and "them." Ensler ironically observes: "Them is always different from us. Them has no face. Them is a little bit deserving of all the bad that happens to them. Them is used to violence—it's in their blood. There are rules about them. We keep them over there, out of sight, conceptual."[17]

There are at least three levels of analysis relevant to this question of "otherness" in the framework of this chapter: firstly, the identification of this strategy of alienation in the philosophical background of violent practices like genocide (for example,

---

13 Alexandra Stiglmayer, *Mass Rape: The War against Women in Bosnia-Herzegovina* (Lincoln: University of Nebraska Press, 1994), 85.

14 In *Rape Warfare* (Minneapolis and London: University of Minnesota Press, 1996), Beverly Allen revises a group of documents that make the genocidal rape strategy explicit, recognizing it as part of the "ethnic cleansing" process perpetrated in Bosnia. Among others, these documents include: the Bassiouni Report, commissioned by the United Nations; the Ćosić Memorandum, which called for a unification of "Great Serbia"; and a variation to the military Ram Plan in which Serbian experts in psychological warfare urged the army to "aim our action at the point where the religious and social structure is most fragile. We refer to the women, especially adolescents, and to the children" (quoted in Allen, *op. cit.*, 57).

15 Amnistía Internacional, *Vidas rotas. Crímenes contra mujeres en situaciones de conflicto* (Madrid: EDAI, 2004), 38.

16 Eve Ensler, *The Vagina Monologues* (New York: Villard, 1998), 58.

17 Eve Ensler, *Necessary Targets: A Story of Women and War* (New York: Villard, 2001), xi.

Bosnia or Rwanda); secondly, the recognition of the elaboration, behind this curtain of alterity, of excuses for political non-intervention in moments of conflict (as happened in Bosnia and Kosovo in the 1990s);[18] and thirdly, the inescapable link between "woman" and "other" that the centuries of discriminating cultural practices have consolidated. All three are applicable to *Necessary Targets* and to the whole of Eve Ensler's dramatic body of dramatic production since the 1990s.

In most contexts of armed conflict, violence specialists have identified a process of alienation employed by enemy forces that comprises not only physical aggression, but also psychological pressure, through the effeminization and exoticization of individuals and groups. Explaining this "us" vs. "them" dialectic, Ervin Staub, Director Emeritus of the Psychology of Peace and the Prevention of Violence Area at the University of Massachusetts-Amherst, comments that members of the opposing group during conflicts are devaluated through negative stereotyping. Aggression by one group against another, he says, *seems* justified if "the other" is identified as a dangerous member of the "out-group," and a collective "them" is defined through racial, religious, class, and gender distinctions.[19] Historian Joanna Bourke further argues that "[r]acism in all its forms (cultural ethnocentrism, scientific racism and broadly-based ideas about 'national character') was a key factor in the prevalence of atrocities in certain theatres of war." Pointing directly at World War II and Vietnam, she also underscores that "[p]rejudice lay at the very heart of the military establishment," and that the soldiers who undertook the most violent actions "had highly prejudicial views about their victims." By dehumanizing the enemies, Bourke concludes, "they all became fair game."[20] Thus, in situations like the Bosnian war, dominant groups elaborate their own discourse of "otherness" to justify their decisions and their possible neglect of other human beings. In order to keep "them" out of sight/merely conceptual, as Eve Ensler put it, the collective "us" constructs a discourse of intrinsic differentiation. In military and political terms, since the Bosnian conflict, this discursive (and actual) fragmentation of national units has been termed "balkanization," and has been repeatedly used in international scenarios. The label has connotations of tribalization and primitivism, and invokes tranquilizing consequences for the in-group, allowing it to feel safe and think "we will never be like them." Mary Kaldor describes this phenomenon in her book *New & Old Wars: Organised Violence in a Global Era*, using it specifically to analyze the late and inadequate intervention of the European Union and the US in the former Yugoslavia.[21]

---

18 Cf., Marta Fernández-Morales, "Communicating the Experience of War. The 'Us' *vs.* 'Them' Dialectic in Eve Ensler's *Necessary Targets,*" *English Studies* 26 (2005): 115–29.

19 Ervin Staub, *The Roots of Evil: The Origins of Genocide and Other Group Violence* (Cambridge: Cambridge University Press, 1989), 17 and 60. Thus, for example, the US forces fighting in Vietnam coined the pejorative term "gook" for the enemy. The elements of racism and sexism contained in the military jargon contributed to blind violence: the term "allowed" the use of emasculating practices such as male castration or female amputation of breasts to destroy the captured enemy. Cf., Mark Baker, *Nam* (London: Abacus, 2001), 50.

20 Joanna Bourke, *An Intimate History of Killing. Face-to-face Killing in Twentieth-century Warfare* (London: Granta Books, 1999), 204–205.

21 Mary Kaldor, *Las nuevas guerras. La violencia organizada en la era global* (Barcelona: Tusquets, 2001), 52–3.

Ever since Simone de Beauvoir, the concept of "otherness" has also been part of debates and theorizations inherent in feminist theory. Repeatedly defined as an "absence" or "lack" in traditional androcentric terms, women have been culturally and socially constructed as "the other" to men (especially heterosexual men). In a dominant discourse stemming from a patriarchal system of thought that equates "masculine" to "universal," everything "female" implies some sort of deviation, which in turn incites discrimination against women. The most radical consequence of the condition of alterity imposed on women is, undoubtedly, violence, which serves as a tool to maintain the patriarchal power hierarchy intact, constructing female citizens as inferior, while keeping them oppressed through fear and abuse.

As a feminist playwright and activist, Eve Ensler concurs with gender violence specialists and asserts that beyond issues of difference among women there is a common trait that unites every female citizen of the world: the threat of sexist aggression. Along these lines, Liz Kelly, Director of the Child and Woman Abuse Studies Unit at the London Metropolitan University, has argued in favor of the conceptualization of violence as a *continuum*. She explains that the term has two meanings that can be applied to feminist analyses of battering, rape, and other forms of aggression for reasons of gender. According to Kelly, the first meaning of the word *continuum*, "a basic common character that underlies many different events," makes the discussion of sexual violence possible: a "basic common character" underlies a variety of forms of coercion and force used to control women in various circumstances across different cultures. The second meaning of *continuum*, "a continuous series of elements or events that pass into one another and cannot readily be distinguished," enables the documentation and naming of a range of abuse that women experience globally.[22] Both of Kelly's arguments reinforce Eve Ensler's belief that all women are included in an "us" which may be potentially victimized within a global system that maintains male domination through diverse forms of violence against women.

With this global perspective, and following the trend of consciousness-raising (C-R) practices in contemporary feminist drama, Ensler has recently published and performed *The Good Body* (2004), where she draws on the C-R tradition started by the early feminist groups of the 1960s and 1970s and goes a step further. The first theater companies born out of the Women's Liberation movement discovered that the threat of violence united all women and put their preoccupation with this violent continuum on stage as a form of protest. Ensler takes this knowledge for granted and moves from protest to transformation; from pain to healing; and from anger to action. Her interview-based plays are the inheritors of the early *Take Back the Night* marches of the 1970s; of performances like *In Mourning and in Rage* (1977), developed in Los Angeles by Suzanne Lacy and Leslie Labowitz; and of the first plays representing the experience of victims, such as the angry *Rape-In* (1970), the revengeful *There's a Wall Between Us, Darling* (1970), or the progressive *Internal*

---

22 Liz Kelly, "The Continuum of Sexual Violence," in *Women, Violence and Social Control* (ed.), by J. Hamner and M. Maynard (Atlantic Highlands: Humanities Press International, 1987), 48.

Injury (1978).[23] Initially, these groups used the actors' and playwrights' experiences about certain areas of female life to create their performances, which were then developed and modified through a process of discussion with the audience *after* the shows.[24] Extending this practice, Ensler opens the scope of the creative process and works to include her potential audience *a priori* in her plays by conducting interviews with all sorts of women in order to compose a realistic collage of their testimonies on stage. Describing her technique to Alexis Greene, Ensler explains that after she talks to the women, she filters their words and picks out a couple of lines that she considers especially significant because they "speak to her."[25]

The consequence of Ensler's selection of material is that she makes her audience gain a real sense of community. Women who have contributed to V-Day highlight this feeling of shared achievement and belonging. A 2007 organizer from Colorado affirmed: "I have come to understand that V-Day isn't a website, or a resource or a movement. V-Day is us, the people who hold the goal of a world without violence deep in our hearts and our vaginas." A participant from Hong Kong also drew on the idea of collective strength in her testimony: "It makes us feel belonging to a very hopeful activity and action, a campaign that is not 'a voice in the wilderness'." A V-Day member from Illinois confessed: "I have never felt as empowered as a woman as I did talking, laughing and moaning in that room with these open, intelligent, vivacious and enjoyable women."[26]

In this framework, humor, which several testimonies on the V-Day website point at, has become a useful tool for Ensler to create community, since it eliminates fear and liberates suppressed memories and taboos. In her 2001 study of this phenomenon, Spanish Professor Asunción Bernárdez states that laughter promotes social bonding and creates a friendly atmosphere. She defends the conception of humor as a political weapon for women which can be specifically implemented through theater.[27] In her interview with Greene, Ensler remembers the moment of revelation when she discovered, after re-writing the first draft of *The Depot*, "that you could make politics funny."[28]

The characteristic twists and turns of Ensler's very personal monologues can be found in *The Good Body*. In this play there is a balanced alternation of humorous and stern pieces, and, just as in *The Vagina Monologues*, laughter helps the audience to accept certain topics that may be unthinkable in other contexts, and therefore, to break through resistance without frightening people.[29] However, the subtext is deeply serious, and the playwright highlights this in her "Preface," where she elaborates on why she is presenting a script "about her stomach":

---

23 Cf. Charlotte Canning, "Representing the Patriarchy and Experience. Plays about Violence against Women," in *Feminist Theaters in the USA. Staging Women's Experience* (London and New York: Routledge, 1996), 146–76.

24 Alisa Solomon, "From C-R to PR: Feminist Theatre in America," in *Contemporary American Theatre* (ed.), by Bruce King (New York: St. Martin's Press, 1991), 231.

25 Quoted in Greene, *op. cit.*, 161.

26 All these testimonies and more can be found at the V-Day website: <www.vday.org>.

27 Asunción Bernárdez Rodal (ed.), *El humor y la risa* (Madrid: Fundación Autor, 2001), 6.

28 Quoted in Greene, *op. cit.*, 159.

29 Ensler, quoted in Greene, *op. cit.*, 172.

It is where the explosive trajectories collide—the Judeo-Christian imperative to be good; the patriarchal mandate that women be quiet, be less; the consumer-state imperative to be better [...] As the world rapidly divides into fundamentalist camps, reductive sound bites, and polarizing platitudes, an exploration of my stomach and the life therein has the potential to shatter these dangerous constraints.[30]

Again, Ensler's perspective is global: she pays attention to the highly diversified forms of violence that women undergo everywhere in order to conform to their cultural roles and to the prevailing standards of beauty.[31] Ensler reveals that women in Africa buy skin-lightening creams to look less "colored"; that mothers in America remove their daughters' ribs so that they will stay thin; and that girls everywhere starve themselves in order to stick to a certain image perpetuated by the mass media. After completing hundreds of interviews, the playwright concludes that most women have been taught to loathe at least one part of their body, and that this is a supreme form of violence and control. A woman obsessed with diets, lotions, and body-building has no time for personal or intellectual development, and no energy for social and political activism. In her seminal study *The Beauty Myth*, American feminist Naomi Wolf called dieting "the most powerful political sedative," arguing that a docile female population feeling sick and anxious is much easier to control than a united, sisterhood- and self-esteem-based female group of citizens.[32] As an exercise of resistance, *The Good Body* is a cry for freedom and a celebration of the potential inherent in women's "docile bodies" to respond to systems of domination. In a direct address in the play, Ensler urges the audience: "Tell the image makers and magazine sellers and the plastic surgeons that you are not afraid. [...] be bold and LOVE YOUR BODY. STOP FIXING IT. It was never broken."[33]

Today, Eve Ensler continues to conceive texts, performances, and initiatives against violence. Her most recent play, *The Treatment* (2006), again brings up the aftermath of an armed conflict in a story where a traumatized soldier tries to redeem himself through therapy. Meanwhile, *The Vagina Monologues* has arrived in Zambia for the first time; Ensler travels around the world to keep an eye on the myriad V-Day projects opened; and more and more celebrities become part of Eve's crusade.

Initially a domestic movement, V-Day is now a globalized entity involving 81 countries and developing programs run by local partners in Africa, Asia, and the Middle East. It includes three types of events articulated around the performance of the *Monologues*, namely: the Worldwide Campaign, the College Campaign, and the Youth Initiative. From these, other branches of work are derived, such as the Stop Rape annual contest, the devising of educational material and programs, the compilation of statistics about gender violence, and the updating of a list of anti-violence resources for women. In 1998, V-Day consisted of a unique gala event

---

30 Eve Ensler, *The Good Body* (London: William Heinemann, 2004), x–xi.

31 The American Society of Plastic Surgeons recorded 11 million operations in 2006, with aesthetics-based breast implants as the most popular type of intervention and Botox as the most demanded in the "injectables market." Cf. <www.plasticsurgery.org/media/press_releases/2006-Stats-Overall-Release.cfm>.

32 Naomi Wolf, *El mito de la belleza* (Barcelona: Emecé Editores, 1991), 242.

33 Ensler, *The Good Body*, xv.

held on Valentine's Day in New York, where a group of film and theater celebrities performed *The Vagina Monologues*. According to the movement's official website, in 2006 there were more than 2,700 V-Day events around the globe.[34] In 2007, a total of 689 universities in 20 countries developed a College Campaign event, and women in nations immersed in conflict, like Afghanistan, Iraq, and Israel, participated in the initiative, generating a worldwide dialogue about the consequences of sexist aggression and the possibility for alternative forms of relationships not only between men and women, but also among women – with themselves and with one another.[35]

The Vagina Monologues as a Feminist Ur-Text, and the Case for V-Day

As a dramatic proposal, *The Vagina Monologues* allows the artist to lead her audience on a journey through a complex gynocentric universe where men are not attacked or neglected; they are simply left out of the equation, because the play is about a universal, female-only "us." It is a radical composition that can be analyzed in the terms proposed by French feminist Hélène Cixous, as an example of *écriture feminine* ("female writing"), and as a confirmation of Cixous's own dramatic politics. For Cixous, *écriture féminine* must be a way to honor the particular voice of women. Writing from their female selves, Cixous contends, women create a gender-marked language articulated as an exclamation, a cry, a howl, a cough, a vomit, a type of music. It is, she says, a voice full of pain and anger, capable of smashing traditional discourse.[36] The key element in this conceptualization of female writing and performance is the body. In *The Laugh of the Medusa* Cixous insists that it is necessary for women to write (from) their bodies to construct a language of their own. In that way, women can recover a body that had otherwise been confiscated by dominant discourse.

The female body's quest for a space of its own in drama is particularly relevant for Cixous. When women write freely and their voice is allowed to take center-stage, Cixous believes, the act of making or going to the theater is revealed as a political gesture with a strong transformational impulse.[37] She writes: "it is high time that women gave back to the theatre its fortunate position, its *raison d'être* and what makes it different—the fact that there it is possible to get across the living, breathing, speaking body."[38] Language and the body become the axes on which the female playwright maps her mission, according to Cixous—a fact that allows it to coincide a hundred percent with Eve Ensler's vision for V-Day.

---

34 See <www.vday.org>.

35 V-Day encourages male volunteers to participate in the initiatives against gender violence through special programs around the re-construction of masculinity, the effects of rape on men, and others. However, the performances, the leading positions, and the main branches of V-Day are women-centered and run by women in all cases.

36 Hélène Cixous, *La risa de la Medusa. Ensayos sobre la escritura* (Barcelona: Anthropos, 1995), 56–7.

37 Hélène Cixous, "Aller à la mer," *Modern Drama* XXVII/4 (December 1984): 547.

38 *Ibid.*

In accordance with Cixous's proposals, the performances of *The Vagina Monologues* expose the female body and its plight in a patriarchal, globalized culture. As an instance of postmodern feminist theatrics, Ensler's piece presents a group of bodies expressing themselves freely on stage—advancing alternative forms of looking at women, a new language formulated exclusively by women, and unuttered questions and reflections surrounding the female embodied experience. In this kind of performance politics, the body raises against invisibility by devising unexpected metaphors for a silenced identity.[39] For Ensler, the vagina symbolizes the essence of womanhood, which is shown as plural and multi-sided, and in constant flux and evolution. In the *Monologues*, the traditional category of "Woman" is transformed into a multiplicity of "women," each with a voice of her own, and the term "vagina" acts as a synecdoche for the whole female being. The repetition of the "V-word" and the unusual topics approached in the play are presented as weapons for women's liberation, because, as Ensler states in the introduction to the play: "as more women say the word, saying it becomes less of a big deal; it becomes part of our language, part of our lives."[40]

This transformational process, which fuses body politics with the deconstruction of traditional androcentric discourse, concurs with Margaret McLaren's proposal for the adaptation of Michel Foucault's philosophy to contemporary gender-conscious theory. Highlighting the certain strategic coincidences between Foucault's thought and the theories developed by the women's movement, McLaren argues that Foucault's ideas provide a useful background for feminism, as evidenced in the work of the critics who "draw on Foucault's work and apply it to women's experience" by adding the dimension of gender to a set of texts that was initially gender-blind.[41] Most prominently, Foucault's idea of "dominant discourse" has been applied to the workings of patriarchy, a system of domination based on heterosexual male control, and perpetuated through practices like an unbalanced division of labor, a constricted distribution of roles for men and women, compulsory heterosexuality, the transmission of degrading images of women, and different forms of violence. Similarly, other Foucauldian concepts like "discipline," "power," and "social norms" can be further illuminated by the addition of the gender variable.

In their introduction to *Feminism & Foucault: Reflections on Resistance*, Irene Diamond and Lee Quinby specify four elements of convergence between Foucauldian thought and feminist theory that will serve as an organizing principle for my analysis of the societal importance of V-Day: 1) the identification of the body as the site of power; 2) the recognition of local and intimate operations of power; 3) the emphasis on the role of discourse to produce and sustain hegemonic power; and 4) the critique of (male) "universals."[42] As we are about to see, all of these are directly applicable

---

39 Laura Borràs Castanyer, "Hermenéutica del cuerpo," in *Escenografías del cuerpo* (Madrid: Fundación Autor, 2000), 9.

40 Ensler, *The Vagina Monologues*, xxiv.

41 Margaret McLaren, *Feminism, Foucault, and Embodied Subjectivity* (Albany: State University of New York Press, 2002), 14.

42 Irene Diamond and Lee Quinby (eds), *Feminism & Foucault: Reflections on Resistance* (Boston: Northeastern University Press, 1988), x.

to the *Monologues* and V-Day with respect to their focus on gender violence as an everyday, systematic form of male domination in the global patriarchal system.

The first argument that Diamond and Quinby identify as common to Foucault and feminism is particularly relevant to the mission of V-Day. In his genealogical work *Discipline and Punish*, the French philosopher discussed the human body as a target for the operations of power, and the seat of "docility," which allows humans to be subjected, used, transformed, and perfected by various systems of domination.[43] For him, systems of domination—one of them being patriarchy, as identified by feminist thought—are built upon a set of discourses and a certain "political economy of the body." On this frame of thought, the dominant group (in this context, heterosexual men) constructs rules and regulations, moral laws, tacit agreements, social roles, and mechanisms of sanction and punishment by which to produce and sustain a determined social order.[44]

In the case of women, the operations identified by Foucault are obvious, since patriarchal mores have historically controlled female bodies, particularly in their exercise of sexuality and/or motherhood. Together with other explicit prohibitions, gender stereotyping, and lines of oppression, violence has been one of the main strategies used to keep female bodies under control. V-Day makes this visible during the performances of *The Vagina Monologues* by dealing with topics of physical/sexual aggression ("My Vagina Was My Village"), biomedical, cultural, and religious abuse ("Vagina Facts" about cliteridectomy and masturbation), and other forms of coercion exerted over women. In response to these kinds of discriminatory patterns, V-Day is conceived as an empowering movement, focused on the possibility of resistance and change in the social and cultural position of women, much similar to Foucault's proposition that the individual has to become a self-determining agent "capable of challenging and resisting the structures of domination in modern society."[45] In the *Monologues* and the activities derived from them, women claim a world where "the shame leaves and the violation stops, because vaginas are visible and real, and they are connected to powerful, wise, vagina-talking women."[46] Foucault's writings may provide a theoretical background for Ensler's emancipatory movement—from victimhood to agency; from silence to control of discourse; and from docility to action.

The second meeting point on Diamond and Quinby's Foucault–feminism axis can also be identified in Ensler's initiative. In fact, the recognition of the local and intimate operations of power is the assumed basis of the *Monologues* and of the V-Day programs in general. Under V-Day principles, there is the understanding that violence is not an isolated phenomenon developed by certain abnormal individuals in extraordinary contexts. On the contrary, it is conceived as an everyday, common exercise of coercion and mistreatment that keeps women oppressed as a group in every single nation in the world. Violence, as we have seen through Liz Kelly's arguments, is a continuum.

---

43 Michel Foucault, *Vigilar y castigar. Nacimiento de la prisión* (México DF: Siglo XXI Editores, 1974), 140.

44 *Ibid.*, 32.

45 Lois McNay, *Foucault & Feminism* (Boston: Northeastern University Press, 1992), 4.

46 Ensler, *The Vagina Monologues*, xxiv.

The internalization of the concept of *continuum* by all women enables them to identify links between "typical" and "aberrant" behaviors, and to locate and name their own experiences in that broader context.[47] There might seem to be nothing extraordinary in rape, battering, or female genital mutilation; nothing strange in the pressure put on women to dress in a certain way, move (or not) in a specific form, and talk (or not) about some topics or others. Patriarchal power is global and structural, and it is reinforced—as Foucault argued about dominant discourses in general—by local and intimate operations of control. The exertion of this kind of sexist "micro-power" over women is not unusual; rather, it has become part of "the norm," and, thus, has become invisible as the breach of human rights.[48] The gender violence expert Miguel Lorente explains that what may be perceived as an extraordinary state when it is experienced just once can become an ordinary, structural condition through its systematic repetition; for women victims of violence, the threshold of tolerance and "normality" is pushed farther every day.[49]

As *The Vagina Monologues* highlights, rape, battering, or sexual harassment happen all the time, and the coercive system that provokes them is maintained not only through open aggression, but also through different types of discourse that sustain the hegemonic position of men over women. Patriarchal discourse in its different forms (biomedical, legal, educational, and so on) maintains its dominance through mechanisms of regulation and exclusion. In his work, Foucault repeatedly points at the connection between knowledge and power, underscoring that certain forms of knowledge (and the circulation thereof) have only been accessible to some members of society. Furthermore, discourse and power inter-relate through the construction of the "true/false" dichotomy, the establishment of taboos, and through systems of dual oppositions, such as "reason/madness,"[50] all of them mechanisms of exclusions to which women have been traditionally subjected. Feminists around the world have insisted on the importance of naming, conceptualizing, and destroying the taboos dealing with female access to traditionally masculinized areas of life and thought. Eve Ensler has made this process of naming one of the defining projects of V-Day:

> Naming things, breaking through taboos and denial is the most dangerous, terrifying and crucial work. This has to happen in spite of political climates or coercions, in spite of careers being won or lost, in spite of the fear of being criticized, outcast or disliked. I believe freedom begins with naming things. Humanity is preserved by it.[51]

---

47 Kelly, *op. cit.*, 51.

48 Argentinian specialist Luis Bonino refers to these low-intensity sexist practices existent on nearly every level of human interaction as *micromachismo* (Luis Bonino, "Develando los micromachismos en la vida conyugal," in *Violencia masculina en la pareja. Una aproximación al diagnóstico y los modelos de intervención* (ed.), by J. Corsi *et al.* [Buenos Aires: Paidós, 1995], 191–208).

49 Miguel Lorente, *Mi marido me pega lo normal* (Barcelona: Ares y Mares, 2001), 23.

50 Michel Foucault, *El orden del discurso* (Barcelona: Tusquets, 1987), 11.

51 Eve Ensler, "The Power and Mystery of Naming Things" (March 20, 2006), <www.vday.org/contents/vday/vworld/vmoments> (accessed 22 July, 2006).

Through V-Day as a realization of *écriture féminine*, victims of gender violence and women in general are allowed to re-appropriate discourse (and consequently, knowledge and power) in their own terms. They take hold of language: they decide what, when, where, and how to speak. They make the fallacies of universality and neutrality collapse, revealing—and we are now moving onto the fourth element of the Foucault–feminist axis noted earlier—the lies behind the dominant (male) discourse. As Cixous postulates for the practitioners of her *écriture féminine*, Vagina Warriors do not take words for granted: they fight for them, empty them of their traditional meanings and give them new nuances to include women's experience. Complementing Cixous, Ensler and other female actors in the *Monologues* occupy the stage with their bodies, using guerrilla tactics developed in feminist theater to put "the language of the dominant to subversive use."[52] In Foucauldian terms, they quit being "docile" and become agents against patriarchy, the dominant order of discourse.[53]

The process of re-appropriating language and demystifying women's bodies goes through different stages in *The Vagina Monologues* until the circle is closed with the birth of Colette, a new member of the V-community that will hopefully live in a less violent world. In the edition of the text taken as reference for this chapter (Villard 1998), the major themes presented in *The Vagina Monologues* can be grouped as follows: 1) declaration of principles ("I Bet You're Worried"); 2) celebratory/ vindicative pieces like "Hair" or "The Vagina Workshop"; 3) denunciation pieces such as "The Little Coochi Snorcher that Could"; 4) unuttered, revelatory questions about vaginas: "If it got dressed, what would it wear? If it could talk, what would it say?"; and 5) vagina facts; that is, historical and current truths about women's bodies and violence.[54] The general approach to these topics is critical but optimistic, placing the emphasis on the possibility of real change and the importance of bearing witness to violence, but also to female courage and pleasure. Along these lines, Navarro has argued that women's verbalization of the violence and the shame they face opens the possibility of healing. The voices in Ensler's play are sometimes bitter, even positively desperate, but there is a common feeling of relief in the act of revelation. Thus, the old lady in "The Flood" confesses: "You know, actually, you're the first person I ever talked to about this, and I feel a little better"; the British woman in the vagina workshop is joyful: "I felt connection"; the outspoken militant shouts "I really like it. 'Cunt.' "[55]

The celebratory mood of the play is particularly reflected in one of its by-products: the book *Vagina Warriors* (2005), which includes a collection of portraits by Joyce

---

52 Janet Brown, "Feminist Theory and Contemporary Drama" in *The Cambridge Companion to American Women Playwrights* (ed.), by B. Murphy (Cambridge: Cambridge University Press, 1999), 167.

53 Foucault, *El orden del discurso*, 32.

54 For an analysis of the contents of each group of monologues, see Fernández-Morales, "El cuerpo-texto y el deseo femenino en el teatro: Monólogos de la vagina," in *Los hábitos del deseo* (ed.), by Carme Riera, Meri Torras, Isabel Clúa, Pau Pitarch (Valencia: Ex-Cultura, 2005), 377–83.

55 Cf., Inga Muscio's manifesto entitled *Cunt* in Muscio, *Cunt: A Declaration of Independence* (New York: Seal Press, 1998).

Tenneson alongside texts by Ensler. In that volume, women who fight against discrimination and sexist aggression are honored, and their value as leaders and their capacity for empowering themselves and others is recognized. In a featured essay that summarizes the main components of V-Day, Ensler states that although Vagina Warriors are always original, they possess some general defining characteristics: they are no longer beholden to social customs or inhibited by taboos; they have a wicked sense of humor; they are done being victims; they are community makers.[56] *Vagina Warriors* includes women of different backgrounds with a common cause: celebrities feature hand in hand with campus campaign directors, Native American leaders, college professors, revolutionaries from Afghanistan, writers, musicians, media CEOs, yoga instructors, or photographers. At the end of the volume, Ensler selects some "Outrageous Vagina Moments," which can be seen as tokens of the achievements obtained by the movement. A brief list with a few representative examples will serve to further contextualize my analysis of V-Day and its relevance in the global struggle against gender violence:

- V-Day's 2002 summit in Sophia, Bulgaria, united women from the Balkans. Women introduced themselves by saying "vagina" in their native languages.
- V-Day's 2003 leadership summit in Kabul. Over 75 Afghan women attended.
- Nine cities (in the USA) were declared Rape-Free Zones by their mayors.
- A preschool-aged girl disabled a potential rapist and made national news as the youngest girl in Kenya to stop rape using self-defense techniques taught at a V-Day sponsored program.[57]

After a decade of history, V-Day is viewed as "a catalyst, a movement, a performance," with the symbolic "V" standing for "Victory," for "Valentine", and, obviously, for "Vagina." Good and bad experiences are collected in the "Success Stories" and "Resistance Stories" sections of the V-Day Internet site, and secondary materials continue to appear.[58] Ensler's mission is clear: in her hands, theater becomes the main tool for a movement of resistance that struggles to return voice to women, providing them and their bodies with mechanisms of visibilization, healing, and empowerment.

On this last point, V-Day strategies coincide with the techniques developed by Augusto Boal in his Theater of the Oppressed Laboratories, originated in Brazil and with branches in different countries today.[59] For the Brazilian dramaturg, as much as for Ensler and Cixous, "theater is necessarily political and a very efficient weapon

---

56 Eve Ensler and Joyce Tenneson, *Vagina Warriors* (New York and Boston: Bulfinch Press, 2005), 5–6.

57 Ensler and Tenneson, 144.

58 In June 2007 the V-Day volume, *A Memory, a Monologue, a Rant, and a Prayer*, was presented in New York through a series of public readings. This collection of writings to stop violence against women features authors such as Michael Cunningham, Lynn Nottage, Susan Miller, and Eve Ensler herself.

59 The US chapter of the Theatre of the Oppressed laboratory was founded in New York in 1990. Boalian techniques of political performance are being used by collectives in Spain, Austria, Sweden, Canada, India, and Turkey. Cf., <www.theatreoftheoppressed.org>.

for liberation."[60] With her C-R approach, Ensler, like Boal, labors for the creation of a new type of audience, one not made of passive spectators. The term *spect-actor*, directly applicable to Ensler's mission as it is realized through V-Day, was coined in the framework of the theory and practice of the Theater of the Oppressed, and it is part of Boal's plan for "transforming the spectator into an actor"[61]—not necessarily a performer on stage (although this possibility is open, too), but an *actor* in life, an *agent* of transformation in their community. What both Boal and Ensler intend to do is to raise critical awareness about certain political and social situations to such an extent that the audience will feel obliged to act on them. They believe in the force of live drama over other forms of art, due to "its immediate contact with the public, and its greatest power to convince."[62]

As daughters of the feminist dramatic tradition, Eve Ensler and V-Day performers and organizers exhibit an explicit "commitment to telling stories of silenced and marginalized women, celebrating women's community and sense of connection through group protagonists, and expressing the moral concerns and societal criticisms that arise from women's experience."[63] As activists, they denounce what Foucault called "the indignity of talking in the name of others," giving the word back to the voiceless.[64] Thus, they continue to gather real testimonies, stories, interviews, and first-hand materials from the thousands of global women that are still searching for a stage of their own—because they know, as actors and writers, performers and directors, grassroots activists and leaders, friends and relatives, and women and citizens, that when it comes to gender violence, silence can be deadly.

Bibliography

Allen, Beverly. *Rape Warfare: The Hidden Genocide in Bosnia-Herzegovina and Croatia*. Minneapolis and London: University of Minnesota Press, 1996.

Amnistía Internacional. *Vidas rotas. Crímenes contra mujeres en situaciones de conflicto*. Madrid: EDAI, 2004.

Baker, Mark. *Nam*. London: Abacus, 2001.

Bernárdez Rodal, Asunción (ed.), *El humor y la risa*. Madrid: Fundación Autor, 2001.

Boal, Augusto. *Theatre of the Oppressed*. New York: Theatre Communications Group, 1985.

Bonino, Luis. "Develando los micromachismos en la vida conyugal." In *Violencia masculina en la pareja. Una aproximación al diagnóstico y los modelos de intervención*, Jorge Corsi *et al.* 191–208. Buenos Aires: Paidós, 1995.

---

60 Augusto Boal. *Theatre of the Oppressed*, New York: Theatre Communications Group, 1985, ix.

61 *Ibid.*, 126.

62 *Ibid.*, 53.

63 Brown, 155.

64 Michel Foucault. *Estrategias de poder*, Barcelona: Paidós Ibérica, 1999: 108.

Borràs Castanyer, Laura. "Hermenéutica del cuerpo." In *Escenografías del cuerpo.* 7–25. Madrid: Fundación Autor, 2000.

Bourke, Joanna. *An Intimate History of Killing: Face-to-face Killing in Twentieth-century Warfare.* London: Granta Books, 1999.

Bourland, Julia. 2000. *"The Vagina Monologues* Creator Opens Up." *Women.com.* <www.women.com/entertainment/interviews/ensler/ensler.html>.

Brown, Janet. "Feminist Theory and Contemporary Drama." *The Cambridge Companion to American Women Playwrights.* Edited by Brenda Murphy. 155–72. Cambridge: Cambridge University Press, 1999.

Canning, Charlotte. "Representing the Patriarchy and Experience. Plays about Violence against Women." In *Feminist Theaters in the USA: Staging Women's Experience.* 146–76. London and New York: Routledge, 1996.

Cixous, Hélène. "Aller à la mer." *Modern Drama* XXVII.4 (December 1984): 546–8.

—— *La risa de la Medusa. Ensayos sobre la escritura.* Barcelona: Anthropos, 1995.

De la Rosa, Mercedes. "Abusos imperdonables." *Magazine*, November 17, 2002, 64–74.

Diamond, Irene, and Lee Quinby (eds), *Feminism & Foucault. Reflections on Resistance.* Boston: Northeastern University Press, 1988.

Ensler, Eve. *The Vagina Monologues.* New York: Villard, 1998.

—— *Necessary Targets: A Story of Women and War.* New York: Villard, 2001.

—— *The Good Body.* London: William Heinemann, 2004.

—— "The Power and Mystery of Naming Things." *V-Day: V-Moments* (March 20, 2006). <www.vday.org/contents/vday/vworld/vmoments>.

Ensler, Eve, and Joyce Tenneson. *Vagina Warriors.* New York and Boston: Bulfinch Press, 2005.

Fernández-Morales, Marta. "'Bits. Fragments. Particles.' Split Identities and Theatricality in Eve Ensler's *Floating Rhoda and the Glue Man.*" The 7th International Conference of the Spanish Association of American Studies. University of Jaén, 2005.

—— "Communicating the Experience of War. The 'Us' *vs.* 'Them' Dialectic in Eve Ensler's *Necessary Targets*", *English Studies* 26 (2005): 115–29.

—— "El cuerpo-texto y el deseo femenino en el teatro: Monólogos de la vagina." In *Los hábitos del deseo.* Edited by Carme Riera, Meri Torras, Isabel Clúa, Pau Pitarch. 377–83. Valencia: Ex-Cultura, 2005.

Foucault, Michel. *Vigilar y castigar. Nacimiento de la prisión.* México DF: Siglo XXI Editores, 1974.

—— *El orden del discurso.* Barcelona: Tusquets, 1987.

—— *Estrategias de poder (Obras esenciales II).* Barcelona: Paidós Ibérica, 1999.

Greene, Alexis (ed.), *Women Who Write Plays: Interviews with American Dramatists.* Hanover: Smith and Kraus, 2001.

Kaldor, Mary. *Las nuevas guerras. La violencia organizada en la era global.* Barcelona: Tusquets, 2001.

Kelly, Liz. "The Continuum of Sexual Violence." In *Women, Violence and Social Control.* Edited by Jalna Hamner and Mary Maynard. 46–60. Atlantic Highlands: Humanities Press International, 1987.

Lorente Acosta, Miguel. *Mi marido me pega lo normal. Agresión a la mujer: realidades y mitos.* Barcelona: Ares y Mares, 2001.

McLaren, Margaret A. *Feminism, Foucault, and Embodied Subjectivity.* Albany: State University of New York Press, 2002.

McNay, Lois. *Foucault & Feminism.* Boston: Northeastern University Press, 1992.

Muscio, Inga. *Cunt: A Declaration of Independence.* New York: Seal Press, 1998.

Navarro Mateo, María José. "La narración de la violencia." *Asparkía. Investigació Feminista* 8 (1997): 17–30.

Smith, Dinitia. 1999. "Eve Ensler: Today the Anatomy, Tomorrow the World." *The New York Times.* <http://talentdevelop.com/EveEnsler.html>.

Solomon, Alisa. "From C-R to PR: Feminist Theatre in America." In *Contemporary American Theatre.* Edited by Bruce King. 227–42. New York: St Martin's Press, 1991.

Staub, Ervin. *The Roots of Evil: The Origins of Genocide and Other Group Violence.* Cambridge: Cambridge University Press, 1989.

Stiglmayer, Alexandra. *Mass Rape: The War against Women in Bosnia-Herzegovina.* Lincoln: University of Nebraska Press, 1994.

Torres Falcón, Marta. *La violencia en casa.* México: Paidós, 2001.

Wolf, Naomi. *El mito de la belleza.* Barcelona: Emecé Editores, 1991.

Index